Beneath
the Badge

Beneath the Badge

A Story of Police Corruption

Herbert Beigel
Allan Beigel

HARPER & ROW, PUBLISHERS
New York, Hagerstown, San Francisco, London

FIRST EDITION

Designed by Stephanie Krasnow

Library of Congress Cataloging in Publication Data

Beigel, Herbert.
   Beneath the Badge.

   Includes index.
   1. Police corruption—Illinois—Chicago. I. Beigel,
Allan, joint author. II. Title.   *incorrect*
HV7936.C85B44 1977   363.2'09773'11   77–5111
ISBN 0–06–010323–X

77 78 79 80 10 9 8 7 6 5 4 3 2 1

To

RICKI-BETH AND JOAN

WITH LOVE

To

EVAN, JENNIFER, AND JILL

WITH GRATITUDE FOR THEIR PATIENCE

To

MOM AND DAD

WITH DEEP AFFECTION

Contents

Foreword

They are not bad men, not evil, venal, or vicious. More than likely they'll buy you a beer, tell a joke, and offer to take your kid fishing. Some are Irish, others Polish, Bohemian, Jewish, Greek, Negro, and most were raised in ethnic city neighborhoods where grandmothers sat on stoops, vendors plied the streets, and the smells of homemade bread and wine drifted from kitchens and mingled with thick mustaches and even thicker accents.

Should you meet any one of them, it would be hard to believe that these men, religious, traditional, patriotic, are capable of being thieves and grafters, and that their crimes have brought them prison sentences.

They are policemen, most of them members of a big city force which, since 1970, has been torn by embarrassing scandals resulting in indictments and convictions of scores of veteran officers.

This is the story of their fall, a look at their intricate shakedown and bribery schemes, the mentality that nurtured such corruption and the environment that sustained it. It is a kind of poetic justice that the story should be centered in Chicago, the town that has always been characterized by outsiders as the "city that works," even though these same foreigners know nothing of payoffs for jobs, contracts, permits, passes, boat slips, votes, and dozens of other commodities.

Indeed, if the city does "work," and payoffs are the grease for its moving parts, then it is only right that the prosecuting cog of Chicago should work, too. Government action since 1971 in Chicago has resulted in the exposure of the biggest police scandal in that city's history, and brought about drastic department reorganization and outward pledges of reform.

But this story, and Chicago's police mess, isn't a local drama, nor a piece of Chicago reminiscent of the Capone days and easily adaptable to a Hollywood set. Police corruption is as universal as the policeman, a concern every time an officer anywhere has to make a decision and apply the law. The facts involve complicated detective work by government lawyers, and communicate the tragedy of policemen who've sullied their profession and destroyed their careers, but those episodes pale beside questions of the morality of the law enforcement officer, and his basic relationship to the law he is supposed to uphold.

Police corruption is a messy, depressing phenomenon, beneath the badge in so many ways. During my time as a police reporter and later as a professional writer, I came to meet several of the tainted police officers in this book. Some, before their problems with the law, were earnest, likable cops, others were self-righteous and smug, and none of them gave me the idea that graft was a way of life for them.

Later I had further contact with them after their trials—those who'd been convicted and were awaiting sentencing, and those who'd turned state's evidence and retained their freedom through immunity. It was then that I had real pity for these men, for they struck me as whipped dogs: bewildered, bitter, unable to believe that something they were taught as rookies—one told me that the first thing he learned on the job was to pay a sergeant $2 a month to forget the mandatory hourly call-in from a beat telephone box—could send them to prison.

These same men had always tried to convince me that money was thrown at them as they went about their day. They were bribed, they insisted, to overlook liquor license violations, speeding tickets, bookmaking joints, prostitutes, or double parking. The public demanded corrupt cops, and it offered "clean" money, they contended, gratuities, favors, tips, gestures of good faith.

But it went much deeper than that, I discovered, and became much more vicious. No probe of police corruption undertaken in the past ten years has been inaugurated over the passage of "clean" money, as dubious as that distinction may be.

Instead, the massive government investigations of organized police scandals, as this book so thoroughly documents, have been based on illegal, aggressive police activities in the areas of bribery, extortion, conspiracy, and perjury. Cops became bullies, demanding "dirty" money totaling hundreds of thousands of dollars. They took it from two-bit tavern keepers and silk-suited syndicate hoodlums; they filtered it from the lowest ranks of the department to the highest levels of command.

Specifically, much of the corruption chronicled here originated in saloons, places where more general nonsense occurs than anywhere, except, perhaps, a bedroom. And police have always found themselves in taverns, on and off duty, and known the places for the vice, the fast action, the low lights and pockmarked characters that they attract.

Any saloonkeeper knows that no matter how clean he runs his joint, he can always use a friend in the local station house. If that means a little cash every month, be it "clean" or "dirty," it is just part of the overhead.

Added to that is action generated by syndicate figures who want police consideration for their places, for overlooking watered drinks, fenced goods, prostitution, and gambling. In no time money is passing from a mob lieutenant to a police lieutenant. No longer is the payoff phenomenon a natural, mutual, big-city reality, but a scandal of damaging proportion which aligns the police with organized crime, and altogether undermines law enforcement.

That is no scenario, in the Watergate sense, no television special or soft-cover best seller, but the guts of the police scandal Herbert Beigel dug into as a fledgling assistant U.S. Attorney in 1971.

His plight may sound romantic, à la Woodward and Bernstein, but it is that only in retrospect. Such investigations usually come to the public eye in their final moments, and most often the credit for the success or failure goes to the top men, the crusading U.S. Attorney, local prosecutor, or a tough magistrate. While it is at those levels that momentum and priorities must be established, the real legwork, the basics of any investigation and its ultimate credibility in court, is done by assistants like Beigel, the nameless, faceless government lawyers, most of them young, idealistic, and aggressive, who track down witnesses and build cases.

Chicago's police scandals have had no Serpicos, no unblemished police officers willing to supply golden information against fellow cops for federal prosecutors. Instead, Beigel and other government lawyers had to scratch for every bit of evidence, court civilian witnesses, beg cooperation from balky FBI agents, and finally, bargain with cornered cops for their testimony.

Once Beigel and others got a toehold—and the dynamics of building a viable court case in such areas are incredibly complicated—their task became one of grooming their witnesses (bag men and vice club members) for the eventual crucifixion of fellow officers in exchange for their own skins. It was a demoralizing, psychologically debilitating exercise for all involved, but one absolutely essential to the prosecution of such massive, ingrained and, sadly, traditional police corruption.

It would be cozy for a lot of readers, police or civilian, to read a story like this with casual detachment, to conclude that this investigation and the bad cops involved were like Al Capone and State Street: of Chicago's making and Chicago's problem. Such an attitude would overlook the fact that police officers throughout the land, be they part of a megapolis or a rural community, have similar powers, a similar weight of discretion, similar pressures and temptations. Only the rules of the game are different with a sheriff who shakes down a country poker parlor or erects a speed trap. That sheriff wears the same badge and fingers the same dough as the vice officers on Chicago's Rush Street, or in Manhattan, or San Francisco's Tenderloin.

The story of *Beneath the Badge* is universal as long as we give police officers the responsibility of the law, and as long as cops are besieged by the pressures of right versus wrong, guilty versus innocent, getting caught versus getting by.

This is not a story of a few bad apples in the barrel, as police officials would like us to believe. As you read this, similar bribery and extortion rings exist in police departments all over the country. Police officers today, like those profiled in this story, are benumbed by a system of justice and a society of values which rewards them not for excelling, for serving and protecting, but for getting by, for trying to avoid being a chump.

One of the policemen who played a significant role in Chicago's corruption probes once told me that he never thought things would go so far, that what he did as a cop for sixteen years would evolve into cold cash and meets with hoods, then finally be replayed in a courtroom with his family in attendance. He had always felt that such dishonor couldn't happen to as decent a guy as him, that it was beneath him, and beneath his badge. He hardly realized that he had long since ceased to carry it, and even longer since stopped trying to understand what it stood for.

Chicago   William Brashler
May, 1977

Authors' Note

Beneath the Badge focuses on the story of one investigation of police corruption which took place in Chicago between 1970 and 1976. It describes many dishonest cops, but dishonest cops do not cause police corruption. The answer to the question of what does, lies in what it is about our law enforcement institutions that so easily permits basic compromises of integrity.

The material in this book is true and is primarily based upon the personal experiences of the authors and their contacts with the police and other law enforcement groups. Where other work or source material has been used, references are noted. Conversations are quoted as accurately as memory allows and elsewhere paraphrased in a way which retains the meaning of the person making the statement. Names have been changed only where unnecessary embarrassment would otherwise result.

This book is directed to the general public in the belief that an enlightened public can effect meaningful change, but it is dedicated to those whose future within a system of law enforcement depends upon their own efforts to solve the problem of police corruption.

Acknowledgments

This book would not have been possible without the cooperation of many who willingly shared their time and knowledge with us.

Our editor, Virginia Hilu, suffered an untimely death shortly before the completion of final editing. Without her, however, the idea of this book would never have come to fruition, and without her dedicated assistance it would not have been possible to bring this entire story to the public. We hope that it is not too late to acknowledge that this book bears the mark of her invaluable aid. We also wish to thank her assistant, Harriet Stanton, and Kitty Benedict, the editor who helped us through the difficult final editing and prepublication process. Special thanks go to Herb Reich of Basic Books, who started us in the right direction and encouraged us to go forward.

We could not have carried on with our professional responsibilities while working on this manuscript without the able secretarial and research assistance of Marcia Binger, Kay Storey, Mary Schmidt, Sue Higgins, and Linda Marquis. A special note of appreciation must be given to Gertrude Anderson, who typed the final manuscript.

ORGANIZATION CHART OF CHICAGO POLICE DEPARTMENT

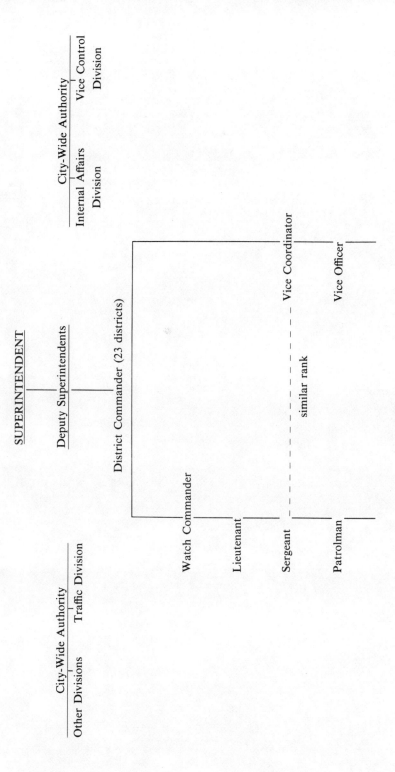

SUPERINTENDENT

Deputy Superintendents

City-Wide Authority

Internal Affairs Division

Vice Control Division

City-Wide Authority

Other Divisions

Traffic Division

District Commander (23 districts)

Watch Commander

Lieutenant

Sergeant

Patrolman

Vice Coordinator

similar rank

Vice Officer

Principal Characters

THE PROSECUTORS

William J. Bauer, United States Attorney (1969–71)
James R. Thompson, United States Attorney (1971–75)
James Featherstone, Chief, Chicago Strike Force (1969–70)
Sheldon Davidson, Chief, Chicago Strike Force (1970–73)
Herbert Beigel, Strike Force Attorney (1970–72)
Dan Webb, Assistant United States Attorney (1970–76)
Allan Lapidus, Assistant United States Attorney (1969–74)
Michael Mullen, Assistant United States Attorney (1972–)
Farrell Griffin, Assistant United States Attorney (1971–75)

THE JUDGES

Richard B. Austin
Abraham Lincoln Marovitz
Edward Robson
Julius J. Hoffman
William Lynch

THE FBI

Charles Bates, Special Agent in Charge, Chicago (1969–71)
Roy Moore, Special Agent in Charge, Chicago (1971–74)
Vincent Inserra, Chief, Organized Crime Squad
Tom Becker,* Special Agent
James Annes, Special Agent

*This agent's name has been changed.

THE POLICE

O. W. Wilson, Superintendent of Police (1960–67)
James Conlisk, Superintendent of Police (1967–74)
James Rochford, Superintendent of Police (1974–)
Mitchell Ware, Deputy Superintendent (1972–)

15TH DISTRICT (AUSTIN) COMMANDERS:

Mark Thanasouras (1967–70)
Victor Vrdolyak (1970–71)

UNIFORMED OFFICERS

Edward Russell, Watch Commander
Matthew McInerney, Watch Commander   Served under
John Foley, Watch Commander   Thanasouras
John O'Shea, Watch Commander

Frank Gill, Lieutenant
James Fahey, Sergeant
Robert Devitt, Lieutenant

VICE OFFICERS

Frank Bychowski, Vice Coordinator (1967–69)
David Holder, Vice Coordinator (1969)   Served under
George Demet, Vice Coordinator (1969–70)   Thanasouras

James Pacente, Vice Coordinator (1970–71)   Served under
                                             Vrdolyak

Walter Moore, Vice Officer
Charles Eckenborg, Vice Officer
Frank Nanni, Vice Officer   Served under
Kenneth DePaola, Vice Officer   Thanasouras
Masanabu Noro, Vice Officer
James Gartner, Vice Officer

18TH DISTRICT (RUSH STREET) COMMANDERS

John McDermott (1960–64)
Walter Maurovich (1964–66)
James Holzman (1966)
Clarence Braasch (1966–70)
John O'Shea (1970–72)

UNIFORMED OFFICERS

James Murphy, Lieutenant
James White, Sergeant ⎫ Served under
James Kinnally, Lieutenant ⎭ Braasch

VICE OFFICERS

William Simpson, Vice Coordinator　　　Served under
　　　　　　　　　　　　　　　　　　Maurovich

Robert Fischer, Vice Coordinator ⎫ Served under
Edward Barry, Vice Coordinator ⎭ Braasch

James Geraghty, Vice Coordinator　　　Served under
　　　　　　　　　　　　　　　　　　O'Shea

John Cello, Vice Officer
Edward Rifkin, Vice Officer
Salvatore Mascolino, Vice Officer ⎫ Served under
Lowell Napier, Vice Officer ⎭ Braasch
Charles DuShane, Vice Officer

THE DEFENSE LAWYERS

James Demopolous
Sherman Magidson
John Muldoon
Gerald Werksman
Alan Ackerman
David Schippers
Eugene Pincham
George Cotsirilos
George Callaghan

THE PEOPLE OF CHICAGO

Herman Ghoulston
Al Brody
Martin Lindstrom
Louis King
Stoyan Kovacevic
Boris Kovacevic
Constantine Sanichas
Tim Powers
Marlin Johnson
Frank Velillari
Bill Gold
Joe Morang
Sheer Folly
Peter Boznos
Sam Crispino

The dilemma of a democratic society is how to give the police sufficient power to perform their role effectively, while at the same time maintaining restraints on the police in order to prevent abuses to democratic principles. Properly controlled, the police become a servant of the criminal justice system; unchecked, the potential abuse of police power could allow it to become master of the judicial system to the demise of liberty and justice.

Allan Edward Bent, 1974
The Politics of Law Enforcement (p. x)

Beneath
the Badge

Prologue

I recognize the badge of my office as a symbol of public faith, and I accept it as a public trust to be held so long as I am true to the ethics of the police service. I will constantly strive to achieve these objectives and ideals, dedicating myself before God to my chosen profession—law enforcement.

—Code of Ethics: International
Association of Chiefs of Police

October 1966

Fall had arrived in Chicago. It was a cold, dry afternoon and, although windy, the bright sunshine made it pleasant to be outside. On the north side, the Lincoln Park Zoo was filled with women and children, strolling around looking at the few animals still outdoors. Nearly all of the visitors had come from the immediate neighborhood or had taken the bus. The south parking lot was empty.

Just after 4 P.M. two cars entered the south parking lot. Each bore the familiar colors and insignia of the Chicago Police Department. They parked side by side. Two men emerged from one, a third from the other. They were young, dressed casually in slacks, sweaters, and windbreakers. One of the men from the first car handed a sheet of paper to the man who had come alone in the other car. "Here it is, Sal," he said. "The arrangements have been made to start the club up again. We have about twenty places marked down to be hit."

Sal took the list, quickly shoving it and his hands back into his pockets. "What do you want me to do, Eddie?" Sal asked.

Eddie pointed to his partner. "Skippy, here, has a lot of experience in the

1

district. So do you. We thought it would be a good idea if you looked it over to see if you want to scratch off some of the bars, or add some we didn't think of."

Sal turned to Skippy and reluctantly took the list out of his pocket, handing it to Skippy. "How are we going to work it, Skippy?"

"Eddie and I will take half of the bars and make the collections from the day shift. You and Lowell will handle the rest on the night shift."

"Let me see the list again," Sal said. He took the list from Skippy. The parking lot was still empty. He walked toward the front of one of the cars and laid the sheet of paper on the hood, holding it firmly with both hands to keep the wind from blowing it away. He ran his finger down the list of names. "Has Lowell seen this?"

"He doesn't care what we decide," Skippy said.

"I don't see any names we should take off the list, but I'm too damn cold right now to think of any to add."

Eddie laughed. "Don't worry about it. It's a good enough start. Besides, we have to meet with Bob and get his approval. He might eliminate some."

"You think so?" Sal said. "None of these bars look like syndicate places." Sal put the list back into his pocket.

"You never know," Skippy said. "Bob has to get the commander's approval. Who knows exactly what he's got going for himself."

"I suppose you're right. He won't want any foul-ups. God, it's cold." Sal opened the door to his car and got in. "Let me know what happens," he said as he started the motor and drove away. A minute later, the second car followed with Skippy and Eddie. The parking lot was empty again.

March 1967

The south parking lot was covered with snow. But it was not empty. One unmarked car with its motor running was in the same spot where Eddie, Skippy, and Sal had met. Two men were in the front seat. The driver looked at the man beside him. "I guess you wanted to stay on as vice coordinator, Bob. But with your promotion to lieutenant, it's simply not possible. You'll have to be in uniform."

"You keep telling me that. I know the rules."

"And rules are rules. You know that too."

"What about our relationship? We've worked together for a long time."

"We can keep it going. You can stay in the Eighteenth District, in uniform."

"I have been offered Commander of Area Two, Auto Theft. I think I would take that instead of being another uniformed lieutenant in the Eighteenth.''

"Frankly, Bob, you have been very valuable to me. Whatever you decide to do, I want you to continue your monthly duties as before and pick up the money.''

Bob turned away and looked out at the deserted parking lot. He could not believe what he was hearing. He had respected the man sitting next to him and had taken many risks for him. Now he was going to another district, but he still was being asked to take the risks. The rest of the guys are right, he thought. He *is* a cold son-of-a-bitch. "I can still do it," he said without turning around.

"Good. But you must understand that we can't split the money the way we used to. I have a new vice coordinator. You know Ed, don't you? I'll have to give him a thousand dollars a month. That cuts down what I can give you. How would four hundred a month sound for continuing to make the pickups?''

Bob knew it was over. He wanted to get out of the car and walk away, but he could not move. "I want five hundred a month," he said.

The driver stared at Bob for a few seconds. "Okay. But I want you to remember one thing. I can't trust Ed too much. I don't want you to give him the details of the big package. I have told him to keep his mouth shut and not ask questions. Don't blow it by volunteering anything. Just show him around the district. Whatever you do, don't give him any idea of how much money is involved. He'll get what he deserves from me and he can pick up some more from the little package. He doesn't need to know any more. Understood?''

"Let's go get some lunch."

Chapter 1

The Struggle

We are not a policy making organization. The FBI is a service organization which is subordinate to the Department of Justice. And that is as it should be. The FBI should never be permitted to become an independent agency, operating without the checks and controls under which it now operates.

—J. Edgar Hoover,
Foreword to *The FBI Story,*
September 8, 1956

If you fellows need a hundred agents, you got them—they'll clean this up in a hurry.

—Charles Bates, Chief,
FBI Office, Chicago,
June 1, 1971

Face it, no one in the Bureau is interested in this investigation and I'm better off working alone.

—Tom Becker, Special Agent,
FBI, October 1971

There are those who say Chicago is a city on the make. Others claim it has already been made, and in the image of the late Richard J. Daley, its Mayor of twenty years. This baron of the Midwest's greatest city presided over a glittering lakefront with its broad expanse of parks shielding the public beaches from miles of towering apartment buildings. The lakefront was there when he took office in 1955. But the skyscrapers, the daring modern architecture born of the Chicago School of the late nineteenth century, and the elevation of the Chicago Symphony to the top echelon of the classical music world arrived only during the Daley years. To many visitors Chicago continues to represent, indeed symbolize, American daring, innovation, and change.

Chicago, the quintessential American city, has its seamy side—slums, racial tensions, financial and political problems. It also has as large a concentration of different ethnic groups as anywhere else in the United States. The great migrations flowed not only to New York and the eastern seaboard, but also to Chicago. Poles, Germans, Italians, Jews, Greeks, Swedes, Chinese, Blacks, Mexicans, Cubans, Hungarians, Puerto Ricans, Irish, Czechs, and Serbians came to Chicago to gain what they hoped would be an endless parade of opportunities.

If Chicago is too complex to define clearly and if the contrasts of newness and decay are puzzling, there is one institution and group that grew with the city and rested secure from examination, variety, and change—the Chicago Police Department. An anomaly in a city which boasts of its novelty and spark, it is a vast bulk of faceless personages, hidebound procedures, and customs and traditions which defy time. Its new headquarters symbolizes the contrasts of Chicago: the modern lobby offset by the drab upper floors of offices and fronting on a decaying area just south of the Loop, surrounded by parking lots, rundown hotels, sex shops, and theaters catering to the growing pornography trade.

Three-quarters of a mile north and just a few blocks south of the Civic Center and the Mayor's offices at City Hall is the place of business of another law enforcement agency, much smaller and of recent origin. On the fifteenth floor of the Federal Building, sharing space with the hundred-man United States Attorney's office, is the six-lawyer staff of the Chicago Strike Force, a division of the Organized Crime Section of the United States Department of Justice.

In 1970 the Strike Forces had been in existence for only a few years. They had been the brainchild of Attorney General Ramsey Clark, who believed that a special team of lawyers could more effectively fight organized crime by concentrating on coordinating the efforts of the FBI, the Internal Revenue Service, the Bureau of Narcotics, the Post Office, the Secret Service, and the Alcohol, Tobacco and Firearms Division of the Department of the Treasury, all of which had long preferred to follow their own idiosyncratic methods of gathering information on those involved in organized crime.

Despite their youth, the Strike Forces had been effective. By 1970 the Chicago office, for example, had accumulated an impressive array of statistics attesting to the many prosecutions brought by its young lawyers. At its helm was James Featherstone, a career government lawyer in his middle thirties. He had not been in his new role long; he hoped to return to Washington soon as a deputy in the Organized Crime Section. In the meantime he had his present job to think about. He had considerable experience in overseeing the prosecution of organized crime cases and little surprised or excited him. Now, however, something new had caught his eye. The present chief of the Criminal Division in Washington, Will Wilson, had begun to show an interest in police corruption. Wilson was an old-time Texas politician brought to Washington by Richard Nixon. Featherstone had no idea why he would have an interest in local law enforcement problems. No matter. Featherstone liked the idea. The police were rarely investigated. This fact alone made the idea worth examining.

Then, there were those articles he had seen in the Chicago dailies a year ago. They had reported rumors of a "$100-a-month club" in which tavern owners were forced to pay monthly stipends to the police for protection. He had originally found the stories interesting, but there had been little follow-up and he did not at that time consider them particularly convincing. Suddenly, in February 1970, things began to happen and his interest was renewed.

On February 13, 1970, the *Chicago Sun-Times* reported that Superintendent James B. Conlisk, Jr., had just demoted the commander of the Austin District (15th) for not getting along with the community. The newspaper reported that Conlisk was also "critical of [the] administration and [its] failure to achieve an acceptable reduction of crime in that area."[1] Conlisk reportedly explained that "Austin residents are entitled to a more professional level of police service than they have been receiving."[2] Conlisk did not define "professional" service.

The dethroned commander was Mark Thanasouras, a department "wunderkind" who, under the previous reign of O. W. Wilson, had progressed from patrolman to captain in just twenty-three months. Considering that many police officers never rise above the rank of patrolman, this was nothing short of phenomenal. Rumor was rampant that Thanasouras had been aided in his rise by political backing from powerful leaders in the Chicago Greek community.

Although the sudden demotion of Thanasouras was newsworthy, this alone was not what caught Featherstone's eye. The *Sun-Times* also reported that Patrolman David R. Holder, the Austin District vice coordinator of vice investigations, had been reassigned to limited duties with the Internal Investigation Division (IID) of the Police Department. The *Sun-Times* said that "it is normal practice to assign policemen under investigation to the IID. The

1. *Chicago Sun-Times,* February 13, 1970.
2. *Ibid.,* March 6, 1970.

investigation began, police said, after some tavern owners complained of police shakedowns."[3]

The background of these complaints received further attention from reporters of both the *Sun-Times* and the *Tribune,* Chicago's largest and most influential daily. It had been a *Tribune* columnist, Robert Wiedrich, who, a year earlier, stated in his column that there existed in Austin a prosperous and widespread $100-a-month club. The column had no special effect on the public or the police at the time it was written; but one year later, with the demotion of Thanasouras and the apparent investigation of Patrolman Holder and the vice squad for shakedown activity, it began to appear that there might be some substance to Wiedrich's report.

Other reporters quickly became interested in the developing story. Art Petacque, a veteran crime reporter for the *Sun-Times,* reported that a group of individuals belonging to the newly formed Tavern Owners Association in Austin had complained to police officials about shakedowns. Speculation followed that Thanasouras's demotion had been directly related to these complaints. The Police Department refused to confirm any link.

Featherstone concluded that there might be a federal violation associated with the reported shakedowns. In response to the severe labor unrest and violence of the 1930s Congress had enacted the Hobbs Act. It made extortion that in any way affected interstate commerce a federal crime. Featherstone reasoned that because taverns sold beer and liquor, much of which was either delivered from or manufactured in states other than Illinois, extortion of a tavern owner would be a violation of the Hobbs Act. Featherstone relayed his thoughts to Vincent Inserra, head of the Organized Crime Squad of the FBI in Chicago, and Leo Petrodi, the agent in charge of investigating Hobbs Act violations. He also made a formal request that the Bureau conduct a preliminary investigation of the newspaper allegations.

The FBI contacted Harry Ervanian, the police officer in charge of the IID. On February 25, 1970, Ervanian told two Bureau agents that he would not furnish copies of his investigative file on alleged Austin District shakedowns. He offered no explanation for his refusal. Ervanian's boss, James Rochford, a deputy superintendent with a reputation for honesty and toughness, was also close-mouthed. He repeated that the IID reports were not available. Rochford implied that Edward Hanrahan, the State's Attorney for Cook County, had directed him to withhold the reports until local indictments could be returned against the implicated officers.

Despite the lack of police cooperation, the FBI was not completely in the

3. *Ibid.,* February 13, 1970.

dark. Unknown to Featherstone, the Bureau had been accumulating since 1968 many details of the "$100-a-month club." Still, it was not until the rash of newspaper stories in early 1970 and a formal request that Featherstone learned for the first time that the FBI had an informant who had been supplying information for several years about police corruption in the Austin District.

The Austin neighborhood had been a close-knit community until the late 1960s, when whites began to flee to the suburbs. Located on the extreme western edge of Chicago, about six miles from the Loop, the Austin District was composed of broad business thoroughfares and quiet, tree-lined residential streets with large, single-family homes, multiple-family dwellings, and small, older apartment buildings. When blacks began moving in from poorer areas on the south side, the whites retained their businesses but moved their residences to the northern and western edges of the area or into the neighboring suburb of Oak Park. Although nearly a third of the residents were black by 1970, they owned only two dozen taverns out of four hundred.

The Bureau's informant began his disclosures following the April 1968 riots after the assassination of Martin Luther King during which he had observed an officer looting stores burned out by arsonists. After he investigated further, he reported to the FBI that many knowledgeable people in the community claimed the officer had underworld connections. When asked by the FBI to pursue the matter further, the informant returned in May 1968 with five pages of information on police corruption in Austin.

He claimed that a lounge on Cicero Avenue was the headquarters for fixing parking tickets and moving traffic violations, and that bets on horses and sports events were accepted from police officers at a tavern located across the street from the police station. He further reported that numerous taverns were being subjected to harassment by the police if the owners did not make payoffs. One owner had supposedly made so many large payments that he ended up in bankruptcy. Another tavern was rumored to be owned in part by Thanasouras, who was suspected by other tavern owners of having muscled in on the previous owner when he refused to make payoffs. Thanasouras's co-owner had complained that his life was in danger if the informant continued his inquiries. Finally, a reliable source claimed that Thanasouras had employed a wiretapper, who was also an officer of the Chicago Police Department, to gather information about top-level police officials so that he could have insurance against exposure.

The FBI had other information tucked away in its files. It learned in 1968 that Frank Bychowski, who was vice coordinator in Austin under Thanasouras, had to give his approval to anyone wishing to run a bookmaking operation.

Also, the Bureau was told of allegations that a man named Joel Stern had served as a police contact for Chicago hoodlums and crime syndicate figures on the west side. Any tavern owner in trouble with the police could receive help from Stern if he would place jukeboxes from a Stern enterprise in his lounge.

The FBI never reported these allegations to the Justice Department, and it never undertook to determine if the information could be corroborated. Featherstone knew that the FBI, like many other federal agencies, jealously guarded its information and autonomy. Still, the Strike Force concept was supposed to reduce this secretiveness. That is why, adjacent to the Strike Force offices, rooms were set aside for agents from the FBI, the IRS, the Secret Service, the Postal Service, the Bureau of Narcotics, and the Alcohol, Tobacco and Firearms Division. This setup was supposed to insure the free flow of information, a unity of effort, and the sensible expenditure of manpower.

Unfortunately, no one occupied the office set aside for an FBI agent on the fifteenth floor. Christy Malone, whom the Bureau had assigned to serve as an intermediary, had not moved from his desk in the FBI's office on the ninth floor. Instead, he occasionally attended meetings with the Strike Force chief to receive specific requests, suggestions, and complaints. Only rarely did he visit the fifteenth floor. Liaison agents from other federal agencies made biting comments about the FBI's failure to cooperate fully.

Knowing that FBI cooperation was as much a myth as a reality, Featherstone was not surprised that it took until March 11, 1970 to obtain from the Bureau a report summarizing the material it had received in 1968 about Thanasouras and the Austin District. That report also contained a recent interview with the informant who had first given information in 1968, apparently the FBI's first contact with him since that time. In regard to the "$100-a-month club" in Austin, the informant named thirteen tavern owners who purportedly had belonged to the club. He did not identify the officers engaged in the collections except to say they were all members of the vice squad.

By the time Featherstone received this information on March 11, another significant development had occurred. On March 5, David Holder and another Austin vice officer, Masanabu Noro, were indicted by a Cook County grand jury for taking money from two Austin District tavern owners and a motorist in an accident case. The two officers were suspended immediately and transferred out of the district along with the already demoted Thanasouras. Ervanian was asked by a *Sun-Times* reporter if the investigation in the Austin District was continuing and he replied, "That's a possibility."[4] *Chicago Today*

4. *Ibid.*, March 6, 1970.

reported that other Austin police officers had been under investigation, but no usable evidence could be uncovered. Featherstone concluded that the indictments of Holder and Noro represented both the beginning and the end of the local investigation.

Thanasouras's bright career had been effectively brought to a close although he had managed to escape criminal prosecution by state authorities. However, with the FBI report of March 11, Featherstone now had information which suggested that Thanasouras's rapid ascent through police ranks might have been paralleled by an equally rapid growth of his involvement in corruption and organized criminal activity. Also intriguing was that before being made commander of the Austin District, Thanasouras had been a watch commander in the 20th District, the infamous Summerdale District where the last major police scandal had surfaced in 1960 when eight officers were found to be involved in a conspiracy to burglarize homes in the district.

As with Austin, the Bureau had information about Summerdale which it had kept secret until the March 11 report. In 1968 it had succeeded in obtaining the cooperation of an ex-police officer who had been heavily involved in syndicate activities in Summerdale after resigning from the department. His story gave Featherstone further insight into Thanasouras's secret career and convinced him of the value and the necessity of launching a full-scale federal investigation into shakedowns in the Austin District during Thanasouras's tenure as commander.

This FBI report also revealed to Featherstone part of the connection between organized crime and police corruption. In the early 1950s, according to the ex-police officer, many independent bookmakers, not controlled by the syndicate, managed successful operations. Most were of the small "walk-in" type, the illicit bookmaking being conducted out of retail stores and other business establishments. At first, tavern owners had been left alone by the police. Gradually, however, the small bookmakers decreased and large bookmaking parlors and wirerooms operating out of the back rooms of taverns took their place. At the same time, the police began to demand payoffs from tavern owners.

As the payoffs became organized, district commanders began to use the vice coordinators to collect money from tavern owners engaged in illegal activity. The vice coordinator might also designate an assistant who would actually make the collections when the vice coordinator was not on duty. The collector, known as the "bagman," split the payoffs with the district commander, giving a percentage of his own take to his assistant. A bookmaking tavern owner divided his profits with the syndicate after making the payoffs. Live and let live was the rule.

Under this system the police raided only bookmakers who were not part of any organized system of payoffs. By the late 1960s, however, few bookmaking taverns were immune from syndicate control, since they lacked the police protection that an effectively organized scheme of payments bought.

Because there were three watch commanders in a district, a rotation of shifts was necessary so that each, if he wanted to be a part, could share in the proceeds collected by the vice coordinator during the day shift. Sometimes, however, the watch commanders would be left out of the action altogether, with the distribution of money going directly from the vice coordinator to the district commander. In return for not participating in these payoffs from organized gambling, the watch commanders were free to take money from "after-hours" operations such as prostitution. They normally did not share this money with the district commander.

The officer on the street would receive payoffs for not arresting tavern owners who had committed liquor law violations. If the payoffs were made at the time of the violation, only the officers immediately involved in the investigation benefitted. If vice detectives came to the scene or a report was written, a larger payoff had to be made, presumably because it was more difficult to engineer a fix once the report had been prepared and filed. The money collected was then divided among the vice detectives and sometimes the watch commander and the district commander.

In 1964 Thanasouras was appointed watch commander in the Summerdale District following his meteoric rise to captain. Shortly thereafter he toured Summerdale, introducing himself to many of the large tavern owners. While the informant did not know what occurred during the next two years, he did find out that in late 1966 and early 1967 Thanasouras met with syndicate bosses on the north side to plan a payoff scheme to protect syndicate bookmaking operations in the district. They decided that a fair take from each bookmaker would be $100 a month. These payments were to be made by tavern owners to a low-level muscle man who then would turn the money over to the police bagman. By the time collections actually started, Thanasouras had left Summerdale to assume his new post as commander of the Austin District.

After his transfer Thanasouras reportedly bragged that a wireroom in Austin would have to pay $1,000 a month if it wanted to stay in business. While this may have been an exaggeration, it was clear that whatever Thanasouras might have lost by leaving Summerdale, he made up for in Austin. The informant stated that between twenty and twenty-five bookmaking operations in Summerdale had been members of the "club," but the money was "chicken feed" compared to more than $3,000 per month Thanasouras was allegedly receiving in Austin. He provided the Bureau with the names of fifteen tavern owners who were members of the Summerdale club.

Featherstone formally asked the FBI squad known as C-4 to interview those tavern owners in Austin and Summerdale who had filed complaints with the IID or who were named in the informants' reports. C-4 generally assumed the responsibility of investigating fraud and labor offenses, including violations of the Hobbs Act.

C-4's chief, Leo Petrodi, greeted Featherstone's request with less than enthusiasm. C-4 had never investigated police corruption. If Featherstone thought police corruption was linked to organized crime, Petrodi believed that Inserra's C-1 squad ought to handle the interviews. Petrodi even dropped hints that the whole thing was a waste of time. Many FBI agents liked the cops and depended on them for information. They would not welcome what could turn out to be a politically explosive investigation on what they considered questionable grounds for federal jurisdiction (the link between taverns and interstate commerce).

There was, in addition, a more basic explanation for the FBI's attitude. The FBI's job is to investigate violations of federal law, not city or state laws. Understandably, the FBI is careful to avoid charges that it has exceeded its authority. The opposite is true of the police, since most federal crimes are also state crimes. The police will start an investigation of any criminal activity even if they ultimately defer to another agency. As a result, most cooperation between the FBI and the police is for the FBI's benefit. If there is no federal violation, the Bureau will not become involved; if there is a federal crime, the police are still concerned and the Bureau will want all the police cooperation possible.

While Petrodi did not like the idea of investigating police corruption, he agreed to supervise the interviews of tavern owners in the Austin District as long as his agents did not have to conduct the interviews or do any legwork. Through Christy Malone, Featherstone turned to Inserra for help and he agreed to assign the required number of agents to conduct *one* interview of each tavern owner, totaling some thirty or forty interviews, during a two-day period. If anything substantial resulted, Petrodi and Inserra said, there would be plenty of time to decide about a further commitment of time and manpower.

Featherstone did not like the idea of "blitz" interviews, but he agreed because he had neither the power nor the desire to fight with the FBI, especially when he was uncertain if any evidence would be uncovered. Featherstone did not believe that the FBI's reluctance at this stage was particularly ominous, but rather a result of a natural, and not necessarily unwarranted, resistance against becoming enmeshed prematurely in a protracted investigation with unpredictable results.

These interviews, conducted during the second week of April 1970, were a disaster. Two agents visited each tavern and asked only two questions: "Did you ever pay the police any money?" and "Did you ever hear of anyone else paying the police?" The agents had no background information. In most cases, they were not even sure to whom they were speaking. If the owner was not available, the agents would ask his identity, note the response of the person interviewed, and move on, making no extra effort to find the owner. There was to be only one interview per tavern.

Only two tavern owners in the Austin District acknowledged that they had paid a police officer. One failed to recall the identity of the officer and the other appeared too frightened even to try and remember. Two witnesses in the Holder-Noro cases declined to talk to the FBI agents at all. Several tavern owners who had complained previously to the IID about police harassment refused to cooperate, saying that they had gotten nowhere and had been subjected to stepped-up harassment since the beginning of the IID inquiry.

The agents could not aid the witnesses in identification anyway. They had no photographs or knowledge of who served on the vice squad in Austin or Summerdale. If a tavern owner wanted to say he never had trouble with the police, the agent could not confront him with the truth. He had no information about the tavern owner's arrest record or the licensing file.

The second question, about knowledge of payments by others, elicited more information, but only because a tavern owner thought that by telling on someone else he might deflect FBI attention away from himself. Several tavern owners, most of them in Austin, stated that others had paid the police and even gave some names. Because this information was being related to interviewing agents at the same time that other agents were questioning the named tavern owners elsewhere in the districts, these new leads were of no use since there were to be no follow-up interviews.

Featherstone received the reports in May. Despite the interview problems, they did furnish material for further investigation if FBI cooperation could be obtained. With no further word from the Police Department or the State's Attorney's office about new indictments, Featherstone could only assume that unless the FBI and the Justice Department conducted their own investigation, no one else was going to step in and fill the void.

Neither Petrodi nor Inserra shared Featherstone's optimism. Petrodi let it be known through one of his agents, Bobby Tompkins, that he had not changed his basic views about the inquiry. Since he had not been willing to have his agents interview tavern owners before, he would certainly not change his mind after the April interviews, which he felt had not unearthed anything of significance. Inserra had been unhappy all along about lending so many agents to the C-4 squad to help in "their" investigation and was unwilling to release men to do more interviews.

Strike Force lawyers later reflected that the Bureau resistance might have had its origin in the same rationale that had led to prior obstruction to Justice Department efforts to launch major investigations that were likely to involve controversy. A case in point was the history of the FBI's involvement in investigations of civil rights violations in the South during the Kennedy years. The United States Commission on Civil Rights had this to say about the FBI response to civil rights investigations:

It has been reported from time to time that the Bureau has little enthusiasm for its task of investigating complaints of police brutality. If the contention is accurate, that fact is, to some degree, understandable. The Director has used the strongest possible language to stress the need for cooperation between the Bureau and law enforcement officials at all levels. Apparently, without this cooperation the FBI could not maintain the excellent record it now enjoys in the enforcement of a long list of federal criminal statutes. Although the Bureau states that it "has not experienced any particular difficulty or embarrassment in connection with the investigation of alleged police brutality," there is evidence that the investigations of such offenses may jeopardize that working relationship.

Still another difficulty may arise from the cooperative relationship between the FBI and local policemen. Although the Bureau has declared that it knows of "no instances of any individuals being fearful to bring complaints to the attention of the FBI," there is evidence that some victims and witnesses, especially among Negroes in the Deep South, are afraid to bring information to the Bureau's field offices. . . . Some of their fears appear to be based upon the fact that agents and policemen often work closely together, and that officials somehow soon learn the name of complainants.[5]

Despite the Commission's comments, it would be a mistake to assume that the apathy of the FBI about an inquiry into police wrongdoing was solely a consequence of the relationship between the two institutions. The Bureau's method of gathering information is also a potential obstacle to the efficient carrying out of a major investigation when there is *no* police cooperation. Agents spend tremendous amounts of time fulfilling informant quotas and writing reports on what informants say. Each agent is assigned many cases to work on, must investigate many alleged criminal figures, all of which requires more report writing, and is subject to immediate reassignment on an emergency call which may take a day, a week, or several months. An agent is at the mercy of his superior's decisions about how time should be spent. The

5. *Report of the Commission on Civil Rights* (1961), U.S., pp. 61–62.

Assistant United States Attorney in charge of an investigation has nothing to say about agent assignment or allotment of manpower.

An even more troublesome problem arises from the FBI's strong desire to produce convictions. This leads to a predominance of investigations into those crimes that experience dictates will result in high conviction rates. FBI involvement in investigations which do not have a proven track record of success is likely to be limited.

The interviews of tavern owners conducted in April 1970 by the FBI produced little more than a thick sheaf of useless reports. A short time later Featherstone was recalled to Washington to take a post with the Organized Crime Section, supervising several other Strike Forces. The new Chicago Strike Force chief was Sheldon Davidson. Davidson was a nine-year veteran of the Justice Department, in his early thirties, and anxious to prove himself as an aggressive administrator. He had built a strong reputation as a tough prosecutor in the Chicago office and was determined to succeed where Featherstone had failed. But Davidson wanted to orient the Strike Force to his goals before undertaking a potentially frustrating investigation into police corruption. The interviews of the Austin and Summerdale tavern owners were stuffed in a file cabinet in the Strike Force office and, for the time being, would remain untouched.

The Investigation Begins Again

In January 1971 Davidson asked Herbert Beigel, a new attorney with the Chicago Strike Force, to look at the April 1970 reports and give him an opinion on what ought to be done next. Beigel took the interviews out of the cabinet and read them, noting that, as Davidson had said, it would probably be better if they did not exist since the witnesses' statements were obviously inaccurate or outright lies.

Neither the FBI, the State's Attorney's office, nor the IID had done anything since April 1970. David Holder had pled guilty and had received a short prison term and a fine negotiated for him by his lawyer, James Demopolous, a close personal friend of Thanasouras. After his conviction Holder resigned from the force and remained unemployed until finding a job as a truck driver. Noro had never stood trial.

The IRS had started its own investigation into police corruption, but its focus was entirely different from that of Featherstone or the Bureau. The IRS was interested in making tax cases against organized crime figures and in developing tax prosecutions against police officers if the amounts of unreported income derived from payoffs was large and the offending officer was heavily involved with the Mafia. The IRS had more than twenty officers listed for investigation, but little progress had been made. Only two agents were assigned to the project and they had been slow to develop informants and leads.

Beigel reviewed the sparse FBI and IRS material and tried to figure out a way to get the investigation off the ground. It seemed to him, as it had to Featherstone, that, although elusive, police corruption was there, waiting to be uncovered. The FBI reports yielded little substantive information, but Beigel was able to reach several conclusions. First, single interviews were valueless. Wholesale denials by tavern owners could not be taken at face value if no follow-up efforts were made. Second and third interviews would let the tavern owner know that the federal agents were serious.

Second, it was a mistake to expect that the Summerdale tavern owners would be cooperative. All were alleged to have worked closely with organized crime bosses in the area. They were less likely to talk than Austin tavern owners, who were, as best as could be determined, paying the police only for protection from arrest for liquor law violations. These relatively minor offenses, however, were not trivial to the owners since they could lead to suspension or loss of a liquor license.

Third, an investigation of police corruption could go forward only with a commitment by the FBI of time and manpower. The Bureau was much larger than the IRS and its jurisdiction was wider.

Finally, the acquisition of photographs and other personnel information about police officers who had been assigned to Austin and Summerdale during the past several years was mandatory. Without this, there was no hope that agents conducting the interviews would know what they were doing or that the persons interviewed would have a reasonable chance of identifying those who had collected money from them.

Within a few days Beigel had concluded his review. He and Davidson decided that there would have to be a meeting of the minds among the Strike Force, the FBI, and the IRS. Davidson and Beigel met with Bobby Tompkins from C-4 (Petrodi's squad), Christy Malone and James Annes from C-1 (Inserra's squad), and Howard Pollitz, the IRS agent who had supervised his agency's work into police corruption. The presence of Annes came as a surprise to the two lawyers. He had not been involved with the April investigation and had been spending his time on gambling matters. He had been a police officer in Los Angeles and perhaps, thought Beigel, had come to the meeting to offer his expertise.

Davidson and Beigel explained their plans to resume the investigation by reinterviewing tavern owners who had seemed to be promising sources of cooperation and also by selecting additional tavern owners to be questioned. The lawyers proposed that this responsibility be divided between the IRS and the FBI, with a full exchange of reports. Annes and Tompkins replied that FBI policy might not allow reports to be funneled to the IRS; however, to the extent that reports would be sent to the Strike Force, perhaps they could be shown to the IRS as long as copies were not made. Pollitz frowned at this last stipulation. He could not understand the problem since he had already agreed to make copies of his reports available to the FBI. Davidson, who had known Pollitz for some time, took him aside and persuaded him that some cooperation was better than none and that he would see to it that copies of important reports would be delivered to him. Besides, argued Davidson, Pollitz had to admit that he and one other IRS agent could not carry out an investigation of police corruption by themselves.

The other problem concerned which FBI squad would actually conduct the required interviews. Davidson leaned toward the C-1 squad under Inserra, but was reluctant to state this view directly to Tompkins for fear of offending Petrodi, whose squad had responsibility for Hobbs Act violations. Davidson therefore suggested that the C-4 squad continue to supervise the investigation through Tompkins, but that Inserra provide the manpower to conduct the interviews. Annes did not object to this proposal but later told Beigel privately that if C-1 agents were doing the work they would ultimately insist on complete control. (This actually occurred several months later when Tompkins told Beigel that he and Petrodi were not interested in the investigation. From then on C-4 involvement was finished and it was with Inserra and his squad that the Strike Force had to work.)

Near the end of the meeting Annes said that he frankly did not believe that the Strike Force would come up with anything significant. He was not convinced that police corruption was as extensive as Strike Force lawyers believed and perhaps everyone might be better off by concentrating on traditional organized crime cases. Davidson pointed out that most of the Strike Force information had come from the FBI and that if the Strike Force believed that corruption was prevalent, it was because the FBI had led it to that conclusion.

Annes was unpersuaded. He did not think that the statements of a few informants and the two days of interviews in April had formed an adequate basis for launching a massive inquiry. The FBI and the Strike Force might be accused of politicking and engaging in fishing expeditions. Davidson and Beigel assured Annes that there was not going to be any investigation for the sake of investigation; if more work produced nothing, it would all be ended quickly.

Davidson and Beigel left the meeting thinking that a beginning had been made. They learned quickly, however, that a plan in theory is not an effective investigation in practice. The most Inserra would do at the outset was assign one agent, Tom Becker,[6] to act as liaison, and three others to work on the interviews. These agents came with severely limited authority since they were to do only interviews specifically requested by Beigel through Becker and Inserra, with Inserra having the right to veto an assignment.

Inserra would not allow the agents to do anything on their own. They could not follow up and they could not conduct an unassigned interview even if, while on the street, they found an opportunity to come up with something significant. The report of the first interview had to be written and an evaluation made before anything further was permitted. This slowed the progress of the interview process and prevented the lawyers from making plans for any extensive future activity.

Becker was a sincere and dedicated agent who had spent his fifteen years with the Bureau talking to informants and keeping tabs on a group of reputed Mafia kingpins. He had never participated in a long-term major investigation of potentially explosive political consequences. He told Beigel that many agents wanted no part of the inquiry and had no idea of how to conduct interviews of basically uncooperative or fearful witnesses. He also said that Inserra was opposed to assigning more agents to the investigation because he was concerned that his gambling projects would suffer.

The IRS did little more. Besides Pollitz, only one other agent spent any time on the investigation. Instead of conducting those follow-up interviews which Beigel had requested and looking for additional cooperative Austin tavern owners, the two agents devoted endless hours to conferences with an ex-police officer to whom they referred in their reports as Confidential Informant CPD-1. Although CPD-1 said many interesting things about Police Department operations and corruption activities, he steadfastly refused to be specific about anything and absolutely declined to give a signed statement or to testify. At Pollitz's request, Beigel asked Becker to relocate the FBI informant who had made the 1968 disclosures about Austin police corruption. The informant could not be found. The FBI had lost track of him.

Between January and March 1971 neither the FBI nor the IRS set aside much time or assigned many men to the investigation. Beigel and Davidson decided to narrow the focus of the investigation to Austin, where the April 1970 interviews and the indictments of Holder and Noro at least provided a

6. This agent's name has been changed. Although he played an important role in the investigation, the use of his real name would give him publicity that he has never desired or courted.

ray of hope. Since it was now clear that the IRS was unprepared to act vigorously, the two lawyers also decided to phase that agency out of an active role in the investigation.

There were other barriers to progress besides the Bureau's lack of cooperation and the IRS's ineffectiveness. Neither the agencies nor the lawyers had any knowledge about police structure, police procedures, or the personnel assigned to the Austin District during the Thanasouras command. They did not even know who was currently on the vice squad in Austin, how long they had been there, or what they looked like. Little was known about how liquor license applications were processed and approved or how liquor licenses were revoked following violations.

In an attempt to solve the personnel information and identification problems, Beigel and Davidson met with the United States Attorney, William J. Bauer, a Republican and a former judge from western suburban Dupage County who had been appointed only six months earlier.

Bauer proved to be helpful. He suggested going directly to Superintendent Conlisk and asking for the photographs and personnel files on all police officers who had served in Summerdale and Austin during the past five years. Although Summerdale was no longer a prime target, Beigel and Davidson still hoped that something might eventually be accomplished in that district and an opportunity to obtain photographs and other information should not be passed up.

A week later Bauer informed the Strike Force lawyers that Conlisk, although worried about a federal "fishing expedition," had pledged his full cooperation and would pass on the desired information as soon as possible. In return he asked only to be kept informed of significant developments as they occurred, including advance warning of grand jury proceedings and indictments.

Conlisk, however, delayed for several weeks after his conversation with Bauer before ordering information about four districts, rather than just the two named by the Strike Force, and the lawyers received no material for two months. The reason for this curious response was not explained until months later, when Beigel and Davidson first met Conlisk at a lunch at the Union League Club of Chicago, a posh downtown private club to which many federal judges, prominent lawyers, and politicians belonged. Conlisk, who had spent his professional life in the Police Department, as had his father, was well liked and had been handpicked by his predecessor, O. W. Wilson. He was quiet, not considered a fighter, and believed to be a partisan of the status quo. He was loyal to Mayor Daley, to whom he owed his stay in office. In an investigation of police corruption, Beigel and Davidson considered him an unknown factor.

At the luncheon Conlisk explained that he had been fearful of the potential broadness and lack of discrimination which could accompany a general federal probe and the possibility that its existence might be prematurely leaked to the press. He did not want his staff to know that he was cooperating in a federal hunt for wrongdoing police officers. Such information might affect his credibility at a time when it was important to solidify it and maintain police morale at a high level.[7] He had requested information about four districts in an attempt to obscure his reasons for seeking comprehensive data for no obvious purpose. Concentration on Austin alone, which everyone knew (since the demotion and transfer of Thanasouras and the indictments of Holder and Noro) could be the place where a large scandal might emerge, would seem suspicious even to his own men. His delay in asking for the information was to give him time to contrive an excuse for the request, an excuse he never revealed to Beigel and Davidson. A request for information about four districts would temporarily prevent anyone from knowing which district was at the heart of interest. This was particularly important if, as he hoped, the federal investigators were unable to turn up improprieties beyond what already had been learned by the IID in 1970.

The IID investigation, which had apparently ended abruptly after the indictments of Holder and Noro, was also of great interest to the Strike Force lawyers. The IID police officers must have conducted numerous interviews. Although Beigel knew that the IID had probably not uncovered major evidence, since only Holder and Noro had been indicted, he asked Bauer to contact Conlisk again to see if a Strike Force lawyer might review the IID files.

Conlisk did not reply for a few weeks and then told Bauer that, although he had no objection, a single file on Austin did not exist. Rather, the IID reports were organized by the names of the officers against whom complaints had been filed. The Strike Force would have to name those officers whose files they wished to review. Whether he would permit copies to be made was another matter. Further consultation with police legal counsel was necessary. He did not want to risk legal exposure if an officer filed suit because information had been disclosed about him to an outside agency without permission. The Strike Force lawyers did not press the copying issue. They knew they could obtain the reports, if necessary, by grand jury subpoena.

Beigel supplied Conlisk with a list of twelve officers who had served on the vice squad in Austin at the time of the IID investigation. Since Beigel now had

7. The Police Department had been undergoing severe criticism from certain groups about alleged police brutality and discrimination in hiring.

the personnel roster of all officers who had served in Austin during the past five years, he was tempted to ask for all the files. He refrained from making this request because he did not want to add to Conlisk's suspicion that the federal investigation was designed only to cause trouble.

One thing particularly bothered Beigel. If the files were organized only according to the name of the officer against whom a complaint had been lodged, how were the interview reports filed on those tavern owners who could not make an identification? To ask Conlisk about this would also risk offending him since he might feel that his truthfulness was being questioned.

Beigel went to police headquarters to look at the files. All were paper-thin except those of Holder and Noro. Even the Thanasouras file was relatively bare, with only a few notations and papers reflecting his rapid rise and fall. If anything worthwhile was to be found, it would have to be in the Holder and Noro files. Beigel sat down at a table in a large conference room and began reading under the watchful eyes of a gray-haired police officer who sat on a stool in the corner with a look of puzzlement on his face. Beigel wondered how Conlisk would now keep the federal interest a secret.

The reports revealed little. A few tavern owners had been interviewed, but with the exception of those named in the indictments returned by the county grand jury, they denied ever having paid the police. One of those listed in the file as not having given any information to the IID had been the first tavern owner to fully cooperate with the FBI. Strangely, she had told FBI agents that all the information given had been previously related to the IID. This contradiction made Beigel question the credibility of the IID investigation and Conlisk's statement that all reports were in files bearing the names of officers. Beigel noticed, as he read the reports, how certain leads had not been followed up and how the investigation from beginning to end seemed to be based on the assumption that only Holder and Noro were involved in illegal activity.

Lie detector tests had been administered to several vice squad officers, but the examiner had concluded that it was impossible to tell if they had answered questions truthfully. Nervousness, lack of cooperation, or some other disability was cited most often as reason for this failure to reach a firm conclusion.

Beigel next contacted the State's Attorney's office and asked for the case files on Holder and Noro. At the same time he inquired if there were any plans to undertake further investigation. He was told the investigation was considered closed. Neither the grand jury testimony nor the slim file on Holder revealed much. Noro had not stood trial because the complaining witness could not be found. The grand jury transcript showed no signs that this witness had been anything but cooperative.

Becker went to find the witness. Much to everyone's surprise, he found him at the address listed in the State's Attorney's file. Becker asked him where he was at the time the Noro trial subpoena had been issued. He replied that he had always lived at the same address and was still waiting for word about when he would be expected to return to court to testify at Noro's trial. He did not understand, he told Becker, why no one had contacted him after his grand jury appearance.

With only Becker devoting all of his time to the case, the IID providing no startling revelations, and the State's Attorney's office apparently out of the picture, the IRS interviews of CPD-1 represented the only new information about police corruption obtained since January 1971. Although his statements were vague and incomplete, they did confirm to Beigel that, however difficult and tedious, the investigation was worth continuing.

CPD-1 was an early-middle-aged man who had spent nine years as a Chicago patrolman, three of them under Thanasouras on the Austin vice squad. Most of what he said was hearsay. Situated at the lowest level of the police hierarchy, he could only guess at the activities of those above him. On the other hand, by his own admission, he had taken part in tavern shakedowns and had some first-hand knowledge about corruption.

The IRS agent who talked with CPD-1 wrote:

"[CPD-1 said] that since he is a former policeman he knows that police 'take care of their own' in more ways than one. Many times, he said, when anyone has turned against the police department by talking, the persons have been gunned down or otherwise disposed of. He cited as an example that he could be shot at in the alley some night while parking his car or he could be driven off the road or a bridge. CPD-1 added that the subsequent investigation by the police would report that he had been killed by unknown assailants and the case would be closed. . . .

"The subject was then told that we were looking into police corruption going on in a certain district; specifically the Austin District. CPD-1 said he figures that is why we were here and added, 'I know what you want—it's there—just dig for it.' The subject continued by saying he would like to help us but he can't and explained that he has to think of the safety of his wife and family. . . .

"Questioned about his work on the police department, CPD-1 said he was a uniformed patrolman for 6 years and then even served as a detective on various assignments when he was offered the job as a vice officer in the Austin District. The witness added that he turned the job down four times before he finally accepted.

"When asked again about payoffs in the Austin District, CPD-1 said, 'Look,

I know what you're after, it's there—just dig for it, but I won't testify because I know what they will do if I talk.' The witness went on by informing us that nobody is assigned to the Austin District without being on the take. . . .

"Referring to Thanasouras, CPD-1 replied that Thanasouras was just another conduit for payoffs that go all the way to the top brass. He said, however, that Thanasouras kept his 'cut' before the 'take' was passed on. The witness stated that Thanasouras is 'out of the take now—he got "dirty" so he got cut out.' . . .

"Next the witness was asked about some of the taverns in the Austin District and he related the following:

1. The restaurant at Lake and Central and another restaurant in the District that burned down were 'torch' jobs. . . .
2. _____ Lounge was a hangout for prostitutes at one time, but feels the owners, the _____ brothers, were not connected with the activity. The witness said he thinks the place is a juice drop for the hillbillies who patronize the place and is controlled by the _____ brothers.
3. When 'cutting the pie' for the take, the police usually meet at [several bars and restaurants were listed].

"CPD-1 went on to say that for a period of time he was one of the chauffeurs for the Police Department Physician when he was on the force and said he knows how the doctor receives his take from individual policemen. On question, the subject told us that if a policeman is sick for more than one day, the man is required to call in and report to the doctor. CPD-1 said even though the man is honestly sick in bed with perhaps a temperature of 102, the doctor will tell the man that if he does not come to his office for a checkup, the doctor will not approve his sick leave. The sick man, according to the witness, will then tell the doctor that when he is well again he will report to the doctor and 'take care of him.' CPD-1 said that when the doctor knows he will be 'taken care of,' he will approve the man's sick leave. CPD-1 let us know that when the man is well again he is obligated to go to the doctor's office and drop a five or ten dollar bill for the doctor.

"The witness next told us about the secretary, a police officer, that every district commander has as an assistant. He said the secretary makes up the watch duty rosters, vacation lists, and assigns days off. If a policeman has a part-time job and wants to stay on a certain watch, the person must pay the secretary up to $100 a month for this special treatment, the subject said. CPD-1 said he had to do the same thing when he worked part time for a paint manufacturer and explained that he and the other policemen feel they have to either pay off or they will be assigned to shifts that will prevent them from earning extra money. This type of 'take,' CPD-1 told us, is split with the commander. The witness told us he did not know how much the secretary kept and how much was turned over to the commander, but figured the commander got the most.

"This same procedure of payoffs, usually dropped in the secretary's open desk drawer, is required for select vacation periods and special days off, the witness informed us. He added that it costs a 'saw-buck' for a certain day off and more for a certain vacation period. . . .

"Questioned about payoffs in the Austin District, CPD-1 informed us that he personally collected from 21 taverns in the District that were booking. The witness went on to tell us that most of the places paid at least $100 a month and doubled when the 'heat' is on. . . . He said the payoffs are collected once a month and all you have to do is find out who the bag men are and follow them on their rounds. The witness also said the bag men always follow the same route. . . ."[8]

Much of what CPD-1 told the IRS agent could not be corroborated. However, he did name the twenty-one taverns that he claimed had made payments to the police in Austin. This specific information was what Beigel hoped would persuade tavern owners to cooperate. If a tavern owner believed that the FBI agent interviewing him knew he had paid off a police officer, it might provide the leverage necessary to force the owner to give information.

All of this was cause for hope, but Beigel knew that, without sufficient manpower, it would be impossible to translate the leverage into usable evidence. Tavern owners had to be interviewed and reinterviewed. Preferably, the same agent should conduct all interviews of a particular witness. Reports had to be carefully drafted and cross-checked for inconsistencies and possible leads. Background information on each tavern was needed and the personnel charts and photographs supplied by Conlisk had to be organized and analyzed.

Despite assurances from Inserra that he would assign more agents to do the interviews, only Becker contributed substantial time to the investigation and his efforts were directed toward organizing and cajoling other agents to do interviews using the background information he had compiled. By the end of May 1971 Beigel and Davidson were beginning to feel the pressure of inactivity. No longer concerned about embarrassing Inserra or Petrodi, they con-

8. This material is quoted directly from the IRS interview report of CPD-1. Minor deletions and modifications have been made to preserve the identity of the informant, which is still confidential.

tacted the head of the Chicago office of the FBI and requested a meeting.

On June 1, Charles Bates[9] came to Davidson's office. He was tall, well-groomed, and conservatively dressed, giving an impression of aggressiveness and confidence combined with an aura that conveyed that he was not a man to tolerate delay. Davidson and Beigel carefully explained to Bates the background of the investigation and the need for experienced agents to handle further interviews. Bates responded that both C-1 and C-4 had many talented and knowledgeable agents who could do more than was expected and do it quickly. He asked Davidson exactly what he wanted. Davidson replied that he was not as concerned with speed as he was with ensuring that the investigation was handled properly. Bates interrupted and said that he had been told before the meeting that the Strike Force needed leads followed up; this could be accomplished very rapidly. "If you fellows need a hundred agents," Bates said, "you got them, they'll clean this up in a hurry."

Beigel and Davidson tried to disabuse Bates of the notion that an investigation of police corruption could be accomplished by simply assigning a battalion of agents to conduct hundreds of interviews in a short period of time. What this investigation required, they explained, was a relatively small and compact group of agents working close to full-time for several months under the direction of Strike Force lawyers. The Bureau's usual method of giving a single agent brief and simple tasks which generally did not require knowledge of the whole case was unsatisfactory in a sophisticated investigation. Instead, all assigned agents should assume the general task of encouraging witnesses to talk by creatively following leads that would develop new information to be used to "turn" uncooperative witnesses. Word of mouth that a tavern owner had paid, a long period of no arrests for liquor violations following many investigations, and hidden or nominee ownership in a tavern which, if known to the state, would be grounds for revocation of the license were some of the situations which, when discovered by an intelligent, experienced agent familiar with the details of the whole investigation, could be used to persuade witnesses to cooperate. More important, it was imperative that each assigned agent know the structure of the Police Department, how the police functioned in the district, and how officers performed their duties. Every agent would have to know who was on the vice squad at what time and under what vice coordinator. Otherwise, how could he persuade a reluctant tavern owner to cooperate?

Bates appeared cooperative. He promised that a special squad of ten agents

9. Bates was later to receive national publicity as the agent in charge of the San Francisco FBI office at the time of the Hearst kidnapping.

would be established within C-1 to work full-time under Strike Force supervision until all that needed to be done was finished. He placed no time limit on the life of this special squad, but indicated he would rely on the good judgment of the Strike Force not to misuse valuable agent manpower. The only caveat was that agents must always be available on short notice for emergency matters and they could not be excused from their obligations to keep in touch with their usual informants and report to Washington in writing as normally expected. Also, all agents must continue to be responsible for those individuals whom they had been assigned to investigate.

The qualifications that Bates placed on his definition of a full-time agent were significant. Nevertheless, Bates had acted as if he wanted to help and the two Strike Force lawyers hoped that, with an assigned group of agents, they could make up for the lack of actual full-time help with continuity and dedication.

All of the agents picked to serve on the special squad were from C-1. Since none had been involved in the gambling investigation or working on a pending investigation, Beigel questioned whether they were C-1's best, but he felt compelled to keep this concern to himself because he was interested in getting the squad together as soon as possible. Whatever their quality, having ten FBI agents to work with was a luxury.

Throughout June, Beigel met with the new squad of agents to explain the reasons for the investigation and the ways in which the Strike Force believed good evidence could be obtained. Although the method was time-consuming and agonizing, Beigel believed it was necessary if any progress was to be made.

In the Austin District there were more than four hundred taverns. Starting with those whose owners were suspected of paying the police, a file was to be developed on each tavern before any contact was made with the owner. Each file was to contain a copy of the city liquor license application, which would disclose those police officers from both the license division and the district who had investigated the applicant and made recommendations to the liaison officer of the city license board. In addition, all police reports on arrests or investigations of violations involving the tavern owner to be interviewed would be requested from Conlisk.

The license investigation information was particularly important. Although the Police Department had a special section to investigate applicants, the district commander was always asked if he had any objection to a specific applicant before it was forwarded to the City Hall liaison officer for review. Often, he would send a vice squad officer, usually the vice coordinator, to conduct another inquiry. Any objection from the district police could cause a rejection of the application. And, because the same district officers who investigated liquor law violations were in charge of day-to-day supervision of tavern activities, the license application was a point at which solicitations for monthly payoffs could begin.

This method of laying the groundwork for the interviews was the antithesis of what had transpired in April 1970, when a flock of agents had invaded Austin on the same day without any knowledge of what they were looking for or how to go about getting it. Although Beigel and Davidson thought this plan was workable, the execution was atrocious. Part of the problem was time lag. Obtaining the required reports from the Police Department took almost as long as the photographs and personnel duty rosters. Leaks were another problem. When reports on a single tavern were requested, the officers involved with that tavern knew very quickly that they were under scrutiny. To minimize this problem the lawyers did exactly what Conlisk had done. Beigel asked Conlisk for more tavern files than he really wanted. This precaution increased the delay.

The major difficulty, however, was the continued intransigence of the FBI. Although Beigel had meetings with the ten agents throughout June, by July only six were doing any work on the investigation and just one, Becker, was working full-time. When the men were assigned interviews, more problems arose. One agent given an assignment by Becker did not carry it out for more than two months. Despite an FBI rule that interviews be reduced to writing within five days, several weeks was the norm.

When the reports finally came in they were deficient in several important areas. Agents consistently passed up important questions or leads worth pursuing. When a tavern owner admitted paying a policeman, the agent often had forgotten to bring photographs or had brought the wrong set. One witness failed to identify any officers, but the agent did not include in his report which photographs he had shown to the tavern owner.

Finally, the agents were not always in touch with the importance of finding out from a witness whether money had been *extorted* from him. Agents often forgot that since bribery was not a violation of the Hobbs Act, the way they reported what the witness had said was critical. Instead of quoting the witness exactly, the agent often paraphrased the tavern owner's words; for example, "The cop and I had a discussion and I agreed to give him a hundred dollars."

Since these reports were to be turned over to defense counsel at trial and could be used to cross-examine the witnesses, it was crucial that the agents report the interviews accurately. Most of the agents assigned to the investigation had never seen a trial or been involved with a significant investigation under the direction of a Justice Department lawyer. Beigel repeatedly had to remind the agents to be specific when preparing their reports. The agents did not like the Strike Force watching over their shoulders so closely and, before long, Becker told Beigel that he could really count on only three agents to work on the investigation.

As the special squad promised by Bates steadily faded into oblivion, so did any hope that significant advances could be made by the fall. By October 1971 most of what the Strike Force had set out to accomplish in June still remained undone. Little new was known about the $100-a-month club. Only a few of the twenty-one taverns named by the informant had been approached. The only prosecutable case that had been developed was against Holder and Noro, the same vice officers indicted by the state eighteen months earlier. Evidence against them consisted only of two witnesses against Holder and one against Noro.[10]

As the lack of progress continued through the summer, Inserra began to drop hints to Becker that the investigation was going nowhere and ought to be wrapped up. Beigel asked Becker to pressure Inserra into assigning more men who *would work* on the investigation, but Becker remained the only agent working full-time. Inserra constantly telephoned Davidson to emphasize the importance of his gambling cases. He also sent Christy Malone to articulate his view that "police corruption had nothing to do with organized crime and was not his concern."

Frustration set in. Becker was trapped in the middle of a steadily growing feud between the Strike Force and the FBI. By October, Becker had thrown up his hands in despair. He told Beigel, "Face it, no one in the Bureau is interested in this investigation of police corruption and I'm better off working alone."

10. Witnesses different from those in the state prosecution were needed to avoid the possibility of a double jeopardy claim by the defendants.

Chapter 2

The End Around Play

I refuse to answer because I sincerely and honestly believe that
my answer may tend to incriminate me.

> —Mark Thanasouras and others,
> December 13–15, 1971

As the middle of October 1971 approached, there was no sign that anyone
except Conlisk, the FBI, the Strike Force, and the U.S. Attorney's office knew
that a large-scale investigation into police corruption was brewing. Despite
earlier disclosures of a $100-a-month club in Austin, the passage of time and
the scarcity of new developments had apparently convinced the media that a
new scandal was not ready to emerge. For the public it was no different. The
largely favorable publicity that had accompanied O. W. Wilson's administration and "reforms" put into effect by him had led most Chicagoans to accept
the notion that the possibility of continued corruption had been reduced.

In reality, many of Wilson's reforms had nothing to do with eliminating
corruption (for example, the new and much heralded communications center).
Some may even have contributed to the spread of police abuses. One of
Wilson's pet projects was the creation of an independent career vice squad,
staffed by officers who enjoyed vice work. Wilson believed:

Officers should be assigned to vice control on a permanent basis and not on a short
period plan of service if effective operation is the sole consideration. Continuity of
service promotes increased efficiency because the officers become more skilled, develop
more contacts, and have available the services of a larger number of undercover
operators. However, it should be remembered that a *certain amount of temptation is
placed in the way of an officer on vice assignment, and appointments on a permanent
basis must be accompanied by some form of administrative check to ensure that an officer
does not succumb to it.* (Emphasis added.)

29

Vice control is sometimes considered undesirable police work, and consideration should be given to the interest and desire of the officers. A permanently assigned officer who is interested in vice control is more likely to do a thorough job than one who is temporarily assigned or lacks interest in the work. Vice assignments frequently have promotional limitations because of the size of the division and the specialized nature of the job. Officers with potential capacities beyond the promotional possibilities of the division should not be assigned, except for experience, but instead, capable officers of limited leadership ability should be selected.[1]

Wilson's acknowledgment that vice duty is filled with "a certain amount of temptation" was completely undermined by his failure to describe what he meant by an "administrative check" and suggestion that the promotionally limited officer is ideal for vice. Wilson also did not recognize fully the very real disadvantages of his reform plan. Vice work *is* undesirable; one officer told Beigel, "If it wasn't for the money, who would want to do it?" While the career vice officer develops more contacts and the department is assured of continuity, both factors can also contribute to the efficiency with which police are able to use the vice detail to extort monthly payments from businessmen and hoodlums. If the Wilson machinery for vice control did not lead to corruption, it certainly fostered it.

Conlisk was not ready to revamp the vice squad structure, and he moved cautiously after the indictments of Holder and Noro and the demotion of Thanasouras. Victor Vrdolyak replaced Thanasouras as commander in Austin. A career police officer in his early forties, he was also the brother of a powerful Democratic-machine alderman, Edward Vrdolyak. Vrdolyak had built a solid reputation as a moderately tough cop who was well entrenched in the police bureaucracy. He had also received some favorable publicity for his efforts to clean up crime during prior commands. His new assignment was viewed by the Strike Force as an attempt to quiet rumors regarding widespread corruption in the Austin District, rather than to stamp it out.

Vrdolyak replaced most of the vice squad officers who had served under Thanasouras. A traditional Police Department practice permitted a commander to have his "own" men join him in a new district. Most of the new vice squad members had served under Vrdolyak elsewhere.

Although officers assigned to vice in the Chicago Police Department are low on the totem pole of rank (they are only patrolmen), they have power and influence. They function entirely in plainclothes and through their vice coordi-

1. O. W. Wilson and Roy Clinton McClaren, *Police Administration,* 3rd ed. (New York: McGraw-Hill, 1972), p. 400.

nator (usually a patrolman, although sometimes a sergeant) bypass the established command hierarchy of the district, responding directly to the commander. Vice officers engage in irregular patrols, check on bars and liquor stores, and follow the activities of local bookies and prostitutes. They have tremendous discretion and shy away from the beats of patrol officers, sergeants, lieutenants, and watch commanders who work on day-to-day crime in the district. The vice officer is a member of an elite group of the lowest-ranking policemen of "limited leadership ability."

The jurisdiction of the vice officer overlaps with that of two other law enforcement units. One is inside the department, the other outside. The Vice Control Division of the Chicago Police has city-wide authority to investigate all forms of vice, but devotes most of its time to illegal gambling, prostitution, and narcotics. In theory, it consults district vice officers and supervises investigations of vice involving more than one district. Vice officers and VCD personnel have to be on continual alert not to step on each other's toes. In the case of tavern investigations, the VCD acts mostly as a coordinator of information. Reports of liquor law violations prepared by a district vice officer are sent to VCD for filing, but the director of the VCD may make his own recommendations to the city board concerning suspension or revocation of a license.

State investigators also operate within the domain of the district vice officer since taverns and liquor stores are licensed by both city and state. A violation can bring an investigation by either or both liquor boards and separate hearings may be held. As a practical matter, however, this rarely occurs. The state cannot begin to cover adequately the more than seven thousand taverns and liquor stores in Chicago. Since the state is compelled to rely on the efforts of the Police Department, this makes the vice squad even more insulated.

If a violation is reported, both the state and the VCD are informed; but if a vice officer decides to overlook illegal activity, it is unlikely that the state will know what he has done or that VCD will react. Protection from the vice squad becomes tantamount to protection from the law.

The complexities of police control of vice, the apparent lack of restrictions on illegal police actions, and the lack of persistence by the IID led the Strike Force lawyers to recognize, even before their difficulties with the FBI, that a successful investigation would have to concentrate on only one aspect of corruption. Finding an "Achilles' heel" was their goal. Both Beigel and Davidson believed that police vulnerability to outside investigation lay in tavern shakedowns because, unlike the case of payoffs from gamblers, prostitutes, and narcotics pushers, it was reasonable to expect that the victims would cooperate. However, with the development of the unanticipated struggle with the FBI and the resulting six months of stagnation, the success of any investigation into police corruption, limited or not, seemed highly improbable.

A New Plan

Although Holder had been indicted and convicted for extortion by the state in 1970 and was no longer on the police force, he was the immediate prime target of the Strike Force. He had been Thanasouras's vice coordinator, and if he cooperated, a case could be made against the former commander. No one believed that Thanasouras had personally made any collections and, therefore, evidence against him would have to come from other police officers. Holder was the logical candidate.

The evidence accumulated by October was sufficient to indict Holder, but it was hardly earthshaking. The principal witnesses were Jane O'Halloran, who owned a tavern in Austin and had been an active member of the Austin Tavern Owners Association, and Bobby Lee Mahaffey,[2] who had tried to start a tavern after his brother, with whom he had worked in another business, was murdered in 1969. Both had been interviewed by the IID.

O'Halloran informed Becker that she had been approached in 1968 by Holder and told that a club was being formed to service the Austin taverns. If she wanted quick service in case of trouble and to avoid problems that could cause the loss of her liquor license, she would be wise to pay a reasonable sum of money once a week—$25. Each week an officer stopped by the tavern to collect the payment. O'Halloran did not remember the names of any of these collectors; all she stated positively was that Holder had made the initial solicitation and occasionally made the collections. O'Halloran either could not or would not identify any of the other officers from photographs. She hinted to Becker that she might not agree to testify if there was ever a trial. The first agent who had talked to her promised she would never have to testify and she wanted no further trouble.

Mahaffey had a small neighborhood bar he affectionately named Up Your Alley. After he applied for his liquor license he was contacted by Holder and told to expect trouble securing his license because his brother had been murdered under suspicious circumstances. Mahaffey asked Holder what he should do. Holder suggested that a several-hundred-dollar cash payment would solve the problem. Mahaffey feared he would not obtain the license he so desperately wanted if he did not pay. Before Holder returned, however, Mahaffey was

2. The names of these witnesses have been changed.

contacted by the IID. He told the interviewing officer what had happened.

When Holder returned a few days later, he was livid. He accused Mahaffey of going to the IID and took him to the district station. In a closed room Holder told Mahaffey that he better keep his mouth shut, talking to the IID would get him nowhere fast, and Thanasouras would never stand for a hillbilly tavern owner causing trouble. Holder intimated that what had happened to Mahaffey's brother could easily happen to him if he did not fall into line. A shaken Mahaffey changed his story at a second IID interview. But a short time later Mahaffey, with his courage strengthened by a friend in the Tavern Owners Association, went back to the IID and told them about the events of the past several days. It was Mahaffey's testimony which had partly led to the Holder indictment by the Cook County grand jury.

Becker and Beigel spent months trying to find Mahaffey and finally located him in a ramshackle bungalow in Cicero, a southwestern suburb of Chicago, not far from the Austin District. Mahaffey, like O'Halloran, was not sure that he could bring himself to face Holder in court. The publicity which was sure to follow worried him. He said he wasn't afraid, but he had his family to consider.

In the third week of October Inserra began to place new pressure on the Strike Force. "I am only willing to take good men off gambling investigations for so long without positive results, before we will have to close the police corruption matter. I need results and, frankly, it doesn't look like we are making any headway."

Becker, in particular, felt the brunt of the pressure to wind down the investigation. He had taken to working alone, developing tavern files himself, interviewing difficult-to-find witnesses, and neglecting to contact periodically his stable of informants. Other agents, with whom Becker had worked for years, criticized his involvement and devotion to what they believed was a meaningless fishing expedition. Because Becker was absolutely essential to the continuation of the investigation (Beigel did not want to lose the expertise he was developing about Police Department operations), Beigel and Davidson met to decide how to avoid a complete collapse of Bureau assistance.

The two lawyers first considered recontacting Bates. The agents Bates had promised were never really produced and the attorneys believed that they had a legitimate complaint to which he might be sympathetic. However, returning to Bates with complaints would only increase the tension that was building between the Strike Force and Inserra. It was clear that Inserra had the power to do pretty much as he liked and that Bates would interfere only to a limited degree. A new conference with Bates was rejected. A solution had to be found which gave Inserra what he wanted. Results.

The only immediate way to give at least the appearance of results was to convene a grand jury and begin subpoenaing witnesses. Until this time there had been no reason to involve a grand jury in the investigation. Indictments were not imminent. Immunity (which only a court could give) had not been contemplated for any witness and, therefore, the grand jury process had little advantage over the effective use of skilled investigative agents. Yet something had to be done to get the investigation off dead center. A grand jury might convince the FBI that the Strike Force did not intend to stop the probe.

Beigel and Davidson finally decided to call a grand jury despite certain risks. Misuse of the grand jury process is a fatal mistake for the careless prosecutor. All testimony given to a grand jury by witnesses who will appear at trial must be disclosed to the defendant's counsel before cross-examination. Since grand jury testimony represents the sworn statements of a witness, any inconsistency between what a witness says to the grand jury and at a trial will be glaringly visible. By using a grand jury the government gives up the excuse often used by a witness that the agent who reported the interview set forth inaccurately the witness's statements. Before the grand jury the words of the witness are actually recorded. There can be no mistake about what he said.

The grand jury was devised to control the unscrupulous prosecutor and to check his power to bring persons to the bar of criminal justice without the approval of lay citizens. As American legal practice developed and the criminal justice system became more sophisticated, it became obvious that, contrary to earlier expectations and with few exceptions, a grand jury invariably carries out the wishes of the prosecutor who orchestrates its proceedings. The secrecy of the grand jury was turned into one of the government's many potent weapons against those it investigates. Courts are reluctant to look at grand jury testimony given before an indictment to determine if the Fifth Amendment requirement of probable cause is satisfied, a function they perform routinely in a preliminary hearing following arrest. The grand jury indictment becomes the constitutionally required determination of probable cause, eliminating the necessity for a judicially conducted preliminary hearing to determine if the arrest was properly made.

The loss by the prospective defendant of many rights associated with a preliminary hearing is also significant. He cannot call any witnesses to testify on his behalf; he cannot cross-examine the government's witnesses; he also has no control over "off-the-record" remarks by the prosecutor which might convince an otherwise unpersuaded grand jury to return an indictment, even though the evidence might dictate that no indictment is warranted. No evidentiary structures of any kind impede the prosecutor. He can present rumors, innuendo, and irrelevant and prejudicial evidence with little fear that a court will later dismiss the indictment. With all the possibilities for abuse of the grand jury process, the ethical prosecutor has a self-imposed burden to determine how far he will go in the presentation of evidence.

Beigel and Davidson knew that their conduct might be observed more closely than usual because of the politically explosive nature of the investigation. They decided to use the grand jury purely as an investigating tool to subpoena only those witnesses who were not expected to cooperate or who would agree to testify only under the pressure which a grand jury's power allows it to impose lawfully. The witnesses who best fit this description were the police officers.

The reasons for calling potential defendants before a grand jury are bound inextricably to the paradoxes of the grand jury process. If the potential defendant testifies truthfully, he may possibly provide evidence against others as well as himself and thereby become the most valuable witness a prosecutor can have —an "accomplice" witness. If he denies any wrongdoing or lies, he can be indicted for perjury, a crime often easier to prove than the underlying substantive offense. An experienced prosecutor also knows that there is a better chance for conviction in a tough case when there is more than one count to present to the jury. Disagreement among jurors is often resolved by compromises of this sort because they do not realize that conviction on one count will carry generally as severe a penalty as conviction on all counts.

If a potential defendant asserts his Fifth Amendment privilege against self-incrimination, the options of the grand jury and prosecutor are more circumscribed, but nevertheless strikingly powerful. The witness can be given "use" immunity, a form of immunity which does not protect the witness from indictment yet compels him to testify. The government simply cannot use his actual testimony or the evidence derived from it against him. The witness can still be indicted if independent evidence is obtained. If the witness does not testify after his grant of immunity, he can be held in contempt and sent to jail until he testifies or until the grand jury is terminated. This act of rebellion can sometimes result in a prison term longer than he would have served if convicted. As courts and prosecutors are fond of saying, "The witness himself holds the key to the jail. He can use it; all he has to do is testify."

An additional wrinkle develops when a policeman or other public official is called before a grand jury. Many jurisdictions, including Chicago, require public employees to cooperate in an investigation or face dismissal. A police officer who is subpoenaed before a grand jury and asserts his Fifth Amendment privilege against self-incrimination can be dismissed from the force.

This traps the "guilty" in a situation from which there is no escape. If the officer admits his crime, he will be indicted. If he lies, he may be charged with perjury. If he refuses to testify, he may lose his job.

Provided they were careful in their selection of witnesses and adhered to procedure and ethics, Beigel and Davidson saw little danger in calling police officers before the grand jury. They also felt they had little choice. Some might even cooperate and provide evidence.

Although Beigel decided to issue subpoenas to all officers who had served under Thanasouras on the vice squad between 1967 and 1970, available evidence clearly implicated only two of them in acts of extortion or attempted extortion of Austin tavern owners. Among the subpoenaed were these two, Holder and Noro, and, of course, Thanasouras.

The Plan in Operation

The normal process for the serving of subpoenas is to use the United States Marshal. Mindful of the promise earlier given to Conlisk not to take significant steps without informing him, Beigel called Conlisk's aide, who had been designated as liaison to the Strike Force, and asked if subpoenas might be sent to the department rather than disrupt police operations by having marshals track down police officers on the job. Conlisk's aide agreed that if copies were delivered to the department he would ensure that the named police officers would appear voluntarily. Holder, who was no longer on the police force, would still have to be served directly.

Although one purpose in delivering the subpoenas in confidence to Conlisk's liaison officer was to avoid publicity, immediately after Beigel informed the department that grand jury proceedings were contemplated the *Chicago Sun-Times* ran a full-page story detailing the nature of the investigation and the Strike Force's plans to call Austin police officers to testify before a grand jury. The reporter was Art Petacque, who together with Robert Wiedrich of the *Tribune* had reported about the existence of a $100-a-month club in 1970. Petacque claimed the Justice Department had uncovered evidence of extortion against as many as thirty police officers and that indictments would be returned within a month. He wrote that the investigation centered on shakedowns of nightclub and tavern owners throughout the city, particularly in night-life and ghetto areas.[3] The following day Petacque reported that "Conlisk has been cooperating with . . . federal investigators and in many instances

3. *Chicago Sun-Times,* November 21, 1971.

IAD and until recently had the job of taking telephone and personal complaints from the public about police misconduct.[10] George Demet, a close
friend of Thanasouras, had been reassigned to the Albany Park District after
Thanasouras's demotion. Another officer was rumored to have been seen in the
company of hoodlums. Three other officers were now off vice entirely, detailed
to police communication at the downtown headquarters.

The flood of publicity and the rush of department reaction continued unabated. Thanasouras was further demoted to a "paper-shuffling job in the patrol
division."[11] When asked by a reporter to comment on his most recent transfer,
he said, "Right now I'm looking over some paperwork concerning crossing
guards."[12] A bar owner told a neighborhood newspaper in Austin that $2,500
was being collected from Austin taverns each week.[13] The *Chicago Daily News*
reported that federal agents were investigating ties between prostitutes and vice
officers (not true),[14] and the *Tribune* said that "$40,000 a month from a single
police district has been uncovered" (also not true).[15] Beigel only hoped that he
could unearth just some of what the press was reporting he already knew.

On December 13, 1971, Beigel stood in the reception area of the U.S.
Attorney's office and waited anxiously for the first witness, Mark C. Thanasouras. Thanasouras appeared with his attorney, William C. Martin, a former
Assistant State's Attorney who had participated in the trial of Richard Speck.
Thanasouras was a tall, ruggedly built man with a seemingly posed expression
of calm gracing his face. Martin motioned Thanasouras to follow Beigel and
Beigel led him into the grand jury room. Under the foreman's lead, Thanasouras took the oath and assumed his seat facing the twenty-five men and women
of the grand jury.

Thanasouras stated his name clearly. He then refused to answer all subsequent questions, including his place of residence and employment. After each
question Thanasouras looked toward his lap to read from a small white sheet
of paper which he had taken from his shirt pocket. All of his refusals were
based upon his right against self-incrimination under the Fifth Amendment.
Within ten minutes Thanasouras was excused, but subject to recall.

Beigel followed Thanasouras out of the grand jury room back to the reception area to see if any of the other witnesses had arrived. Several officers were

10. *Chicago Daily News,* December 29, 1971.
11. *Chicago Sun-Times,* December 7, 1971.
12. *Ibid.*
13. *The Austinite,* December 15, 1971.
14. *Chicago Daily News,* December 13, 1971.
15. *Chicago Tribune,* December 15, 1971.

waiting together with a man who nodded at Thanasouras as he walked out the door. This man then jauntily walked over to Beigel, held out his hand, and said, "I'm Jimmy Demopolous. What's your name?"

Demopolous, several FBI reports had stated, was a good friend of Thanasouras and of the police in general. He was short, tending toward pudginess, and combed his black hair straight back and close, reminding Beigel a little of George Wallace. He was in his middle thirties, but looked five to ten years younger, and said everything with a smile, his eyes darting over Beigel's shoulder into space. He spoke quickly, but aggressively, interrupting frequently to make a point with an outstretched hand and a mischievous glint in his eyes. He stood very close to Beigel, exuding camaraderie although this was their first meeting.

Demopolous told Beigel that he represented all officers who had been subpoenaed to testify that day, including Holder and Noro. He complained that Holder had been under a tremendous strain, having had difficulty finding and holding jobs, and asked if Beigel didn't agree that inasmuch as he had already been convicted once there was no point in putting him through the mill all over again. As for the others, Demopolous said, they, like Holder, would "stand on their rights."

Beigel looked suspiciously at Demopolous, and replied that although he could appreciate that Holder had been through quite a bit, it had nothing to do with the federal investigation and he, as well as the others, would have to appear before the grand jury. Demopolous jerked his head nervously as Beigel spoke. He became visibly agitated, and grabbed Beigel by the elbow. He said that if he insisted on calling his clients before the grand jury despite his knowledge that they would not answer any questions, Beigel would be abusing his professional responsibility and also would be in violation of the Canons of Ethics. "Take my word for it, Herb. It's improper. I know you wouldn't do the wrong thing." Beigel responded that the witnesses would simply have to appear. Demopolous let go of Beigel's elbow with a start, shook his head in almost mock disgust, turned around, and stalked back into the reception area, where he sat down next to Holder and whispered something in his ear.

Before Beigel called the first of Demopolous's clients he confirmed that there was no ethical prohibition against calling witnesses under these circumstances. Still, as Demopolous had promised, each witness refused to answer any questions other than his name—that is, all except one. Barry J. Miller had been subpoenaed because a tavern owner had told Becker that a cop whose name he thought was Miller had shaken him down for $50. The only Miller listed on the computer printouts provided by Conlisk was Barry J., and although Beigel did not know if he had served on the vice squad under Thanasouras, he was also subpoenaed. When Beigel met Miller in the reception area Demopolous pulled him aside to say that Miller, whom he represented, would also refuse to answer any questions. Beigel ignored Demopolous and led Miller into the grand jury room. Miller proceeded to answer every question asked of him. By the time he had finished it was clear that Miller never had anything to do with either Thanasouras's vice squad or a $100-a-month club. He had served in Austin only a few months after Thanasouras assumed command. What puzzled Beigel was why Demopolous had asserted that he represented Miller and that Miller would be uncooperative. It was to serve as a sign of later Demopolous' maneuvering.

Beigel had known going in to the grand jury that it was unlikely that anything substantive would develop immediately. Still, the total failure to obtain testimony from the vice officers was a setback. A few tavern owners who had been particularly troublesome during interviews by FBI agents were also subpoenaed. Although there was little real hope that they would testify truthfully, Beigel and Becker had agreed that some tavern owners should be called to maintain the credibility of the investigation on the street. Otherwise, the word would spread that the FBI could be ignored without consequence.

Beigel had hoped that one or two of the subpoenaed tavern owners would assert their Fifth Amendment privilege, thus enabling immunity to be given. Although Beigel had no great interest in catching tavern owners in a lie that would permit perjury indictments (since that would shift the focus of the investigation from the police to the "victims"), the threat of perjury together with the granting of immunity might cause reluctant witnesses to testify truthfully. In addition, an immunity proceeding would generate further publicity which, Beigel hoped, would lead the public to believe that the Justice Department was ready to fight lack of cooperation from witnesses.

Unfortunately, few of the tavern owners came to testify with legal counsel. They failed to realize, even after repeated warnings, that lying to the grand jury was improper and dangerous. Most of them were still in business and either openly sympathized with the police or feared the police more than the federal government. A few of the witnesses who were subpoenaed that first week did wilt a bit under the pressure and name other tavern owners they believed to be paying for protection, although continuing vehemently to deny paying themselves.

The nearly complete lack of response by the vice officers foreclosed the possibility of new leads from that quarter. Beigel had expected a few of the police witnesses to "take the Fifth," but not every vice squad member. Neither Holder nor Noro testified. Noro was represented by Demopolous and Holder had nothing to lose by remaining silent.

By not responding to Beigel's questions the other vice officers were in danger of being suspended or discharged from the force under Chicago Police Department Rule 51. This rule, as mentioned earlier, required all police officers to cooperate fully in any investigation and to answer all questions concerning their official duties. Beigel realized that if Demopolous had convinced him to forego his clients' appearances before the grand jury, he would have removed the risk of their suspension or discharge under Rule 51. Ironically, these officers could have answered most of Beigel's questions without much difficulty or fear. What only the Strike Force knew and what the officers could not possibly guess, especially after reading press accounts of the investigation, was the lack of sufficient indictable evidence possessed by the government at that time. To that extent the grand jury was a chimera and a fighter without a knockout punch.

The Aftermath

The grand jury had been distressed to watch public servants marching brazenly in and out of the grand jury room saying nothing like many of the mobsters portrayed in movies or seen on television during congressional hearings. The foreman of the grand jury asked Beigel what his next steps were and all he could respond was that the investigation would continue and more witnesses would be called. The grand jury was scheduled to last at least eighteen months and already many grand jurors were bored.

The consequences for the police officers who had invoked the Fifth Amendment were immediate and serious. Although Rule 51 theoretically subjected them to disciplinary action, grand jury proceedings are secret and, unless the officer admitted that he had refused to testify, it seemed technically impossible for anyone to lawfully find out what happened unless there was an indictment or a trial. Even then, if the officer decided to take the stand in his own defense, his failure to testify before the grand jury might remain undiscovered.[16]

It was possible that the IAD might interview the subpoenaed officers after their grand jury appearances. Even there, the officers could place the burden of proof on the department or the Corporation Counsel's office, which normally supervised disciplinary investigations of police officers in Rule 51 violations. Without access to the grand jury transcript the city might be powerless to act. Beigel decided to see whether anything could be done to avoid the

16. Taking the stand would preclude anyone from assuming that the officer had refused to testify before the grand jury. The assertion of the Fifth Amendment privilege was not admissible evidence.

prospect of repeated Rule 51 infractions without running afoul of the grand jury secrecy rule.

Demopolous, reacting prematurely to the spreading rumors that his clients had taken the Fifth, filed suit in federal court requesting an injunction against the Police Department. If granted, this injunction would prohibit the department from taking any disciplinary action against the officers who had appeared before the grand jury and refused to testify. Demopolous first appeared before Judge Julius Hoffman in connection with three of the officers, Noro, Demet, and Thanasouras (although he had not represented Thanasouras before the grand jury). Hoffman denied his request for a temporary restraining order and set the case to be heard in a full-scale hearing on December 27. Conlisk asked the Corporation Counsel's office to give an opinion on whether he could lawfully suspend any of the officers prior to that hearing. He did this even though he did not know, except by inference from Demopolous's suit, that the three witnesses had refused to answer questions or what questions Beigel had asked.

Despite Conlisk's request, nothing occurred before the 27th, when Demopolous appeared before Judge Richard B. Austin, to whom the case had been assigned. Demopolous asked Austin in loud, serious tones to enjoin the department from taking disciplinary action against any of the vice officers who had appeared before the grand jury, including, strangely, Barry J. Miller, who had testified fully.

Although the United States was not a party to this lawsuit, Judge Austin requested that Beigel appear. Austin asked Beigel when he arrived in court to recite those questions which the officers had refused to answer and their exact responses, if any.

Beigel began to read the transcripts. The newsmen present recorded furiously everything he said although all officers had recited the same eighteen-word refusal to every question after "State your name, please." The repeated litany droned on for thirty minutes. First the question, then, "I refuse to answer because I sincerely and honestly believe that my answer may tend to incriminate me."

Judge Austin had insisted on having this testimony read into the record because he had concluded that he could determine whether the department had a right to suspend an officer for asserting the privilege against self-incrimination only if the questions asked related to his official duties. By bringing this action Demopolous had made public what might have otherwise remained secret.

After the hearing was completed Judge Austin denied the request for an injunction, stating that, because all of the questions had focused squarely on matters related to the officers' performance of their official duties, the department was entitled under the Constitution and Rule 51 to initiate disciplinary proceedings. Austin commented: "They cannot come crying now. When they signed up for the job, that was the law. They took the job pursuant to it." Within a week of Austin's ruling Conlisk suspended the officers who had refused to testify.

Beigel had been puzzled by Austin's ruling that the grand jury testimony could be read in open court. He reviewed the Federal Rules of Criminal Procedure and the relevant cases. In short time he came across a little-invoked rule which authorizes the disclosure of grand jury testimony in any proceeding "preliminary" to a judicial proceeding. This meant that if the Corporation Counsel opened up an investigation each time an officer was subpoenaed before the grand jury, disclosure might be made to his office pursuant to this rule since his administrative investigation could be considered as preliminary to a judicial proceeding. On the basis of this reasoning and supported by further research, Beigel agreed to a request by the Corporation Counsel to initiate a procedure which, with the approval of a federal judge, would allow the Corporation Counsel to gain access to those questions related to official police duties which a witness refused to answer. This method of disclosure would work as long as the Corporation Counsel had actually instituted an investigation which could lead to suspension or discharge of the officer.

Judge Austin's order affirming the right of the city and the Police Department to take action against any officer who did not cooperate with the grand jury, along with the procedure which allowed disclosure of grand jury testimony under specific circumstances, practically guaranteed that, in the future, any police officer called before the grand jury would testify rather than risk being suspended or discharged. The die was cast. A police officer appearing before the grand jury found himself in a terrible quandry if he had anything to hide.[17]

Conlisk was clearly worried. But instead of opening a legitimate full-scale investigation of his own, he merely ordered several demotions, transfers, and suspensions of the officers who had refused to testify before the grand jury. On December 30 he changed heads of the division of which the IAD is a part; demoted the commander of the Town Hall District, which had been rumored

17. What many officers failed to recognize was that there was a strong legal argument that their testimony could not be used against them, including any leads developed from their answers. No officer or attorney ever argued this point during the investigation. (For a detailed discussion of the applicable legal principles, see Herbert Beigel, "The Federal Investigation of Police Corruption," *Northwestern Journal of Criminal Law,* June 1974).

inaccurately to be an immediate target of the Strike Force; and kicked upstairs the commander of the Eighteenth, a district known for its night life and singles bars and long thought to be a hotbed of corruption. Conlisk said, about these changes, "The dynamic society in which we live today necessitates ensuring the continuing viability of the department. It [the changes] further strengthens the command of the Chicago Police Department."[18]

The demotions and transfers were futile efforts. The problems were not of Conlisk's making. The crux of these problems lay in the lack of an independent managerial class in the police hierarchy and the overall civil service concept of police selection and promotion which pervades law enforcement everywhere.

In a system in which supervisory personnel are promoted solely from the ranks a true managerial class never emerges. This inbred leadership fosters in the command structure attitudes which are closely allied with those of the lowest-ranking patrolman on the street. The commonality of experience tends to prevent the controls, checks, and restraints on power which are necessary if abuses are to be prevented.

The civil service system also inhibits change. Because it is supposed to be a citadel of fairness, hearings must be held and evidence of malfeasance presented before disciplinary action is taken. The offense must be extremely serious before anything more than a slap on the wrist is given. The more serious the complaint, the less likely it is to be proved or the less willing someone may be to testify if it means exposing others.[19]

Superintendent Conlisk was a product of these traditions. He had spent his life as a police officer, as had his father before him. He must have been influenced by what was going on around him. If the public knew that it was easy to fix a traffic ticket and was not interested in doing anything about it, then Conlisk may have also felt the same way. If there was a $100-a-month club in the district where he served as a patrolman, he would have had to engage in some strained rationalizations to maintain his ideals about police work. As a career police officer trying to move ahead and to perform in accord with what was expected, both his desire and ability to lobby for meaningful reform had to have been affected.

The changes which Conlisk made two days before the start of 1972 were

18. *Chicago Sun-Times,* December 31, 1971.

19. Other views of the influence of civil service can be found in James F. Ahern, *Police in Trouble* (New York: Hawthorne, 1971), pp. 208–209. The Knapp Commission thought that the superintendent of police in New York did not even make much use of the few options for demotion and transfer open to him. Knapp Commission Report (1972), pp. 219–220. See also Ramsey Clark, *Crime in America* (New York: Simon & Schuster, 1970), pp. 146–150, for some observations on the stagnant leadership of police forces.

symptomatic of the malaise which had gripped the Chicago Police Department —transfers and demotions from command but not from rank were reactions, not actions. Simply because an old district commander was replaced did not mean that methods and procedures would be altered. It was likely that the new commander had been reared in the same traditions as the old. These actions by Conlisk could not have a significant effect on the real problem now facing the department by virtue of the federal investigation—the exposure of widespread corruption in the law enforcement system of the second-largest city in the United States.

The Struggle Begins Again

After the grand jury proceedings were under way there was a momentary spurt of activity by the FBI. Agents who were assigned originally to Becker's special team, but who had never done any work, reappeared suddenly, ready to accept assignments to interview tavern owners. Nevertheless, the Strike Force lawyers could not shake the gnawing feeling that this renewed FBI enthusiasm might be shortlived. This led them to abandon, for the moment, the previously planned canvassing of every Austin tavern and to concentrate on those tavern owners who they suspected had paid the police for protection. This revised approach called for developing the evidence necessary for a few quick indictments which, in turn, might encourage more people, including honest police officers, to come forward with new evidence. In conjunction with interviewing tavern owners it was also necessary to continue the grand jury hearings to give Inserra the feeling that positive action was continuing and to keep the public interested in the investigation through the publicity the grand jury sessions generated.

This publicity gave the investigation strength and credibility. Corruption began to be exposed by the press. A former Chicago policeman told the *Sun-Times* how lawyers and policemen routinely schemed to fix tickets in Chicago Traffic Court through faulty testimony.[20] In an unrelated matter Conlisk suspended a captain following an investigation of alleged payoffs to police from operators of illegal cabs (the FBI had been secreting this information in its files for some time). The newspapers also reported that cops paid politicians to achieve quick promotions and upgrades in rank. Finally, the *Chicago Tribune* claimed that a former vice coordinator in a south side district had once been informed by the local alderman that he wanted his share of all

20. *Chicago Sun-Times,* February 5, 1972.

payoffs taken in.[21] The FBI earlier had received information similar to this when a bar owner had alleged that an alderman was scheming with a distributor of concession machines to extract payoffs from tavern owners in exchange for permitting "after-hours" operations and the granting of licenses to stay open to 4 A.M.

As more and more policemen were called to the grand jury, tavern owners began reluctantly to reveal what had been happening. This increased rate of success in getting tavern owners to talk, however, was offset by Inserra's repeated requests to save the agents' time and simply call all witnesses before the grand jury. But for Beigel there was simply no substitute for hard work by agents on the street. Unfortunately, the agents, with the exception of Becker, refused to devote the time necessary for effective investigation.

At the end of January there were still no indictments. Agents assigned to interview tavern owners often went about their tasks in odd ways. Some looked for owners early in the morning, when it was likely that the taverns would be closed. Others interviewed witnesses as if they were informants and failed to pay attention to important details. One agent, although assigned to one owner, decided to interview another across the street when he found his subject not at the bar. He did not know that this owner had been interviewed an hour before. His interview, which was written up before the duplication was discovered, revealed a plethora of contradictory statements which, if the tavern owner had testified, would not exactly have done wonders for his credibility.

Inaccurate newspaper stories continued. Beigel and Davidson believed that only the FBI could be the source of the leaks. Stories appeared about an agent who had talked to an informant in another district which the Strike Force had not even thought about investigating. Another story claimed that the probe had expanded into a detailed investigation of the relationshp between crooked cops and crooked lawyers. In reality, the Strike Force had evidence about only one lawyer whose card an Austin vice squad officer had passed out to those he arrested.

The attorneys were also hit with a steady barrage of statements from FBI personnel designed to pressure them into making these reports come true by returning indictments. In every meeting Inserra emphasized the importance of returning indictments immediately. Without them, he said, Washington would refuse to release further agent manpower.

The investigation lurched like a wounded animal. The only real encouragement came from the almost accidental discovery of cooperative witnesses. The

21. *Chicago Tribune,* January 4, 1972.

mere presence of the FBI in the Austin District caused tavern owners to come forward. One was an immigrant from Yugoslavia who told an agent, for whom he had become an informant on what was happening in the Chicago Slavic community, that he had been recently shaken down by a lieutenant and a sergeant.

In the past this information would have been considered irrelevant to the subject matter of the contact, namely, the possibility of violent demonstrations by Yugoslavs. Even if reported, it would have, in all probability, been buried away in FBI files. Beigel, however, had prepared for this when he realized how secretive the Bureau could be and that agents often picked up stray information from informants and other contacts. With Becker's help he was able to persuade Inserra to send a memo to other squad chiefs requesting that they alert their agents to forward any information about police corruption to C-1. The agent had already interviewed the Yugoslav when he heard of Inserra's request, but he immediately forwarded a copy of his "302" to Becker. The shakedown was described in three lines at the bottom of page three of a five-page interview. But it was there.

Another tavern owner, never interviewed by the FBI although he had operated one of the better-known police hangouts in Austin, read the newspaper stories and called the FBI. Louis King said that his bar, The Scene, had been subject to harassment ever since he had put in an application for a license to stay open until 4 A.M. Because of the payoffs he had to make he finally closed his business in disgust. After several interviews he agreed to tell his whole story.

Thus the investigation managed to stay alive. Indictments had to be returned shortly, however, if the investigation was to continue and the investigators so desperately required were to be made available. It had been nearly two years since Featherstone had decided to see if evidence could be found of a $100-a-month club. The Strike Force was still searching.

Yet the police were clearly frightened. Conlisk was under increasing pressure. The department was rapidly descending into chaos; morale was sinking. Demotions and transfers occurred almost weekly, accompanied by front-page stories. Even if indictments which could be returned did not involve the $100-a-month club, they might serve as a breakthrough. In Chicago, as in most other cities, it was not every day that police officers were indicted.

Chapter 3

The First Indictments

Q. Did you ever accept any money from any employee or agent of a tavern or business while in the performance of your duties as a Chicago police officer?
A. Not that I can ever recall.
Q. As a Chicago police officer, have you ever at any time accepted any money from anyone to overlook a duty that you had as a Chicago police officer?
A. Did I—oh, boy, 20 years. Now we are going back 20 years. Did I ever? Not that I can recall.

—Excerpt from the grand jury
testimony of Robert Devitt

Even with the grand jury proceedings and FBI involvement shakedowns were still occurring with depressing frequency in Austin. The extortion of the Yugoslav tavern owner was one example. Wholesale extortion from a chain of liquor stores was another. Tavern owners were harassed frequently. One had placed a coat rack in front of a window and was arrested for violation of Chicago's open-view ordinance which requires that the entire bar must be visible from the street. Another owner was cleaning up after hours while a few friends kept him company. He was busted for keeping his tavern open after the legal closing time. With dismaying regularity cops would routinely enter a tavern and check the IDs of all customers, making people wary of coming back.

The brashness of the police in ignoring the federal investigation made Beigel determined to continue the probe and return indictments. If more cooperation from the FBI could be obtained, he intended to expand the investigation to other districts. If only a small amount of what the many old FBI and IRS

49

reports contained was true, the extent of police corruption was staggering, extending even to other political institutions with which the police dealt.

The problem, of course, was to return indictments. By February enough evidence had been obtained for possibly eight or nine, most of these against low-level vice officers who had collected money from tavern owners. The Strike Force still had been unable to develop evidence against officers in higher levels of command. None of the cops who had taken the Fifth Amendment during the December grand jury had come forward to cooperate. Furthermore, as the months rolled by, fewer officers took the Fifth for fear of being suspended or discharged under Rule 51. Those who testified steadfastly denied ever taking any money or knowing anyone who did. The police had closed ranks in a conspiracy of silence and evasion.

Beigel and Davidson were also worried about the strength of the evidence. The worst thing that could possibly happen would be to return indictments that would not lead to convictions. In 1968, after the Democratic Convention, Thomas Foran and his staff of assistant U.S. Attorneys had developed several cases of police brutality. Not one officer was convicted.[1] If this happened now, the investigation not only would be stopped dead, but its critics might claim that the inquiry had been politically motivated.

The weakness of the proposed cases was that in each situation an officer would be charged with extorting money from one or possibly two tavern owners on only one or two occasions. The tavern owners had paid money to avoid arrest for liquor law violations, but there was little or no independent corroboration of their testimony. At trial, the chances of conviction would depend solely on whom the jury chose to believe. Because there had never been a conviction of a police officer in the United States District Court in Chicago for wrongdoing which he had committed during the course of official duties, the attorneys were not optimistic about their chances for many convictions.

The Strike Force attorneys had two choices, either return indictments now and take their chances, or wait in the hope that stronger evidence would be developed. Any more delay, however, could be disastrous. The FBI and Beigel's superiors in Washington were becoming anxious. The longer the investigation continued without the return of indictments, the more likely it was that people would believe that it had been engineered as a political scheme to embarrass Mayor Daley. In light of these pressures and with the continuation of the investigation at stake, the attorneys had to find out if juries would convict.

1. 1975 reports emanating from congressional hearings indicated that Hoover had directed the Chicago FBI office to find evidence that would exonerate the accused police.

The only officer against whom there was a strong case was David Holder. Unlike other officers who shook down tavern owners, Holder did not go out of his way to be nice to the victims. He spent little time chatting with the owner and made few promises about the valuable services the police could provide for a small monthly fee. At the least sign of resistance, he would emphasize what would happen if the bar owner did not pay. What he said to Mahaffey was repeated to almost every other bar owner he asked for money.

Holder was a big man, well over six feet tall, broad-shouldered and hulking. He carried himself like a street fighter. His hair was cut short without sideburns or waves, almost in a crew cut. He wore ill-fitting plain suits, tight in the waist and loose everywhere else. When he smiled, the spaces in his teeth made even a show of friendliness seem ominous. He had been an officer for thirteen years and a vice cop for four before the IID investigation ended his career. He looked as if he had seen everything.

Holder had been Thanasouras's vice coordinator, but judging from the appearance of the two men and their backgrounds, one would doubt they had much in common. Whereas the smooth Thanasouras, with the aid of political friends, had risen quickly through the ranks, Holder had no special connections. While Thanasouras was rumored to be something of a swinger and was often seen partying in Greek Town at belly dance restaurants, no one ever recalled seeing Holder except in his role as a vice cop. When Holder was off duty, he acted as if he were still at work. Unlike other cops, he made shakedowns when he was presumably off duty.

Holder was married and had a son who had just turned twenty and had recently joined the Police Department. He liked to talk about the possibility that his son would some day join the FBI. Nothing upset Holder more about his state court conviction and resignation than the possibility that his disgrace would prevent his son from becoming an FBI agent.

Because Holder had been Thanasouras's vice coordinator and because his shakedown activities were so blatant, Beigel believed that if anyone had funneled money to Thanasouras, it was Holder. Since Holder had been disgraced by the local investigation and might want a chance to redeem himself, Beigel thought it might be worthwhile to talk informally to him before indictment to see if he could be persuaded to testify. Holder's cooperation might lead to a breakthrough and the gathering of evidence against officers higher in rank than patrolman. If he cooperated, Beigel would recommend immunity.

During the second week of February Becker met Holder outside his house in the northern section of Austin, a predominantly white neighborhood that had resisted the racial changes to the south and east. Becker met with Holder in his FBI car and asked him if he would be willing to talk with Beigel. Becker told Holder that he had a right to have Demopolous present. Holder shook his head. "He framed me good on the state charge; what do I need him for now." Becker asked Holder what he meant, but Holder did not want to elaborate, saying only that he had not been warned that a heavy fine might be imposed.

Holder then rambled on about his fear that "the hillbilly tavern owners are out to get me" and that "now that I'm off the force, I'm an easy mark." Holder also vowed that he was "never going to rot another day in jail because I almost got killed during the few days I spent at Cook County Jail." As Becker continued to press him, Holder softened. He said that he would meet with Beigel as long as Becker would tell no one. He did not want the bar owners to think him weak for talking to a prosecutor.

Three days before the scheduled meeting Beigel was at the Strike Force office working late when the telephone rang. A man whispered that he had information to give about police corruption. He would not say more on the telephone, except that he was a police officer and would come to a private meeting. Beigel suggested his office on Sunday night, the day before the meeting with Holder, and assured him no one else would be present.

On Sunday night at nine o'clock Beigel met the anonymous caller in the lobby of the Federal Building. He was of medium height, stocky, and gray-haired. On the elevator he fidgeted nervously, tugging at his collar as he stared at the elevator door in silence.

In Beigel's office James Barley[2] took a chair and lit a cigarette. He began to talk slowly and quietly. He had been a cop for twenty-three years. His father had been a factory worker with little income but knew, through neighborhood clubs, the committeeman and alderman of his ward. When he returned from the service in 1949 with little money and no job, his father's offer to get him on the police force seemed interesting. The several cops who lived in his neighborhood were treated with respect and appeared to have a relatively easy life.

Barley became a beat patrolman and walked the streets for five years. During that time he learned that success as a police officer went hand in glove with keeping quiet about what went on, whether it was watching other officers pick up cases of liquor from tavern owners for the commander's stock or hearing about shakedowns of teenage burglars for their loot in exchange for not making arrests. When he first learned of these activities, he naively asked his sergeant why these things happened. The sergeant told him this was the

2. This officer's name has been changed.

way it had always been and if he kept quiet and played by the rules he would get his share.

During his first five years Barley was happy just to walk his beat, accept a few gratuities from some of the businessmen he knew, and have his lunches free at a neighborhood diner. When he switched to patrol car, his partner initially impressed him as a straightforward and honest cop. At their first auto accident investigation he saw his partner take one of the drivers over to the opposite corner under a street light. He could not hear the conversation, but he saw that it was very animated. Then something which looked like money was passed to the officer by the driver. After Barley had interviewed the other driver and returned to the squad car, his partner told him that they would write it up charging the driver Barley had interviewed with running a stop sign. Barley said that his driver had clearly been at the intersection first and that he claimed to have come to a complete stop before proceeding. His partner took a bill out of his pocket. "Don't be a sucker, Jim, there's ten bucks in it for you." Barley took the ten dollars.

From then on Barley got used to the idea that a cop was pretty much entitled to what he could get. No one sat around and theorized why payoffs and shakedowns were okay, but it was clear to him that everyone accepted the idea the police deserved extra money and that the public was happy to pay it. Those cops who wouldn't take money or accept favors were allowed to go their own way as long as they kept quiet. If not every officer took money, few ever dared break the conspiracy of silence.

Barley had never been a vice officer. He had been offered that position ten years earlier and had turned it down. He figured he was doing all right as it was and that vice was a dirty business, involving shakedowns of a size with which he was afraid to become involved. Barley said that he was happy with "the couple of grand in extra money" which he made every year from small shakedowns, favors, and gratuities.

Barley, now on his fifth cigarette, puffed nervously. "I read about your investigation in the papers and I figured that somebody ought to tell you what really goes on in day-to-day stuff. Sure, tavern shakedowns are big and a lot of money changes hands. But a small fry like me took in thousands over the years and I didn't have to even try very hard for it."

Barley was now the secretary at the ———District. It was the softest job in the department and the center of payoffs within the district. If any cop wanted a favor, such as a day off, a new assignment, or a special shift, the secretary was the man who handled it. It cost money to the cop who wanted the favor, "a few bucks here, a few bucks there." In the end, the secretary did pretty well and the commander relied upon him. It was a job of discretion.

Beigel asked Barley if he had any personal knowledge of a $100-a-month club or payoffs from organized crime. Barley said he knew pretty well that those things went on and who was involved, but did not want to get into specifics. "If I did, and it came out, the best I could hope for is that I'd be drummed out of the force. I got five kids. I need my pension. It wouldn't be worth it."

Beigel explained that if no one came forward corruption would never be eliminated. Barley replied, "Look, I feel a little guilty about the money I took. But that's all. Sure, I'd like to see the payoffs end. But that's not going to happen in the few years I got left on the force. I just didn't want you guys to think that there aren't any of us who realize what we're doing."

Barley looked at his watch and said, "It's ten-thirty. I told my wife I was going out for a drink with a buddy. She's going to be wondering where I am." Barley got up, put on his coat, and left.

Beigel stayed in his office for an hour after Barley left trying to understand what made an essentially honest man so passively accept the way things were. He thought about how the development of a corrupt attitude began in what a cop experienced on the street. He remembered the three nights he had once spent with a police officer on patrol in another city, when he learned law enforcement is only one phase of police work. Indeed, the officer had called himself a "keeper of the peace." "My job," he said, "is to make sure people keep their heads on and stay out of trouble. If I stop things before they get a chance to start, then I'm getting somewhere. Like keeping kids from hanging out on corners. When you've done this as long as I have, you learn that a guy with nothing to do is getting ready for trouble."

All cops are concerned with power and control. They want to master every situation. This attitude leads to actions which often go far beyond what is necessary to the investigation of crime. The "keeper of the peace" idea is so much a part of the police officer's self-image that it is understandable why he often resists the controls and checks of outsiders—the courts, other law enforcement agencies, or other governmental institutions. What the patrol officer Beigel accompanied did with youths on street corners and warring spouses would not necessarily be sanctioned by the law or by the courts which interpret the application of constitutional rights. The cop may feel isolated and unsupported from the very beginning of his career. Soon he may conclude that he is above the law.

Beigel had Barley on his mind the next morning when Holder walked in the door with Becker. Like Barley, Holder was initially reluctant to talk about the corrupt activities he had witnessed in the Police Department. After Beigel explained that this was a strictly off-the-record conversation, Holder began to speak quickly, brokenly, and bitterly about the treatment he had received from the department during the investigation which had led to his earlier indictment. He ranted and raved against his fellow vice officers, with the exception of Noro, who he claimed had received a bum rap and was an honest cop. He complained that Thanasouras and Demopolous had set him up. Although he made a point of not denying that he had been involved in collections from tavern owners in Austin, he stated repeatedly that his role was peripheral and that unnamed others had gone uncaught and were the real masterminds.

Beigel told Holder that, of all the cops being investigated, the Strike Force had the most evidence against him. He was in deep trouble and the result would be a penalty not nearly as light as the one he had received two years before.

Holder said there was nothing more anyone could do to him and that he didn't "give a damn" about a bunch of hillbillies. Collections from tavern owners were "nickel and dime" activity. Tavern owners wanted to pay. "Shit, they get favors, they don't get arrested, and they keep their licenses. You fellows should be spending time looking into the real corruption with narcotics and hoods rather than wasting time on tavern payoffs."

Beigel told Holder that the only witnesses who would talk were tavern owners and that if Holder knew anything which would lead to the cooperation of dope peddlers, bookies, and organized crime figures, he should let him in on it. Holder shrugged and said that he didn't understand why the "Feds" were picking on him.

Beigel could see that his hard approach was not working. He spent the next hour trying to convey to Holder some measure of sympathy for his ruined career. Holder gradually became friendlier and talked freely about his life as a cop and how easy it was to make an extra buck. However, he still would not be specific. He said he would like to help, but if he did, he'd soon be found dead in an alley somewhere.

Beigel did not believe Holder's fear was genuine. After all, he had never risen above the rank of sergeant and probably would have little personal knowledge about the activities of higher-ranking officers. What surprised Beigel, however, was Holder's reluctance to talk even about the vice officers with whom he served and Thanasouras. Perhaps it was due to the same conspiracy of silence Barley had alluded to the night before.

It was obvious they were getting nowhere. In a last-ditch effort to get Holder to be more cooperative, Beigel set forth the specific evidence the government had collected against him. He told Holder that his only chance was to give detailed and truthful testimony against those police officers with whom he had worked, including Thanasouras.

Holder said that he had spent so long with the Chicago Police Department and its lawyers it was laughable to think that anybody's word meant anything. He had first believed the lawyers at the State's Attorney's office were honest; but too many cases had been fixed and too many cops had changed their testimony easily. Crooks had always told him you could rely on the Justice Department to keep its word, but still, he said, "You never know."

Beigel tried to convince Holder that it would be better to cooperate than to be indicted on possibly six or seven counts of extortion under the Hobbs Act. The penalties for conviction were considerably more severe than what he had faced in state court for solicitation of a bribe. It was also possible that other evidence might be found against him. If no deal was made now, it might never again be possible.

Holder listened, occasionally interrupting with "I know all about that. I'm no dummy, you know." Finally he said that although he might be willing to take his chances that Beigel would deal fairly with him, there was nothing the government could do which would sufficiently assure him and his family that they would not be maimed or murdered if he talked. There was no way Beigel could guarantee Holder's safety if he cooperated and testified even though, as with all witnesses who testify for the government, all possible steps are taken to protect them. This protection can range from bodyguards to a complete relocation of the witness and his family, including a change of name, job, and Social Security number.

The "limited" guarantees available to Holder did not convince him to change his mind. He kept pointing out how this or that person who had testified had been disposed of either before or after the trial. Beigel could not really disagree with him. Beigel knew, as did many others, that witnesses had been murdered despite use of the most sophisticated methods of protection available, even though in many cases the witnesses had failed to carry out the protectors' instructions.

By 3 P.M. Holder was simply repeating that he wished the Strike Force investigation well but it would have to do without him. All he would say was, "You keep looking and you'll find it with or without my help. It's all there for anybody to find who looks for it." Looking for corruption was one thing, Beigel said, but obtaining the cooperation of witnesses was another. Holder replied, "Mr. Beigel, you really have me by the balls, but I'd rather not be dead."

The next day Demopolous telephoned Beigel. He said Holder had told him about the meeting and he was troubled that Beigel had not asked him if he wished to be present. Beigel apologized, explaining that Holder insisted that he was no longer represented by Demopolous. Demopolous replied, "You know that's ridiculous, Herb. I represented every vice officer before the grand jury and I still do. In the future I would appreciate being accorded the courtesy one in my position is entitled to."

If Demopolous did represent all vice officers, he had an enormous conflict of interest. If there really was a $100-a-month club and if several of the vice officers he represented were involved, it would mean that each had information to give about the other. By advising all to take the Fifth in the grand jury Demopolous was caught squarely in the middle of a conflict since his representation of one could affect his advice to another. He also claimed to represent Thanasouras, against whom several of his other clients, including Holder, might offer evidence. Under these circumstances his representation of the vice officers might be interpreted as an attempt to insulate Thanasouras from adverse testimony at the expense of his other clients.

Beigel explained all this to Demopolous, concluding, "Frankly, Jimmy, you are buying yourself a lot of trouble. Holder himself is suspicious of your relationship with Thanasouras and he was not exactly happy about your representation of him on the state charge. He says it was a frameup with him being the scapegoat."

Demopolous was not convinced, replying sharply, "You take care of your business and I'll take care of mine."

Beigel tried to mollify Demopolous. As long as Demopolous continued to represent Holder, it would be difficult for Holder to decide to cooperate. He told Demopolous that he appreciated his right to advise his clients as he thought best but was only trying to help him avoid trouble. Beigel agreed to forewarn Demopolous if any of his clients came to talk to Beigel.

Shortly after Demopolous's phone call Holder telephoned. He said that Demopolous had told him to keep his mouth shut. He really wanted to cooperate but was afraid that something would happen to him or his family. It sounded like a copout to Beigel. There was no need to call him to repeat what he had already said. In the future, Beigel told Holder, he should have Demopolous convey his messages. Holder was silent for a moment and then said, "I understand." Beigel never spoke with him again.

Soon after this incident Beigel received a phone call from another police officer, Robert Devitt. Lieutenant Devitt had served in the Austin District, as a sergeant, until 1968. During the FBI's canvass of the Austin taverns two owners had stated that Devitt had extorted money from them. These extortions had occurred in 1964 and 1965 and were now unprosecutable because of the five-year statute of limitations under the Hobbs Act. Without evidence of more recent wrongdoing Devitt could not be brought to trial.

Beigel had subpoenaed Devitt to the grand jury to shed some light on what was going on in Austin during the time he was working there.

On the telephone Devitt was almost too polite. He understood he had been subpoenaed and, of course, would be happy to appear but, "What's this all about anyway? I've been a cop for twenty years and I was never mixed up with shakedowns of tavern owners." Beigel told Devitt he would be happy to discuss the matter further with his attorney. Devitt replied that he did not need an attorney. If he had to, he would come to testify alone.

On the day he was to testify Devitt came, unaccompanied, in uniform, with his sidearm hanging at his belt. Beigel advised him of his rights and told him he was a potential defendant. Devitt still did not request to meet with an attorney.

Beigel asked Devitt, as he had asked all officers who had testified before him, if he had ever taken money from any person in connection with his duties as a Chicago Police Officer. He also asked Devitt about certain taverns, including those where the FBI had not uncovered payoffs but suspected them. Beigel followed this procedure with any suspected officer so that the officer would not necessarily know who had talked to the government.

It was difficult to pin Devitt down. Yet his testimony provided a good example of how a witness can be too careful in his responses, a maneuver which can destroy credibility rather than enhance it.[3]

Q. Do you ever recall making an arrest at Al's and Don's Parkside Tavern for failure to report a fight which had occurred at the tavern in the year 1966 or 1967?

A. That is so far back. I can't remember what happened last year, Mr. Beigel. You are asking me about things that happened five, six years ago. I can't—I don't even remember the streets. I haven't even been out there. Five or six years ago—

Q. So you don't recall that arrest?

A. I don't recall it, no. I can't remember things that happened last week. We are talking about things that happened six and seven years ago, you know. I mean—. . . .

3. The following are verbatim excerpts from Devitt's grand jury testimony.

Q. Do you know an individual by the name of Thomas McCauley[4] who is associated with that tavern?

A. The name doesn't strike me.

Q. Did you ever accept any money from Thomas McCauley?

A. I don't recall even the man. How do I accept any money from him?

Q. Did you ever accept any money at all from anyone at all associated with the tavern located at 5208 West Chicago Avenue?

A. Not to my knowledge. . . .

Q. Let me ask you this again, Lieutenant Devitt. While assigned to the 15th District of the Chicago Police Department, did you ever receive money from any person for any reason in connection with your position as a Chicago police officer?

A. Well, that is a real broad, broad question, isn't it? Did you ever receive —will you please try that again?

Mr. Beigel: Will you read the question, please.

(Question read)

A. (the witness) There is no way you could answer that. It is too general a question. That is too general a question.

Q. (Beigel) Other than your salary?

A. Well, I had special employment at the White Castle—

Q. The question, if you recall, was only in connection with your position as a Chicago Police Department officer.

A. I can't recall.

Q. Did you ever accept any money from any tavern owner while assigned to the Austin District?

A. Ever accept any money from a tavern owner while assigned—that is so far back I can't remember at all, and that is the God's truth. I can't remember.

Q. You can't remember?

A. No.

Q. Whether you ever took a bribe or not?

A. A bribe?

Q. Yes.

A. For what? To do what?

Q. For anything.

A. To overlook my official duty?

Q. That is correct.

A. Never took a bribe to overlook my official duty. I was never in a position.

4. This was a witness who had told the FBI about a payoff.

In my position I didn't have—I wasn't in a position where I could, let's say, determine whether or not somebody was or wasn't under arrest. Well, that is not exactly right. What I am trying to say is that I never had final decision on any tavern case in the district.

Q. So is your answer to the question no?

A. My answer to the question has got to be what would anybody give me any money for?

Q. Is it yes or no?

A. It would have to be not to my knowledge. I can't recall taking any money from anybody.

Q. Have you ever taken any money from any employee of any tavern in the Austin District?

A. I can't recall ever taking any money from anybody either—boy! . . . .

Q. As a Chicago police officer, have you ever at any time accepted any money from anyone to overlook a duty that you had as a Chicago police officer?

A. Did I—oh, boy, 20 years. Now we are going back 20 years. Did I ever? Not that I can recall.

Devitt's actions in the grand jury surprised Beigel. The other cops had testified matter-of-factly and calmly with the studied pose of respect, integrity, and righteousness that typically characterizes police testimony in court. Devitt's behavior had been threatening; he had even screamed at times. The jurors were shaken by his departure from what they expected of a police officer.

Devitt's startling abandonment of the traditional police method of testifying led Beigel to consider again whether there was some way in which Devitt could be held accountable for the shakedowns, despite the statute of limitations. The answer lay in the crime of perjury.

The crime of perjury occurs when the witness falsely testifies. It makes no difference that he is being questioned about a crime committed far in the past, the prosecution of which is barred by the statute of limitations. If Devitt either had asserted his Fifth Amendment privilege or had admitted taking money from tavern owners, he could not have been indicted at all. But he lied. Even his refusal to deny categorically that he had ever taken money did not preclude a perjury charge if the government could prove, on the basis of the circumstances surrounding the shakedowns, that he must have remembered and therefore was lying when he claimed he did not.

When the grand jurors met to vote on whether Robert Devitt should be indicted for perjury, his manner of testifying badly damaged the credibility of his testimony. That would turn out to be very unusual. In the trials that were to follow the government lawyers repeatedly faced their greatest obstacle when they had to convince the jury that the relaxed, confident, smooth, and articulate testimony of a police officer did not mean that he was telling the truth.

The First Indictments

By the second week of March twenty-nine present and former police officers had appeared before the grand jury. Fourteen had refused to testify. Thirteen of the fourteen had been suspended by Conlisk and the fourteenth had resigned. Eight of the twenty-nine were named in indictments that Beigel had prepared to submit to the grand jury. Only two of the fourteen who had refused to testify were in this group, Holder and Demet. The government did not have sufficient evidence of wrongdoing against the others to warrant indictment.

On March 30, 1972, the grand jury returned nine indictments, charging eight officers with extortion, perjury, and attempted extortion. It was the largest number of police officers indicted at one time since 1960, when eight policeman were charged in connection with burglaries in the Summerdale District.

Once the indictments were announced, they were subjected to a certain amount of political maneuvering. The United States Attorney, James R. Thompson,[5] went out of his way to avoid being critical of the department. He told reporters that he had met with Mayor Daley "to assure him that this is not an indictment of the Chicago Police Department, but of the individual officers who have gone beyond their duties and become outlaws."[6]

Conlisk also issued a statement saying that:

Three of the eight indicted officers were suspended previously and charges are on file with the Chicago Police Board seeking their dismissal from the department.

Until today, the department had no information of misconduct regarding the five other officers. As a result of these indictments, I have ordered the immediate suspension of these five officers, and charges will be filed with the police board seeking their dismissal.

One of the men was a former police officer who resigned from the department in 1970 while charges were pending seeking his dismissal. He was convicted in the Circuit Court of Cook County on evidence obtained by the department.

No one deplores more than I the violation of a public trust. The police department

5. In November 1971 Thompson, then First Assistant, had replaced Bauer, who was named a federal district court judge.
6. *Chicago Today,* March 30, 1972.

has cooperated fully with federal authorities in this and other investigations. The department has sought to root out any misconduct by its personnel. Nothing has a higher priority. We shall continue to do so.[7]

Who were these indicted officers, the men who were finally exposed to public scrutiny after more than two years of government investigation? Not the ringleaders of massive corruption schemes, nor even commanders who knew about the shakedowns and tolerated them; they were the rank and file who had used their position to take money from both willing and unwilling businessmen.

1. Sergeant George Demet, suspended for taking the Fifth in December 1971, was charged with extorting $50 a month from Louis King, the owner of The Scene, in exchange for not ticketing the cars of customers and not engaging in general harassment.
2. David Holder was charged with extorting $25 a week from the owners of Lynch's Lounge from 1966 to 1969; $100 from the licensee of Up Your Alley in December 1969; $100 a month from the owners of a bowling alley; and attempting to extort money from the owners of a tavern known as the Club Cabana.
3. Patrolmen James Gartner and Kenneth DePaola, former vice officers under Thanasouras, were charged with extorting $300 in July 1967 from another King tavern known as the Questionmark.
4. Patrolman Frank Greenwich, assigned to the Vice Control Division as a license investigator, was charged with extorting $500 in August 1967 for an after-hours license and later more money from Louis King in connection with the operation of The Scene. He was also charged with perjury.
5. Lieutenant Robert Devitt was charged with perjury.
6. Lieutenant Frank J. Gill was charged with extorting $300 from the owners of Chicago-Oak Liquors in July 1971, and with perjury.
7. Patrolman James Pacente, former vice coordinator of the Austin District under Victor Vrdolyak, was charged with extorting $200 from the owners of Chicago-Oak Liquors in connection with their license application, and with perjury.
8. Patrolman Walter Moore, a black vice officer in Austin, one of the few who had not been transferred after Thanasouras's demotion, was charged with attempted extortion from two black tavern owners in Austin in July and October 1971 of amounts ranging from $50 a month to $1,000.

7. *Ibid.*

These indictments were at best a grab bag, a motley conglomeration of charges following fourteen months of active investigation. Not even Noro was indicted,[8] and one case involved only attempted extortion. Nevertheless, they were still indictments and the press began a stream of publicity that was to continue unabated for the rest of the year.

8. The witnesses against Noro could not say that he actively participated in the shakedowns so Beigel decided to ignore him for the moment.

Chapter 4

The Reluctant Commitment

I guess one might say the FBI is the last bastion of idealism.

> —Roy Moore, Special Agent
> in Charge, Chicago FBI,
> April 1972

The return of the historic indictments did not prevent Beigel and Davidson from recognizing two sobering facts which could turn those first indictments into the "last hurrah" of a moribund investigation. First, the FBI had never completed its assigned tasks in Austin. Second, Beigel had not been able to convince Holder to cooperate and had found no other officer to testify about the $100-a-month club.

There was one encouraging sign. A growing number of FBI agents, who had heard stories about corrupt police activities, were beginning to seek out knowledgeable informants who would provide information to the Strike Force even if they would not testify.

Three Incidents of Corruption

John Osborne had served on the C-1 squad for several years. Something of an expert on the fringe elements of Chicago's north side society, he had become acquainted with pimps, prostitutes, pornographic bookstore owners, homosexuals, and assorted outcasts. His fellow agents often kidded him about the company he kept, but just as often he managed to produce interesting, if not always useful, information.

Shortly after the March indictments Osborne told Beigel that vice squad officers in the 19th District (Town Hall), including the vice coordinator, were organizing monthly payoffs from numerous tavern owners, particularly the proprietors of hoodlum-controlled gay bars on Clark Street in the new "singles" neighborhood known as New Town. Osborne had received most of his information from informants who were not directly involved, but he had interviewed a homosexual who claimed to have specific evidence of corruption. He was even willing to meet with Beigel, although he made it clear to Osborne that this did not mean he would testify before the grand jury.

Ted Marshall[1] was approaching thirty, and had kicked around the Chicago gay community for about ten years. He had first tried his hand at acting, but without success, finally settling on working the bar in some of the gay establishments that had sprung up on the north side during the late 1960s. One of these was The Unicorn.[2] Marshall told Beigel he had first worked there in early 1971. It was a small bar in the New Town area that catered mostly to a sedate homosexual clientele. It had no entertainment and served primarily as a watering spot for homosexuals who wanted a friendly place to pass the time.

It was clear to Marshall that The Unicorn had mob connections. The man who hired him said he was the manager and owner, but he did not appear to have complete control of the tavern's operations. Every month another man well known around the neighborhood as a "juice" collector stopped to examine the books. Afterward, large cash transactions would take place near the entrance to the bathroom in the rear of the bar.

One morning when the manager was away Marshall stole a look at the books, which were kept behind a false wall at the end of the bar. From his past jobs Marshall had acquired a passing familiarity with bookkeeping. As he looked at the columns of numbers, he suspected that all was not proper since the cash receipts recorded did not come close to what he had observed to be the actual revenues. Marshall concluded that the meeting he witnessed each month was the end result of a simple "skimming" operation. In Beigel's office he took a piece of paper out of his shirt pocket which he said contained copies of entries in The Unicorn's books. According to Marshall, the amounts recorded were at least 20 percent below the actual receipts of the tavern.

Now that Marshall realized that The Unicorn was operating as a front, he began to watch the customers more closely. Each Monday, just after the bar opened, a blue Oldsmobile[3] pulled up in front of the bar. The driver, a middle-aged man, never got out of the car. Instead, the manager would go outside and talk to him for a few minutes through the window. With the manager's back

1. His name has been changed.
2. The name of this bar has been changed.
3. The type of car has been changed.

to him and the driver's face obscured, Marshall could not begin to figure out what was being said. After several weeks of observing this routine, Marshall finally heard the owner address the driver as "Sergeant" and realized that the driver was probably a cop. He talked to several friends, giving them a description of the driver, and soon learned that he was a vice cop who had raided several other gay bars during the past several months. Marshall concluded that in addition to being under control of the mob The Unicorn was paying the cops for protection. It suddenly dawned on Marshall why, unlike other gay bars where he had visited and worked, The Unicorn had been remarkably free from police harassment.

Marshall said he would be willing to look at some photographs in an attempt to identify the officer involved. He also agreed to keep his eyes open and relay information to Osborne and the Strike Force, but that was all. "Gays' lives aren't worth a damn," he said.

Another FBI agent on the opposite side of Chicago, in the far south side district of Grand Crossing, had grown tired of gambling investigations. After the first police indictments were returned, Bill Hermann, an agent for twenty years, asked Becker if he might do a little poking around in Grand Crossing. He knew the people, he said, and was friendly with many of the tavern owners. Perhaps, on his own, he could see if there was any evidence of police shakedowns. Becker was elated.

Within a week Hermann found a bowling alley whose proprietor, Jack David, told him that for two years he had been giving money to the cops for protection. The protection symbolized the changing character of the neighborhood and had nothing to do with liquor violations.

The owner told Hermann that, a few years back, he had begun to experience increasing difficulty with neighborhood kids who would come to bowl, have a few drinks, and then get rowdy. Fights became more frequent. The neighborhood was in the throes of racial change and David and his partner, both white, were fearful that the blacks of the area resented their continued ownership of one of the district's most popular spots. Naturally, David said, he began to feel that the police were the only available protection against vandalism and dangerous scuffles at the bowling alley.

Soon David began to wonder if the police were truly on his side. When he called them after a fight broke out, he found them unsympathetic. He complained to no avail. When incidents were about to explode, he would telephone the district station. It was often an hour before anyone showed up, too late to stop the fight or prevent the damage. Sometimes the police would not come at all.

After several months a plainclothes officer visited David. He said that he understood David was dissatisfied with the service he had been getting from the police. David told the cop that this was an understatement and that he might as well close up his business if things did not improve. The cop said that the police could not be everywhere at once and if David wanted prompt service he would simply have to show his gratitude. After a brief discussion the cop summed up the situation bluntly. "For protection against the criminal elements in this community" it would cost $100 a month. David, believing that he had no choice, agreed. The payments began shortly thereafter. Police service improved immediately. He could now rely on the police to do a job for which he thought he had already paid through his taxes.

David, although open and candid with Hermann, was desperately afraid. When David told Hermann that the payments were continuing and that the current collecting officer was the third in two years, Hermann asked if he would be willing to look at photographs. David thought this over for a moment. "You know, I didn't like the idea of paying the cops for what they're supposed to do anyway, but I've had a good business here, and I would hate to louse it up. Besides, if I identify anybody, look what will happen to me. The cops will stop responding to my calls, and I'll be right back where I started." Hermann said that he understood, but it was also important to try to stop this type of activity. David nodded his head in agreement, although he was hardly enthusiastic.

Becker and Hermann went to Beigel to discuss how best to handle David. Some thought was given to asking Conlisk for photographs of all officers in the Grand Crossing District, but this idea was rejected. David might not identify anyone; a request for photographs might be leaked to the press; fear would likely sprout in Conlisk's mind coupled with a suspicion that the investigation was going off in all directions. The resolution of the David matter could be delayed for weeks. Becker then suggested that David be approached with the idea of participating in a setup of the cop at the time of his next collection visit.

Hermann went back to David. After considerable cajoling and a promise that the FBI would protect him, David agreed to cooperate. David told Hermann that the collections were usually made on the second Friday of each month in the late morning. The FBI and the Strike Force began to prepare for the next collection day.

On April 14 Bill Hermann and a black FBI agent, Sherman Noble, met David at the bowling alley shortly after it opened. They gave David $100 in marked bills and began bowling.

About 11:30 A.M. Hermann and Noble observed a balding white police officer enter the bowling alley and approach David, who had come out from behind the counter to greet him. David was clearly nervous, but put up a good front and appeared to engage in a friendly conversation with the officer for a few moments. David then reached into his back pocket and removed the marked bills and handed them to the officer. The officer said goodbye, put the bills in his pocket, and walked toward the door, not even glancing over at Hermann and Noble. After the officer left the bowling alley Hermann and Noble quickly ran after him and found him starting to get in his squad car. They stopped him and said that he was under arrest, flashing their FBI credentials under his nose. In the squad car two other officers sitting in the front seat looked on in shocked disbelief as their fellow officer, Sergeant Robert Crowley, thirty-six, was informed of his rights by Noble. Crowley was searched and taken before a magistrate who set his bond at $4,500. Crowley said nothing to the agents. Within a month he was indicted for extortion. The other two officers were questioned by the FBI and released. Before the grand jury they would not or could not identify the significance of a list of addresses on a piece of paper found in Crowley's shirt when he was arrested. None of the persons at these bars and other businesses would say that Crowley made collections from them.[4]

About the time of Crowley's arrest, Becker told Beigel that he had run across a tavern owner in the northwest side district of Shakespeare who was complaining that he was being pressured to make a payoff. His license was being threatened in connection with a revocation proceeding arising from an arrest several months earlier for keeping a house of prostitution. Beigel invited the owner to his office. The bar owner told Beigel that, after the arrest, he had engaged a lawyer who had been recommended by another cop and who was a member of a politically connected downtown law firm. Although no officer had actively solicited him for a payoff at the time of the arrest, the arresting officer had said to him that if he wanted to save his license it would probably cost him a "bundle." Now, the bar owner told Beigel, the officer's statement was coming true. His lawyer was demanding a $2,000 cash payment to represent him at the upcoming hearing. With the owner's consent, arrangements were made for him to call his lawyer to discuss the proposed fee and to tape the conversation.

On the telephone the bar owner complained to his lawyer that he could not understand why the legal fees were so steep. His friends had told him that

4. Crowley was later convicted and given a jail sentence. He never talked.

lawyers generally charged only about $500 for the half-day hearing. Why was this one so expensive? he asked, and why did the lawyer have to have it all in cash? The lawyer responded that it was not easy to save a license and that his services were worth every penny he charged. He was not just any lawyer. "When you get this far, there are people you got to take care of." Although the owner pressed the lawyer for more details, he would not be more specific about whom he had to take care of. All the lawyer would say is, "I need the money in cash the morning of the hearing. If you want to talk more about it, come to my office. I don't want to say more on the telephone."

After the telephone conversation the owner got cold feet. He told Beigel that his license was at stake and that it was his only livelihood. He did not want to offend his lawyer with more questions than he obviously wanted to answer. If it took $2,000 to keep his license, he was simply going to have to pay it.

Beigel did not press the issue. There was no way of knowing if the lawyer's statement that people had to be taken care of meant payoffs or was simply a convenient way to justify an exorbitant fee. Whether or not a payoff was involved, it was clear that the lawyer's statement encouraged the owner's acceptance of the idea that corruption was a way of life.

These three incidents convinced Beigel that the roots of police corruption run much deeper than the presence of "unenforceable" laws and regulations. Underlying almost every kind of corrupt police activity found during the investigation was the need of the public for service and the freedom of the police to decide whether to provide it.

The name of the game is service. Like a neighborhood patrol officer who performs many non-law-enforcement functions ranging from arbitrating domestic disputes to chasing kids off street corners, all police frequently find themselves in situations requiring the exercise of discretion which they can use to extract money in return for performing a service. The possibilities for harassment and withholding services are enormous.

For example, a Chicago west side community leader told Beigel that after a "block club" had been established to keep a black neighborhood in good condition and to reduce the incidence of crime, the police actively and openly transported prostitutes and drug addicts from another part of the district to this block. The police then began to profit from the deteriorating social environment which they had in part created. As the situation worsened, more people asked to be protected. This gave more power and discretion to the police, facilitating bribery, extortion, and other corrupt activities. In Austin the incidence of extortion of tavern owners was highest in that part of the district where racial change was occurring the fastest.

Despite the clear indication that the roots of police corruption can be found in the power the police wield and in the ways in which it is used, certain police leaders believe that cynicism, not power, is the true breeder of police corruption. One career police official has said that "it seems rather futile to try to convince police to be honest when better educated, better paid, and more respected members of the criminal justice community are involved in graft, bribery, payoffs and other forms of corruption."[5] If cynicism is the cause, efforts to clear up the police are doomed to fail unless other institutions are reformed at the same time. This destructive point of view leads to a belief that this "so's your old man" defense excuses the failure to implement meaningful change. The dishonesty of others becomes a license for dishonesty by all.

The police utilize the full extent of their power and discretion. The general public encourages this by accepting blindly the idea that the police must have unchecked authority if crime is to be controlled. What Jack David brought home to Beigel was that this power and discretion was often used not to enforce the law but to extort money from people who either wanted to avoid the law or who desperately needed more of its protection. The Shakespeare bar owner summed it up best: "It looks to me like I *gotta* pay off to get a fair hearing before the liquor board and I *better* pay off in the future if I want to avoid arrest for keeping a few girls around the bar."

A Missed Opportunity and an Extortion that Didn't Work

Despite the comparatively minor nature of the activities which formed the basis of the March indictments and the lack of charges against a central ringleader, the media paid considerable attention to the investigation and to Edward Hanrahan, the State's Attorney, who decided to take the side of the police. He was under considerable fire from blacks and civil rights groups for his police advocacy role following a 1969 incident during which several Black Panthers had been shot down by the police after they burst into their apartment during the early morning hours. But he never tired of defending the police. He entered the fray with vigor.

He criticized the *Chicago Tribune,* which had traced the recent history of police difficulties, saying that the series "is being published on the newspaper's front page, but far less publicity is being given to the two or three killings, the six or seven shootings, and the 30 or 40 armed robberies which shatter the peace and safety of Chicago every day."[6] Before the Chicago Chamber of

5. William H. Smith, "Deceit in Uniform," *The Police Chief,* September 1973.
6. *Chicago Tribune,* May 11, 1972.

Commerce, Hanrahan came prepared with statistics, noting that the police being investigated represented less than two-tenths of one percent of the police force and that "neither the apostles nor Ivory Soap has ever claimed a better record for integrity."[7]

The explosion of press reaction following the indictments was also the result of an unprecedented attack on the Police Department from other quarters. A report had been made public on March 23 by the private Chicago Law Enforcement Study Group charging that the Chicago police kill an excessive number of civilians and get away with it. U.S. Representative Ralph H. Metcalfe, a disaffected Daley supporter, had also launched a scathing attack on the department for police brutality and its harassment of blacks.

With Hanrahan vigorously defending the police and Mayor Daley besieged with demands to take action, the public debate reached new heights. It was only natural that questions would be raised about the good faith and integrity of the federal prosecutors.

This reaction was not surprising, but was completely contradicted by the facts. Investigations into corruption and political malfeasance had been receiving top priority in the U.S. Attorney's office for some time. In addition, those who suggested that politics was behind the police investigation chose to ignore an important reality—the Strike Force was headed and manned primarily by Democrats. Despite the many politically motivated activities of the Nixon administration, this investigation had more difficulty garnering support from inside the government than outside, beginning with the intransigence of the FBI. Indeed, the biggest fear of the leaders of the Organized Crime Section of the Justice Department in Washington, often expressed to Davidson and Beigel, was that an unsuccessful investigation would lend credence to charges that it was a political vendetta.

Although the arrest of Sergeant Crowley in the Grand Crossing District was a spectacular coup, Beigel knew that its impact would fast fade unless new avenues of investigation opened up. Despite the indictments, Inserra did not promise that the FBI would be more cooperative. Becker confided to Beigel that Inserra preferred to wait until convictions were obtained before committing himself and his men.

The indictments presented another unexpected liability. The little FBI assistance Beigel had managed to extract in the past now had to be deployed to complete the investigations of the indicted officers. For example, proof of a Hobbs Act extortion requires establishing a connection between the extortion

7. *Ibid.*

and interstate commerce. It was therefore necessary to procure the records of the taverns and the distributors to establish that the shipments of liquor came from outside Illinois. Beigel found it nearly impossible for his small force of agents to concentrate on the time-consuming task of record gathering. Beigel worried not only about from where help was going to come to continue the investigation, but also that he would not have time to gather the evidence necessary for the trials.

Toward the end of the first week of April, Beigel returned to his office one afternoon feeling depressed about what had just happened in court. Judge Austin, to whom two of the police cases had been assigned, had made it clear that he would not tolerate any delays. He set the trials for the middle of June. Beigel did not know how he could possibly be ready in time, but did not protest because he feared this might be interpreted as a sign of weakness in the cases. The defense attorneys did ask for more time, but Austin would not budge.

When Beigel entered his office, Becker was waiting for him with new information. A fellow agent whom Becker knew casually had told him about his relationship with a tavern owner who ran a bar on the north side in the Rush Street nightclub area. During the past several months the bar owner had confided in him how, for several years, he had been making sizable payments to the police in that district. This agent had put none of this in writing because he considered the bar owner a friend rather than an informant. Since the return of the indictments, however, he had reconsidered the significance of what he had learned and thought that Becker ought to know about it. A meeting was set for that afternoon with the agent.

The bar involved was a well-known spot near Rush and Division. It catered to singles, sailors, and prostitutes, and was surrounded by a mixture of fancy French restaurants, discotheques, B-girl strip joints, both respectable and pornographic movie theaters, and expensive nightclubs. Near the main strip were luxurious brownstones, highrise apartment buildings, and the mansions of Astor Street. To the west was a deteriorating area with a high crime rate. The population of this area was a mixture of the older establishment, young professionals, secretaries, and career women, living alongside homosexuals, drug addicts, and criminals. As a result, by 1972, Rush Street was declining as a sophisticated nighttime area. The clientele of the better bars was now primarily depressed singles looking for company and out-of-town businessmen looking for action. On weekends teenagers swarmed into the neighborhood.

The agent had known the bar owner for two years. He lived in the neighborhood and often went to the bar on Friday nights for a drink. Slowly, they struck up a friendship. In January, as the agent was sipping his last drink for the night, the bar owner bitterly complained that his payoffs to the police were getting out of hand. He had been paying for several years to avoid police harassment and to get police service if trouble occurred. He hadn't mentioned it before because, he explained, it had been valuable to have police cooperation, especially when he had to be on the lookout for underage drinkers, when one mistake could cost him his license. But recently "the ante had gone up" and it was "getting hard to pay the freight." Worse still, he said, two groups of officers had to be paid, a bagman from the 18th District vice squad as well as a uniformed patrolman. Payments to the vice squad did not protect him from harassment by uniformed officers and vice versa. The agent asked the bar owner if he knew others who were paying. The bar owner replied that he believed most of the bars in the area and throughout the district were paying to one or both of the "clubs." He had even heard rumors that the district commander had his own "club" for Mafia-owned big-time nightspots.

Beigel asked the agent whether the owner was still making payments. Thursday was pickup day and, the agent said, there was one coming up in a week. Beigel turned to Becker and said, "Why don't we try the same thing we did with Crowley?"

Beigel asked Becker to speak to the bar owner, but Becker thought the other agent should be the one to attempt to set up the arrest since he had a close relationship with the bar owner. The agent agreed to talk to the bar owner.

Within two days Becker told Beigel the agent had changed his mind. He was in favor of the plan but did not want to be involved because of his relationship with the owner. Becker was reluctant to approach the bar owner because he was desperately trying to help the few agents left to complete the preparation for the trials of those already indicted. Becker said he would assign another agent to meet the bar owner and set the plan in motion.

This new agent, with whom Beigel had little experience, went to the bar owner as planned. He was accompanied by the first agent, whom Becker had convinced to help make the introduction. After the owner's agent friend left, the new agent proceeded to tell the owner that he should stop paying the police, that the FBI was investigating police corruption, and there was soon going to be no need for protection. Although the agent also told the owner that he wanted to be present on Thursday when the pickup was made, the damage was done.

Because of the agent's advice, probably given for no reason other than to establish rapport, the bar owner, three days prior to the collection date, refused to pay another officer who came to collect on behalf of the vice squad. On Thursday the uniformed bagman did not appear. This refusal of the bar owner to make the payment on Monday, especially in view of the regular payments for several years, had alerted the police that something was amiss. The arrest, which Beigel hoped would be more spectacular than the Crowley coup, never materialized.

Davidson and Beigel went to Inserra and told him what had happened, being careful to avoid criticism of the agent who had muffed his assignment and to extend every possible deference to Inserra's complaints of insufficient manpower to carry out his gambling investigations. After a half hour, during which Inserra stared at the ceiling and looked puzzled, he asked Davidson what he wanted. He replied that he wanted one agent to follow up the incident which had just occurred in the 18th District and to see if there was anything worthwhile pursuing. Inserra said he thought the request was reasonable, but that he was not going to overextend his personnel. The Austin investigation was time-consuming. However, if the Strike Force wanted one agent to do a couple of interviews, he would agree. "I have just the man for you," Inserra exclaimed. "He'll do the job and he'll do it quick. He's my ace gambling man and he's aggressive. His name is James Annes."

Beigel knew Annes, as did Davidson. Annes was the former Los Angeles policeman who had been skeptical about the Austin investigation in January 1971, when Davidson and Beigel had first tried to coordinate FBI and IRS efforts. Davidson grimaced when Inserra mentioned Annes, but Beigel had worked with Annes on a gambling investigation which had resulted in the indictment of more than twenty bookmakers engaged in an interstate sports betting operation. Annes had received a personal letter of praise from Hoover and was considered bright and ambitious, even though he was occasionally too cocky. In addition to knowing from first-hand experience that Annes was a competent agent, Beigel believed that Annes's police background might make him work harder to find out whether police corruption was as extensive as the lawyers believed.

At his first meeting with Annes in April, Beigel described the procedures which Becker had used in the Austin District. Annes, who was accompanied by his partner, Duane Hill, listened with a skeptical look on his face. When Beigel finished his explanation, Annes replied, "Your Austin investigation was penny ante; if you want something accomplished, let me do it my way. What we need is a few quick turnovers, a couple of indictments, and we'll be off and rolling." Annes also insisted that the cases in which he would participate had to be stronger than the indictments returned in Austin.

Beigel said to Annes, "Sure, I know this is your career case. But we're out to make decent cases; no case is a sure thing."

Annes retorted, "This is your career case, not mine. If there's anything to be found, Hill and I will dig it up. But I still think it's a waste of time."

"We'll see," Beigel replied.

Beigel, Annes, and Hill finally decided that, because of the "limited" nature of the preliminary inquiry, they would first contact the taverns which had been named as possibly belonging to the "club." Prominent on this list was Dan Farrington,[8] who owned a popular singles bar on Rush Street.

On April 16 Annes and Hill went to see Farrington. They were greeted by a stone wall of silence and denials. Annes returned to Beigel and insisted that "Farrington is lying through his teeth" and should be subpoenaed immediately before the grand jury. The subpoena might scare him into telling the truth. Beigel persuaded Annes to do a few more interviews. "We might as well see if there's anything worth pursuing before getting bogged down with subpoenas and the grand jury."

Every owner interviewed, while denying payoffs, mentioned that it was common knowledge throughout the Rush Street area that owners were paying cops for protection and better service. The reports and the numerous leads developed made it clear that a thorough investigation of police corruption in the 18th District should not be passed up.

Beigel and Davidson returned to Inserra with a request for more men, but they were summarily rejected. Inserra said, "I can't afford more men, and besides, I talked to Annes and Hill and they agree they can handle the investigation by themselves."

Beigel and Davidson then decided to ask Conlisk for photographs of officers in the 18th District. The request was processed as before, but this time they did not receive a critical comment from Conlisk, although his aide said to Beigel, "Jesus, don't you guys ever stop?"

Despite the lack of agents and the difficulties encountered by Annes and Hill in getting the Rush Street tavern owners to talk (they seemed more close-mouthed than their Austin counterparts) some progress was made. On April 18 Bob Wiedrich of the *Chicago Tribune* devoted his entire column to the new federal investigation in the 18th District. Its impact began to loosen the tongues of some owners. Several came close to admitting membership in various "clubs," but all still refused to identify any of the officers involved. Beigel thought the photographs might help, although he recognized that the lack of identifications probably had nothing to do with an inability to remember the collectors' names.

8. His name has been changed.

In the midst of this slowly developing story two breaks occurred. In early May a former 18th District vice officer told Annes he was willing to give a statement concerning what went on during the years he had served there. This officer had resigned from the department under less than honorable circumstances. He had become involved with members of the Democratic machine in the ward run by Edward Vrdolyak and had been caught arranging stag and sex parties for well-connected politicians. He was indicted in federal court (since many of the girls had come from out of state) and had pled guilty. He received probation and the department asked him for his resignation.

His life was shattered. When Beigel met him he was a pathetic middle-aged man who wanted no further trouble. He was cooperative, although almost embarrassed by his inability to tell only a few stories about the activities of vice officers in the 18th District who for years had managed a "club" of tavern owners who paid them each month. Although his information was not useful for obtaining indictments because he had left the vice squad more than five years before, it opened the door. He had confirmed the existence of at least a "vice club" and convinced Annes that perhaps the corruption about which the Strike Force had been talking was really there. Annes and Hill followed up his information by contacting those tavern owners about whom they now had specific information. Like the informant information used by Becker in Austin, this officer's statement made it harder for tavern owners to lie and get away with it.

The case of Dan Farrington was a classic example of how this cooperative former officer's statement had made easier the task of convincing witnesses to talk. On May 31, 1972, a sheepish Farrington came to Beigel's office with Annes and Hill. He was a thin, pale-faced man who was now suddenly apologetic for the off-handed way in which he had brushed off the FBI agents when he was first contacted in April. He told Beigel he was now ready to tell all, but "going into court is another matter altogether; I'm not making any promises." Beigel replied, "Neither am I, except that to cooperate can't hurt you."

Farrington told Beigel that he had lied to the FBI agents in April when he denied ever paying any money to the Chicago police. He still feared reprisals against him and his business if he cooperated, but realized he could no longer convincingly stand behind denials.

In July 1967 Farrington and his partner Bob March[9] had opened their tavern on Rush Street. During the first six months of operation the police stopped by several times to check patrons' identifications. As the visits in-

9. His name has been changed.

creased, Farrington began to feel he was being unnecessarily harassed, since he had always been very scrupulous about checking IDs so that no one under age would be served.

After about eight months Farrington was arrested for serving liquor after hours. He felt this arrest was a setup. He had been hearing rumors that the 18th District cops would make harassment arrests unless the owners agreed to monthly payments. The next day a friend who managed another Rush Street bar and who worked part-time at Farrington's tavern told him that he knew someone who could "help him."

A few days later his friend arranged a meeting with a sergeant at a restaurant down the street. The officer told Farrington that "all your troubles will end if you start paying monthly." After that Farrington received a call around the middle of each month from an unknown person who would tell him that the pickup would be made that night. As promised, an unmarked police car would pull up in front of the bar and Farrington and March would go outside and give $300 in cash in an envelope to the driver. Each month the driver was a different person and was always in plain clothes.

The payments continued throughout 1968 and into early 1969. When Farrington's business had dropped off so much that he could no longer afford the payments, he told his anonymous caller he would make it up when business improved. After that, no further attempts were made to collect any money.

Similar statements from several other owners convinced Beigel that there was large-scale corruption in the 18th District. The problem was, as it had always been, to obtain the necessary FBI commitment. Inserra was essentially uncooperative and Charles Bates had been recently replaced by Roy Moore, an unknown quantity.

The appointment of James Thompson as U.S. Attorney was also a factor to consider. Thompson had been cooperative with the Strike Force and had seemed enthusiastic about the return of the first indictments. However, he was also very interested in launching his own investigations and it was not clear how much active support he would lend to the Strike Force. Beigel and Davidson decided to meet with Thompson.

Thompson was a big, strapping man with straight blond hair. His warm, friendly smile masked the intense seriousness with which he pursued his job. However, he was not overbearing, had a scholarly background, and seemed to downplay politics. He was the perfect U.S. Attorney in the Watergate atmosphere—a Republican who wanted to clean up political corruption and who had never been tainted by charges of dishonesty or double dealing.

Thompson listened quietly as Davidson and Beigel explained the history of the investigation, concentrating on the problems with the FBI. Davidson emphasized particularly the potential in the 18th District and the Strike Force's hope that, if the investigation was expanded, "we will eventually be able to indict some officers closer to the top of the police hierarchy."

Thompson indicated that he was personally interested in the police investigation and that it should have top priority. "It's ridiculous that you should have so much trouble with the FBI, especially when they are pressuring us every day to devote more time to this and that minor investigation. Who do you want me to call for more help for you fellows?"

Davidson suggested a personal meeting with Roy Moore. Thompson had only briefly chatted with Moore and thought the meeting would be a good way to find out what he was like.

Only occasionally is an FBI agent thrust into the headlines. If he makes a spectacular arrest, his name will be mentioned. If there is a controversy, he may be asked to comment. Hoover had generally frowned upon personal aggrandizement and resented it when an FBI agent was personally praised; he wanted the FBI as an organization to receive the credit. Becker used to tell Beigel that he would be happy if his name never got in the papers.

It already appeared that Moore was more prone toward using the press than would be normally consistent with Hoover's policy. Shortly after assuming his new post and after the first indictments, Moore announced to the press that the FBI was on the verge of cracking a police "hit squad" which had been responsible for the murders of several black businessmen during the past year. Moore had said that the murders were connected with drug trafficking and indictments were imminent.

The story caused a great stir. Moore's statement that the murders were associated with drug pushing was probably accurate, as was his announcement that there was police involvement in the murders. His statements were, however, grossly premature. A federal grand jury was nowhere near returning indictments. It was even possible that, because of lack of evidence, no indictments would ever be returned. Moore was in danger of being embarrassed by his press statements if indictments did not materialize.

When Beigel walked into Thompson's office for the scheduled meeting, Moore was standing near the window with another man. Thompson and Davidson had not yet arrived. Beigel introduced himself. Moore turned away from the window and introduced the man next to him as his chief aide. The agent said nothing except "Nice to meet you." He was totally expressionless.

Beigel did not want to engage in any substantive conversation until Thompson and Davidson arrived, so he remained silent. Moore said in a distinct

Southern drawl, "I've invited Vinnie Inserra to the meeting and some of my other squad heads. This seemed like a good time for all of us to get acquainted." He then began to tell a few homespun tales about other cities where he had been stationed. As suddenly as he had started, he stopped and turned to look out the window, saying to Beigel, "You know, I am increasingly amazed and gratified by the character and makeup of the FBI. Did you know, for instance, that many of our agents originally intended to go into the ministry or the priesthood?"

"No, I didn't know that." Beigel had no idea what Moore was driving at. "It's true, believe me."

"Why do you think that is?" Beigel replied, since he could think of nothing else to say. He wished Davidson and Thompson would arrive.

"I guess," Moore said with a loud sigh, "one might say the FBI is the last bastion of idealism."

Before Beigel had a chance to answer, Davidson and Thompson walked in. Several other agents entered the office, including Inserra. Beigel and Davidson eyed one another nervously. Why were these agents present? Thompson had said nothing about it.

Moore began the meeting by saying that Inserra obviously knew more about the investigation than anyone else. The other three agents were present, Moore explained, because he thought it would be valuable to involve as many knowledgeable people as possible in discussing an investigation of this importance. "I am relatively new to Chicago," he said, "and you'll forgive me if I am not completely up to date on how the police work in this city. I have been briefed by Vinnie, however."

Beigel and Davidson were still suspicious about the presence of the other agents, all of whom were chiefs of FBI squads in Chicago. These men knew nothing about the investigation. One squad concerned itself with bank robberies, another with interstate transportation of stolen goods, and the last with theft from interstate shipments.

Beigel reviewed the progress of the investigation, including a rundown of the indictments returned and the possibilities for further indictments. Beigel peppered his narrative with frequent compliments to Inserra and his men and Inserra nodded approvingly. Beigel also explained how he hoped to obtain the cooperation of one or more of the indicted Austin officers so that cases could be made against higher-ranking officers.

Davidson added that some problems had been experienced "in moving along the investigation as expeditiously as we would all want" because sufficient FBI manpower was not available. They had not brought this to Moore's attention earlier, Davidson said, because the FBI was doing a spectacularly effective job, especially in view of tremendous pressures it was under as a result of the demands of other important investigations. As long as this investigation was limited to Austin, the Strike Force felt that the manpower problems could be handled.

"But now," continued Davidson, "and I'm sure Vinnie would agree with me, with the possibility for a significant new investigation in the Rush Street District, some arrangement has to be made at the top. Too many agents are required and both Vinnie and I need some direction from you. I feel that it is imperative that the FBI cooperate in a coordinated effort to organize an expanded investigation of police corruption throughout Chicago."

Moore had followed along with no visible signs of displeasure until Davidson had mentioned the word "expanded." Moore shifted in his chair and looked sideways at Inserra, who was now leaning forward on the couch and appearing less relaxed. Still, Moore and Inserra said nothing.

Beigel resumed and described what he had learned from the Rush Street bar owners who had cooperated. Moore and the others continued to listen without interrupting, occasionally smiling faintly, but mostly staring at an ornate chess set on a table in a corner of Thompson's office.

Beigel felt as if he were arguing a case to a jury in which each juror was making a concentrated effort to refrain from displaying any feeling about the case, one way or the other. This lack of response tempted Beigel for an instant to launch into a tirade about the lack of FBI cooperation and Inserra's resistance to the repeated requests for more agents to work in Austin. He controlled his impulse when he saw Inserra sitting on the couch scrunched uncomfortably between two other squad chiefs. He realized that an outburst would do the investigation absolutely no good.

After Beigel finished, Moore said his narrative confirmed his impression that everyone was working well together and was devoted to a fruitful end to the inquiry. However, Moore said, he had several concerns which he wanted to discuss. "First, can you get convictions of those you have already indicted and, if you do, will they stand up on appeal? Second, should we waste time on hundred-dollar extortion cases when we have murders to investigate?"

Beigel was a little taken aback by Moore's questions and asked him what reasons he had for thinking that the convictions might be reversed on appeal. "Naturally, Mr. Moore, we hope to get convictions, but it is unusual for police to be indicted in this district. It's impossible to tell how juries will react; but if we do win convictions, I see no reason why they should be reversed."

Moore replied, "Well, you lawyers obviously know more about this than we, but isn't it true that the taverns do not conduct business in interstate commerce. We need that to use the Hobbs Act."

Moore's statement revealed either a profound ignorance of the law or a cover for some unarticulated concern about the investigation. Beigel and Davidson reminded him that the Hobbs Act embraced the extortion not only of businesses engaged directly in interstate commerce but also of those which sold goods manufactured out of state and delivered into the state. Davidson added that the evidence justified the indictments and the state had done nothing about the corruption.

Moore agreed that "we should never be afraid to go forward," but still, "we don't want to unnecessarily impair our relationship with the police, upon whom all of us depend, and of course our credibility. Murder is one thing. Tavern shakedowns are another."

Moore turned to Thompson and said this was as good a time as any to mention the problems which his squad chiefs had encountered in regularly obtaining the full cooperation of some of the Assistant U.S. Attorneys on cases important to the Bureau. Moore acknowledged that Thompson's men were overworked. Nevertheless, he wished that Thompson might "encourage [his] staff to be a little more cooperative in some of the cases that might not seem as exciting as the political ones."

Thompson, who had said absolutely nothing since the meeting had begun, lurched forward in his reclining chair as Moore finished his statement and said, "If there are any specific complaints about the way my assistants are handling investigations in areas in which you are interested, I would be happy to hear them." He continued, "But the purpose of this meeting is not to have a general complaint session. Ways to improve the efficiency of federal law enforcement do not concern the Strike Force here. This meeting was called to talk about the police investigation."

Moore stood up abruptly and with a strained effort to control his anger said, "Part of the investigation of police is the hit squad. What about the investigation of the hit squad? When are those indictments going to be returned?"

Thompson replied calmly, "When the Assistant United States Attorney in charge of the investigation has enough evidence to present to the grand jury, which I understand that he does not yet have." Thompson's answer sounded to Beigel like a veiled reference to Moore's earlier statement to the press that indictments were imminent.

Davidson was upset. "Are you saying, Mr. Moore, that you will not investigate Hobbs Act violations because of FBI relations with the police?"

Moore blanched. "We always carry out our responsibilities." Davidson began to worry that Moore's obviously bitter feeling about how his "pet" case was being handled might lead him to withhold support from the police corruption investigation.

But Thompson was firm. He was not about to trade a quick indictment in the "hit squad" case for men to work in the 18th District. Thompson told Moore that he considered the police corruption investigation a top-priority matter. "If the necessary Bureau assistance is not forthcoming, I will take my request to Washington."

Moore sat down in his chair and turned to Inserra. "Vinnie, how many agents can you spare to look into this Rush Street business?" Inserra coughed and replied, "I think I could spare three or four besides Annes and Hill and, if absolutely necessary, more later." Moore turned back to Thompson, "Well, Jim, I think we can accommodate you. But please realize that this is a strain on Vinnie's squad. All I and the other squad chiefs hope is that your men will also accommodate us and move our cases faster."

Thompson replied, "Roy, you know that I want us to work closely and accomplish a lot. We're all interested in the same thing."

On this strange note the meeting ended. Beigel and Davidson felt as if they had spent the last half of the meeting in a corner, watching two fighters in the main event. But if more help was to be available, their discomfort was immaterial. The main objective had been to get things moving. Any commitment by the FBI, reluctant or willing, was a victory.

Chapter 5

The First Trials

"You're a one-eyed jack around here, but I've seen the other side
of your face."

> —Rio (an outlaw) to Longworth (a crooked
> sheriff) on the eve of Rio's trial, from the
> movie *One-Eyed Jacks*

On June 14 Beigel appeared before Judge Richard B. Austin to present the case
of Walter Moore, who was one of the Austin vice officers indicted in March.
The courtroom, located on the twenty-fifty floor of the Federal Building, was
large, high-ceilinged, and dimly lit. Counsel, jury, and spectators were sepa-
rated from the judge by an enclosed area for the court reporter, marshal, and
clerk. The rows at the back were filled with old-time courtroom watchers,
friends and relatives of the defendants, and people intrigued by the oddity of
a cop on trial. The press reporters sat ready to record every important word.
Artists were present to sketch the events and the main characters for the
evening television news.

As Beigel waited for Judge Austin to take the bench, Davidson was downstairs in his Strike Force office preparing to begin another grand jury session
in connection with the Rush Street investigation. The outcome of Moore's trial
and those that followed could have a significant effect on that grand jury and
the credibility of the entire investigation. Judge Austin, himself, considered the
cases important. He was the judge who, the previous December, had denied
Demopolous's bid to prohibit the Police Department from suspending or
discharging officers who "took the Fifth" before the grand jury. When he
learned that the Moore case and one other had been assigned to him, he lost
no time scheduling them back to back.

83

In another courtroom, a few days later, Sergeant George Demet, friend and associate of Thanasouras, was scheduled to go on trial before Judge Abraham Lincoln Marovitz, a veteran judge and popular friend of many prominent Daley Democrats in Chicago. During these last two weeks of June four police officers would have their fates decided by three juries and two judges.

The Trial of Walter Moore

Judge Austin took the bench at 10:15, fifteen minutes late. He was a man of slight physical proportions, nearing seventy, but in good health. He conducted his courtroom as a forum for cynical justice, shooting frequent barbs at lawyers, defendants, and witnesses. He had once been a prosecutor and was suspicious of defense attorneys. But everyone agreed that he conducted a fair trial and would not tolerate distortion of the evidence by either side. He often went out of his way to rule for the defendant on procedural and evidentiary matters to avoid being reversed by the court of appeals if a conviction won.

During his days as a State's Attorney, Judge Austin became well known after successfully prosecuting a cop who had turned murderer. He was nominated for Governor of Illinois, but lost the election. Many believed he had a grudge against the Daley administration for allegedly stabbing him in the back during the campaign.

Recently he had crossed paths again with the Daley administration when he ruled that the city had discriminated in its selection of sites for public housing. In early 1972 the simmering tension between Judge Austin and the local Democratic machine had exploded over a minor incident. The prestigious suburban Olympia Fields Country Club, to which Judge Austin belonged, was raided by the Sheriff's Office of Cook County, ostensibly for a minor violation of a county ordinance. Miffed by this raid, Judge Austin never let an opportunity pass to make snide and sarcastic comments in court about the pettiness of local politicans and law enforcement.

The defense attorney, Gerald Werksman, was a veteran criminal defense lawyer in Chicago, a former Assistant United States Attorney, and a Columbia Law School graduate. Although he was personable and easy to get along with, on this first day he was uncharacteristically tense. He sat next to Moore thumbing randomly through a pile of papers and nodding impatiently every time Moore leaned over to whisper something to him.

If Beigel could have selected which police case should be the first to go to trial, it certainly would not have been Moore's. It was an unusual case with weaknesses which Beigel was not confident could be overcome. Moore was a

black officer who had served under Thanasouras and, remarkably, had remained a vice officer even after Thanasouras had been demoted. He had
resigned from the force shortly after his indictment in March. The case against
him had been built solely by Becker, who had found witnesses by interviewing
bar owners along Madison Street, one of Austin's principal thoroughfares.

The four-count indictment against Moore involved two taverns, the Chez
Herman and the Unique Lounge. Moore was charged with attempting to
extort $50 a month from Herman Ghoulston, owner of the Chez Herman, and
a monthly payment and a single balloon payment of $1,000 from Al Brody,
owner of the Unique. Like the other officers who had been suspected of illegal
activity, Moore had been subpoenaed before the grand jury. He had not taken
the Fifth, however, but had answered all questions, vigorously denying any
wrongdoing. From these denials, the fourth count of the indictment arose,
lying before the grand jury about the alleged attempted shakedowns.

Even after Becker had taken the statements of Ghoulston and Brody, there
remained a serious question whether they would testify. Beigel had not called
them before the grand jury because he was reluctant to upset them unnecessarily or prematurely, thereby running the risk of inconsistent statements due
to lapses of memory. And Becker visited Ghoulston and Brody weekly after
the indictments were returned to preserve the rapport which he had carefully
nurtured prior to the indictments.

Two weeks before the trial began Ghoulston had second thoughts about
testifying. His wife was upset, and his friends had been needling him for
cooperating with white prosecutors against a fellow black. Al Brody, a poor
man who had saved money from his factory job to buy the Unique Lounge,
was still holding that job to make ends meet. He was now worried that his
testimony would lead to further police harassment which would destroy his
new business.

Both tavern owners had resisted Moore's attempts to collect money. If they
were now afraid to testify, it might mean that the other tavern owners might
be even less willing to testify. Beigel told Becker he wanted to meet Ghoulston
and Brody again; not at his office, but where they lived and worked. Perhaps,
if he talked to them on their own ground, he could convince these two strug-
gling black businessmen that it was worth helping a white prosecutor in his
attempt to convict a black police officer who, until his indictment, had done
well in a department which black groups had frequently accused of discrimination.

Becker and Beigel met Brody at the Unique Lounge at 10 P.M., ten days
before the trial. The bar, like the outside, was hot. The few customers cooling

off with a beer looked at Beigel and Becker, who were obviously out of place, with quizzical expressions as Brody led them to a booth in a dark corner toward the rear. Brody spoke only when absolutely necessary and then with the fewest words possible. Beigel told Brody that the trial was scheduled to begin in a week and that he would make every effort to arrange things so that Brody would not be too inconvenienced.

Brody said, "I told Tom that I would always be truthful about what that cop did to me, but I am just barely keeping this bar alive. I don't know if I can come down and testify. I can't get off my factory job and I can't afford to leave the bar in the evenings."

Brody's face showed his fear, and Beigel responded, "Look, Al, I know this isn't any picnic. Only one other bar owner will testify against Moore, and frankly, he's wavering. He thinks, naturally, why does he have to be the one. If you don't testify, the other guy will probably say what the hell, why should I, and then Moore will get off. If that happens, there will be nothing to stop a cop from coming here and causing you trouble any time he wants."

Brody leaned back and stared out toward the front door of the lounge through which he could see a police car parked across the street. "You know, Mr. Beigel, I bought this lounge with my last dime and if it goes under, I'm through. As it is, I'm never home. I got no life and I work my butt off all day at the factory. If this bar closes, that's it." Brody paused and stared, so it seemed, right at the police car. "I guess, though, you got your job to do, and you wouldn't be out here if you didn't need me. I come this far with you. I might as well go all the way."

Beigel's feeling of relief was shortlived. Although no one else had been a part of the conversations between Moore and Brody, Brody's barmaid had been in the tavern on two of the nights when Moore had made his visits. She could corroborate Brody's testimony on the events surrounding the attempted extortion. When Brody brought her to the Strike Force office several days later, she said, "I told you all I know, but I've decided I'm not going to testify." She paused for a moment. "My brother was killed a couple of years ago and they caught the guy who did it. I came down to testify at that trial and sat in a room for three hours waiting, just waiting. Then this State's Attorney, young like you, came out and said, 'We don't need you any more.' I said to him, 'What do you mean?' He said, 'The case is over, that's all. I'm sorry you had to wait. But you can go home now.' I found out later that they did that plea bargaining stuff and gave the guy probation for manslaughter. Well, I'm through waiting."

Beigel explained that this time her testimony and cooperation would not be wasted. If there would be no trial, it would be only because Moore pled guilty. He would not be given a deal which would make her look foolish for cooperating. "There are many reasons why what happened in your brother's case happened. Some are good, some are bad. But none of them apply here. Al's going to testify and we need you to back him up."

She took a tissue from her purse and wiped a tear from her cheek. "I'll do what I can for Al."

Herman Ghoulston lived in an old dilapidated two-story wood frame house about five blocks from the Chez Herman. The morning following the meeting with Al Brody, Beigel and Becker drove out to the house to meet with Ghoulston. His wife and two of his children, a boy about ten and a girl of five, were also there. Ghoulston was friendly and outgoing. He lost no time in telling Beigel that he was glad he could help the government because "those cops do nothing but get on your back."

Ghoulston then took Beigel by the arm and led him and Becker into the dining room, leaving his wife and two children in the living room. As they left one room and entered the other, his expression changed. "You know," he said, "a lot of my friends keep telling me that I'm just helping Whitey give us the shaft again. They say what do we care about that. My wife, too. She doesn't think my testifying is such a good idea. I just don't know what to do."

Ghoulston, Beigel, and Becker walked out of the dining room and into the front hall to get their coats. "Why don't you come down to my office tomorrow," Beigel said. "We'll talk some more."

Ghoulston's wife appeared in the hallway and looked inquiringly at the three men. Ghoulston said nothing. "Well, Herman," Beigel said, "ten in the morning. Tomorrow. Okay?" Before Ghoulston could reply, his son came running up to Becker and said, "Hey, man, are you an FBI agent?"

"That's right," Becker said.

The boy looked as pleased as a boy could be. "Did you tell him, Pop? Did you? That's what I want to be."

As Ghoulston smiled at the boy, his resistance appeared to melt away. He turned to Beigel and said, "I'll be there tomorrow. You can count on me."

Beigel and Becker at one table and Werksman at the other watched Judge Austin conduct the main examination of the prospective jurors. The attorneys would not be allowed to pose any questions directly to the jury. Instead, they were required to submit their proposed questions to Austin. The only question submitted by either side involved whether any prospective juror was related to anyone in the tavern business. Judge Austin was already prepared to ask each juror the standard background questions including whether a relative or friend worked for the city or the Police Department.

The rigid procedure employed by Judge Austin in the selection of a jury made it nearly impossible to get a prospective juror excused for cause. Since preemptory challenges (excusing a juror for no legally acceptable reason) were limited to six for the government and nine for the defense, jury selection was unlikely to be protracted.

Neither attorney used all of his allotted challenges and no one was excused for cause. Those who were challenged had relatives or friends either in the tavern business or the Police Department. Beigel excused one woman whose brother had once served as a police bodyguard and a man who worked for the Chicago Park District.

As Beigel rose to give his opening statement to the newly empaneled jury, he realized he did not have any solid impression of them. They were a nondescript mixture of men and women, city and suburban residents, blue- and white-collar workers. They listened attentively as Beigel described what the government intended to prove and to Werksman, who told them to keep an open mind and not to judge the evidence until all had been heard.

The prosecution's first witness was Herman Ghoulston. Under Beigel's lead, Ghoulston explained that he had been the owner of Chez Herman for the past two and one-half years. On July 5, 1971, Ghoulston testified, he arrived at the tavern at about 10 A.M. to find two police officers talking to his oldest daughter. Ghoulston identified one of the officers as Walter Moore. Moore responded to the identification with a look of sublime indifference.

Beigel then asked Ghoulston to relate the conversation he had with Moore. Ghoulston's voice dropped suddenly. Worried that Ghoulston was losing his nerve, Beigel walked back to the end of counsel's table, about thirty feet from the witness stand, to force Ghoulston to raise his voice. Ghoulston spoke louder. He testified that Moore had told him that his license had been altered and that he was under arrest. Beigel produced the license. It had indeed been changed; the typed expiration date had been scratched out and a new one had been inserted. But Ghoulston said he told Moore he had not done anything to the license.

Ghoulston then testified that he was forced to spend about two hours at the police station before he was released on bond. The next morning, July 6, Ghoulston and his wife went to the State of Illinois Building and City Hall. He learned that nothing was wrong with his license that the change had been made by the licensing authorities because a clerk had inadvertently typed the wrong expiration date on the license.

Ghoulston returned to the tavern. Five minutes later Moore came through the door and said he would like to see Ghoulston for a minute. They went to Moore's car parked at the corner. Ghoulston continued, "Well, he said he got a little deal going out here in this here district. We want to get $50 a month from each tavern owner. And I said to him, 'If you want a raise, you better see Mayor Daley.' Then I got out of the car." Moore said he would see him later. Ghoulston returned to the tavern and told his wife and daughter what had occurred. Ghoulston never saw Moore again.

Ghoulston's testimony was so disarmingly simple that there was little Werksman could do with him on cross-examination. He took Ghoulston back and forth over the events of July 5 and 6, but Ghoulston did not deviate from his direct testimony.

Ghoulston's wife and daughter supported his account of the basic events of those two days, but neither had been a party to the critical conversation in Moore's car. Beigel felt that their testimony would be of some value since it might help to counter Werksman's argument that Ghoulston had made up the story because he was angry at Moore for arresting him. He also realized, however, that this supporting testimony would not be enough to ensure conviction. Cross-examination of Moore would have to establish that Ghoulston's arrest had been set up to make him vulnerable to a later shakedown attempt. Ghoulston set the stage for this when he said, "I thought if I don't pay—it ran through my mind if I don't pay, they are liable to send somebody in to kill somebody and set me up to close my tavern."

Before he would need to worry about Moore's testimony, however, Beigel had to present his evidence in connection with the attempted extortion of Al Brody, the owner of the Unique Lounge. After Brody took the stand, he told, in a quiet, unassuming voice, how he had held down a full-time job for the past three years while he worked hard to make his tavern a success.

Brody testified that, in September 1971, while he and his associate, Catherine Walker, were working in the tavern, Moore arrived dressed in plain clothes. He took Brody aside and told him that his boss had sent him to talk. Brody testified, "I asked him about what. He said most of the places around there was paying off and I wasn't. And I asked him what did he want, and he said $50. And I said, 'Is that a year?' He said, 'No, that's a month.' Then I said, 'Well, I don't have no $50.' I said, 'Look at my customers. I don't make that kind of money.' Then he said, 'Well, I'll just have to go back in and tell my boss. There is nothing I can do if you haven't got it; you haven't got it.'"

A week later Moore returned. Brody again told him that he didn't have any money. Moore said, "You are sure you can't get any?" Brody said, "No, you can see what kind of a business I have. I don't have no money." Moore replied,

"Well, you will just have to suffer the consequences."

It was not long before Brody saw Moore again. On October 17, 1971, a fight broke out between two customers just outside the front door. One of the men was armed with a knife and, as Brody came to investigate, he saw him cut off the bottom part of the other man's ear. Brody closed the front door as the two men continued to scuffle outside. The police arrived shortly thereafter. Brody later heard that the man had died as a result of the beating.

A week later Moore came back. Catherine Walker was behind the bar and Moore asked Brody to come out to his car. In the car Moore told Brody that his "boss had sent him to talk" and that he could get things straightened out for Brody, "since all of the papers and everything have to go through the boss, and the boss sees to it that they don't get downtown."

"How much?" Brody asked Moore.

"A thousand dollars and eighty dollars a month," Moore said.

"If I had a thousand dollars, I could come downtown myself."

The papers to which Moore was referring included the report written by the officers who had investigated the fight on the 17th. If the report stated that the fight began in the tavern, Brody could lose his license. A tavern owner is required to report promptly any disturbance. Since Brody had not done so and since the police had accidentally come upon the fight in the street while on patrol, an unfavorable report could put Brody's license in jeopardy. Nevertheless, Brody testified that he did not pay Moore any money. He simply did not have it, he said, and waited for his tavern to be closed.

As with Ghoulston, Werksman could make little headway on cross-examination. He did get Brody to admit that during one of his talks with Moore he had told Moore that he had paid other police officers. Beigel could not see how this helped the defense since it was obvious that Moore had not asked Brody whom he had paid and had not made a report of the conversation as required by department regulations.

After Brody stepped off the witness stand, Beigel called Catherine Walker, who confirmed that the last critical conversation between Brody and Moore had taken place in Moore's car. Beigel hoped that the jury would recognize that this was highly unusual if the conversation was as innocent as Moore would have the jury believe. She testified clearly and forthrightly and later told Beigel that she had been so surprised the case had actually gone to trial that she changed her mind about the treachery of all prosecutors.

The testimony of Catherine Walker concluded the prosecution's case. Becker was now a bundle of nervous energy. He was concerned that since neither Ghoulston nor Brody had paid any money to Moore, the jury might say, "What's the big deal?" or even worse, doubt the truthfulness of the two tavern owners.

Werksman began Moore's defense by calling several character witnesses to the stand. Three police officers, including a captain and a lieutenant, testified about Moore's reputation for honesty and integrity. A minister testified that he had known Moore since childhood and that he was "a very fine young man." A final character witness, John Kozaritz, turned out to be an unexpected bonus for the prosecution.

Kozaritz was the vice coordinator of the Austin District. He vouched for Moore's good reputation. However, Werksman also asked Kozaritz about the duties of a vice officer, and this allowed Beigel to cross-examine on subjects other than the defendant's character.

Beigel outlined for Kozaritz the circumstances surrounding Ghoulston's arrest, and then questioned him about proper police procedure in that situation. Kozaritz testified that there had been no need for Moore to arrest Ghoulston for the alleged tampering of the license. A citation was the routine action, followed by further investigation. This admission by a police officer who was also Moore's witness could help Beigel convince the jury that Moore's arrest of Ghoulston had been nothing more than a setup to get him to agree to a later demand for protection money.

Then Walter Moore took the stand. He had a round, cherubic face, looking considerably younger than thirty-seven. He spoke pleasantly and sincerely and was the model of propriety.

Q: (Werksman) With whom do you live?
A: (Moore) I live with my wife, my son, and my younger sister.
Q: Where are you presently employed?
A: Finkel and Son. That's a steel mill.
Q: How long have you worked there?
A: Since about April 24 of this year.
A: And what are your duties there?
A: I'm a machinist's helper.

Moore recounted his entire employment history, telling how he had served for three years with the army before receiving an honorable discharge, was a high school graduate, had worked as a repairman, assistant lab technician, and janitor and had served in the Police Department for six years.

After becoming a police officer Moore spent six months in a patrol car. He was then assigned to the tactical squad. In November 1969 Thanasouras approached Moore and asked him if he wanted to become a vice officer. "I was the second black vice officer in the Fifteenth District, at which time I refused. . . . The main reason that stood out mostly to me, I felt I had only been on the job for a short time." This statement gave the impression that Moore had had no great desire to become involved in "dirty" police work. When asked a second time, however, he had agreed to become a vice officer.

Werksman interrupted the narrative to ask Moore if he had received any awards or commendations. Moore had won several commendations and once had even been designated the patrolman of the month after his apprehension of a murder suspect.

Finally, Werksman brought Moore to more recent events and the incidents at the Chez Herman and the Unique Lounge. Moore's explanation of what had happened was consistent with what he had told the grand jury. Moore said that he had noticed that the license in the Chez Herman had an original expiration date in June and that a new date had been inserted—September 30, 1971. Moore admitted that Ghoulston denied tampering with the license but said he arrested him anyway, ostensibly so that "we can check this out; verify what you are saying." Moore said he told Ghoulston at the station that he would have to lock him up because he "had never seen a discrepancy like this one."

Moore then departed completely from Ghoulston's testimony. On July 7, as he was passing by Chez Herman, he noticed it was closed. When he saw Ghoulston's daughter standing in the doorway, he asked her where Ghoulston was and she replied he would be back later. Moore decided to return to the tavern later that day because he couldn't understand why it was closed. When he came back, Ghoulston was there. He told him that he didn't have to close: "The license—if it's like you say it is, it's valid. When you go to court they will throw it out of court. It's as simple as that." Moore denied asking Ghoulston for money and testified that he learned later that the license was indeed valid.

Moore next testified about the Brody incident. He first met Brody after making a premises check and noticing that the cigarette machine license had expired. Because Brody was not there, he returned later in the day. "Well, like I say, I wasn't sure whether or not I had ever met Mr. Brody before, and I went there to meet him personally. And the main reason, I was one of the black officers assigned to the black area, and I wanted to give my people service. This is what I wanted to do and create a decent relationship like that."

Moore acknowledged that he went to the Unique Lounge in October on assignment by the vice coordinator because there had been a fight and he had to find out if it took place in the premises or on the street. Moore then carefully related his version of the conversation with Brody. He explained to Brody that he had an obligation to notify the police in case of any disturbance. Brody, who he said had been drinking, told him that he had heard that if he dropped a few dollars to the cop in charge, he could take care of it. Moore testified that he told Brody that wouldn't do any good. Moore admitted, although so casually that it could easily have been missed, that he did not write up a report even though the visit had been part of an official investigation and department rules required it.

Moore finished his direct testimony by again stating he had never asked Brody or Ghoulston for any money and that he had told the complete truth. He had testified well, without brashness or overconfidence. He was a believable witness, but Moore had made one significant mistake. Beigel went after it as he began his cross-examination.

Q: (Beigel) Mr. Moore, you have testified here today that after you took Mr. Ghoulston down to the police station, you saw him on the 7th of July, is that your testimony?

A: (Moore) The next day.

Q: The next day. So it would be the 6th of July; isn't that right?

A: Yes.

Q: And where did you see him?

A: At the premises.

Q: At the tavern, is that right?

A: Right.

Q: But when you first arrived he wasn't there, is that right?

A: That's right.

Q: And what time of the morning was it then when you arrived?

A: It is hard to say, sir. Morning hours. I don't know exactly what time it was.

Q: And were you just driving by, or did you go there specifically?

A: No, I was making other premises checks along that same street. In fact, I was heading for Mike's Tavern and I believe that is in the 5900 block on Madison. That is where I was headed.

Q: And then you stopped back again at the tavern, is that right?

A: Yes sir. I was curious about this license.

Q: To find out what had happened, is that it?

A: Yes sir.

Q: Well, you had made an arrest, had you not?

A: Well, just like I said, I was trying to develop a rapport with my people in the area. I was there as their officer. I was there to give them service. Mr. Ghoulston thought I was harassing him and I wanted to make it very clear that I was not harassing him.

Q: But of course, you made an arrest then instead of issuing a citation.
A: That's part of my job, sir. I have that option.
Q: That doesn't establish too good a rapport, does it?
A: Well, sir, I did the best I could under the circumstances.
Q: Wouldn't it have been better to issue a citation and investigate further?
A: Sir, I was following instructions.
Q: You have heard the testimony of Officer Kozaritz, haven't you?
A: Yes, I did.

Beigel next questioned Moore about a glaring inconsistency between his grand jury and trial testimony. In the grand jury Moore had sworn that, on the same day as Ghoulston's arrest, he had gone to the tavern to return his license. He said that he did not see Ghoulston then or ever again. At the trial, however, he admitted seeing Ghoulston the following day. Moore explained this discrepancy by saying his memory had been faulty in the grand jury because he did not have the arrest report to refresh his recollection. This excuse was clearly fabricated since the arrest report had been written on the day of the arrest and would obviously have made no reference to a subsequent visit. A shaken Moore would not admit that his grand jury testimony was false.

Moore regained his composure as Beigel moved on to other subjects, but lost it again when forced to concede that all of the critical conversations had taken place in the privacy of his car even though, by his own testimony, there had been no reason for it. While he continued to insist that he had done nothing wrong, the impact had been made, at least on Werksman, who several times futilely objected that Beigel was harassing Moore.

When Moore left the stand Beigel whispered to Becker, "What do you think?"

"I don't know," Becker said. "I guess it's a question of who the jury believes."

Werksman pulled out all stops. In his closing argument he kept asking, "Where's the evidence? Where's the evidence?" Werksman cited to the jury the high reputation of the FBI, then ironically jabbed, "Isn't it odd that they have no physical evidence to back up Ghoulston and Brody?" He also tried to portray Ghoulston and Brody as bent on revenge because of the troubles at their taverns. He closed his argument with an old-fashioned "support the police" refrain. "If you pass judgment on or discredit a police officer doing his duty, then you are taking away from the policeman that responsibility and you are handcuffing him."

Beigel attacked the "logic" of Werksman's argument. He pointed out that physical evidence does not usually exist when the crime consists of privately made threats. He argued that since there was no evidence Ghoulston and Brody had paid Moore, this proved they were telling the truth.

"If those witnesses were really out to get Moore and lie to do it, they certainly would have gone all the way and said that they *had* paid Moore. The fact that they candidly acknowledged to you that they had not paid him is a sign that they are telling the truth. And remember, an attempt to extort money is just as serious as the extortion itself. Because Moore did not succeed in getting these tavern owners to pay him does not make him any less guilty."[1]

Since credibility was the main issue and Werksman had spent so much time on the supposed revenge motive, Beigel stressed to the jury that neither Ghoulston nor Brody lost his license. Beigel asked the jury to use common sense in evaluating the evidence.

"If you do that, you will find that there simply was no reason for Ghoulston and Brody to lie. Moore, on the other hand, had every reason to be less than candid and to deny trying to get money from these two tavern owners. Mr. Werksman has talked about handcuffing the police and taking away their discretion. But no man is above the law."

The jury retired to deliberate at 2 P.M. on Friday afternoon and the judge announced that if no verdict was returned by 4:30, he would lock up the jury for deliberation during the evening and weekend. Any verdict returned would be announced on Monday morning.

Four-thirty came with no verdict. When Beigel left the courtroom he saw Moore and his wife pacing the halls. Moore smiled at Beigel. He seemed resigned to the result, whatever it would be. Since he had resigned from the police force after his suspension, he probably would never again be a policeman regardless of the verdict. But this had been his choice. He could have remained as a suspended officer, and, if acquitted, would still have had the chance to be reinstated. Beigel was puzzled why Moore had decided to quit the force immediately after the indictment. The case against him had not been that strong.

Beigel returned to his office. At 6 he went home. The pressure of waiting was great. Davidson had observed, probably accurately, that an acquittal in

1. Because of the unavailability of a complete transcript of the closing arguments, the quotes are paraphrased.

this first case would hurt the investigation, both because the FBI would surely increase its resistance and because the public might also lose confidence in the integrity of the Strike Force's efforts. Davidson knew that the Moore case had not been as strong as he would have liked, but he had still hoped for a quick verdict. When it did not come, he walked around the fifteenth floor asking everyone what they thought. Beigel decided it was better to be alone with his family.

That night Beigel learned the jury had reached a verdict, but he would not know what it was until Monday. He spent an anxious weekend.

On Monday morning Beigel walked into court at 10 and found it again packed with spectators. Judge Austin came in and promptly called the jury into the courtroom. They looked at the defendant, an action that many lawyers believe always signals an acquittal on the theory that jurors will not look at a person they have just convicted. The clerk opened the sealed verdict and gave it to the judge. Austin looked at it and handed it back to the clerk. Moore, who had risen when the jury walked in, remained standing. The clerk began reading.

"We the jury find the defendant, Walter Moore, guilty on Count One of the indictment. We the jury find the defendant not guilty on Count Two of the indictment. We the jury find the defendant guilty on Count Three of the indictment. We the jury find the defendant not guilty on Count Four of the indictment."

The jury had convicted Moore of attempting to extort $50 a month from Ghoulston and Brody, but acquitted him of the later attempted extortion of $1,000 and $80 a month as well as perjury. Although this verdict was seemingly inconsistent and clearly the product of a compromise, it was legally valid. One possibility was that a deadlock had occurred in the jury on Moore's guilt and that dissident jurors had been persuaded by the others to vote guilty on half the counts. A more likely possibility was that all jurors had felt Moore was guilty of at least one of the attempted extortions, but could not agree on which one. But guilty was guilty.

Moore accepted the verdict without any show of emotion, but his wife began to cry. Moore and the attorneys approached the bench. Austin said he saw no reason why Moore should not be sentenced immediately and asked for arguments from the attorneys. Werksman pleaded for probation, citing Moore's excellent background and unblemished police record. Beigel simply said, "The Hobbs Act carries one of the highest penalties among federal statutes. Congress intended that such conduct not be tolerated."

Austin asked Moore if he had anything to say. Moore said, "I've been a good policeman to the best of my ability, but unfortunately it wasn't good enough."

Austin sentenced Moore to two years in prison, although he recognized that Moore was "on the bottom rung of a ladder that escalates. . . . He would not have been the ultimate repository of whatever were the emoluments. . . ." Beigel was struck by Austin's comments since there had been no evidence at the trial that Moore had received money.

Austin allowed Moore to remain on bond pending appeal. The first cop convicted of police corruption in this investigation had not even been charged with receiving money nor had it been shown that he was part of some larger conspiracy. But the ice had been broken.

Beigel's colleagues rushed to congratulate him. He hardly heard what they were saying. He was thinking of the trial which had just begun before Judge Marovitz and the new trial which would soon begin before Judge Austin.

The Trial of George Demet

As Beigel was preparing for the second police trial before Judge Austin, Assistant U.S. Attorney Allan Lapidus stood before Judge Marovitz ready to present the government's case against Sergeant George Demet. When it had become clear after the meeting with Roy Moore and other FBI agents that there would be at least an initial effort to investigate the Rush Street District, Davidson and Beigel realized that they no longer could handle everything alone. They went to Thompson for help. He assigned Lapidus to work on the Austin investigation and to try one of the first three cases. Lapidus was an experienced trial lawyer. He had been actively involved in a previous investigation of frauds by lawyers who coaxed police officers into filing false accident reports to insurance companies. He was no stranger to illegal police activities.

The Demet case was simple yet unusual. Although the FBI had heard continuous rumors of Demet's close ties with Thanasouras and that he had been involved in large-scale shakedowns of both taverns and wirerooms, by the beginning of 1972 it had found only one tavern owner who said that he paid Demet any money. His name was Martin Lindstrom, owner of Marty's Lounge in the northwestern all-white section of the Austin District. Lindstrom's name had originally surfaced in 1971 when both CPD-1 (the ex-police officer informant of the IRS) and several other tavern owners had told Becker that they had heard Marty's was one of the taverns belonging to the $100-a-month club. At first, however, Lindstrom, proclaimed self-righteously that he had never paid any money to the police. Becker ordered the police file on Marty's Lounge to see if he could establish that Lindstrom knew more than he claimed.

These records revealed that in 1966 Marty's had been raided for violation of Chicago's open-view ordinance. This law, of which only a few tavern owners were aware, required that there be a clear view of the entire bar from the street. Supposedly, the law was designed to prevent illegal activities in the bar by allowing everything to be visible to someone who looked in the window from the street. One of the arresting officers was George Demet. This arrest was followed by another a short time later, by Frank Bychowski, (Holder's predecessor as vice coordinator) for taking bets from customers. That charge was dismissed.

The records showed no further investigations by the police for the next six years. This pattern supported Becker's suspicion that Lindstrom had not been honest with him. Two quick arrests followed by peace suggested that Marty's Lounge was enjoying police protection. Becker went to see Lindstrom again. This time, with the police reports in hand, Becker had the advantage. Lindstrom admitted reluctantly that he had paid $75 to Demet on six different occasions in 1966 and 1967. Lindstrom pleaded with the FBI and later Beigel not to force him to testify before the grand jury or at a trial. He feared that his business would be closed by the police and that his friends would believe he was a "fink." Besides, he had a son in college. "What would he think?" Lindstrom told Becker.

Beigel could do nothing with Lindstrom. The payoffs he had made to Demet were beyond the statute of limitations. Because Demet had taken the Fifth before the grand jury, Lindstrom's testimony could not be made part of a perjury charge, as in the case of Lieutenant Devitt.

Despite this setback, other evidence was eventually uncovered. Louis King, owner of two taverns in the Austin District, had called the FBI early in 1972 after reading one of Bob Wiedrich's columns in the *Tribune* encouraging witnesses to come forward. When Beigel first met King at his home in suburban Niles, King seemed less enthusiastic about talking. He acknowledged that he had called originally because he felt it was his "citizen's duty," but he also had many friends in the Police Department whom he did not want to hurt. King said he was now out of the tavern business. He had undergone a series of operations which had left him partially disabled. He wanted to move to a milder climate.

Beigel told King that it was too late to back down. King's wife took Beigel's side: "Louis, this is no time to get cold feet." After Beigel assured him that he would not be the only one to testify against policemen, King agreed to tell his story.

King was a veritable gold mine of information about police payoffs. During the past five years he had paid a license investigating officer and numerous members of the Austin District vice squad for protection to avoid arrests for liquor law violations. Among those whom he paid was George Demet.

The case against Demet was based solely on credibility. Would the jury believe that Demet extorted money from Louis King? Unlike the Moore case, there would be no possibility of a jury compromise since there was only one count in the indictment. Lapidus, although concerned with what seemed to be a wild gamble in this case, had been encouraged by the conviction of Moore. Now it was at least known that a Chicago jury would convict a police officer for official misconduct.

While waiting for Judge Marovitz to enter the courtroom Lapidus looked at Demet sitting across the room next to his attorney, Jim Demopolous. Because Demet had not testified before the grand jury, Lapidus had no idea whether he would decide to testify in his own defense at trial, or what the defense strategy might be. Unlike state court criminal cases, neither the government nor the defense was required to disclose potential witnesses. A federal criminal trial still retained the element of surprise which laymen always expect will occur. No one was to be disappointed. The Demet trial would have one major surprise before it was over.

King was the first witness. A plain-looking man of about forty, medium in height and stocky, he acted like a typical bar owner—friendly, outgoing, and engaging. He began by acknowledging that he knew Demet, identifying him as the man sitting at defense counsel's table wearing a green tie and blue shirt.

Demet was a big man with broad shoulders and a square, rugged face. But now he seemed shrunken. His eyes were glassy and the way he slumped in his chair made him look much smaller. His appearance reminded Lapidus of the story Becker had told about his first meeting with Demet prior to the December grand jury. Becker had asked Demet if he preferred to cooperate with the investigation rather than face possible indictment. Demet's only response, delivered in a voice of utter dejection, was "Why did this have to happen just before I was to take my lieutenant's exam?"

Demet never took that exam. After he asserted his Fifth Amendment privilege before the grand jury and Demopolous lost in his suicidal attempt to have Judge Austin restrict police disciplinary action, he was suspended. Now he was unemployed and broke. Lapidus turned back to King.

Q: (Lapidus) Mr. King, directing your attention now to December of 1969, did you have a conversation with Mr. Demet?

A: (King) It was the latter part of November or December, yes, I did.

Q: Where did that conversation take place?

A: At The Scene.

Q: What was Mr. Demet wearing at that time?

A: Plain clothes.

Q: What time of day or night was that conversation?

A: It was late. It was between 12:00 and 2:00 A.M.

Q: Who was present at that conversation, sir?

A: Demet and two or three other police officers. I don't recall who they were.

Q: Do you recall any employees of your tavern who were present in the vicinity at the time?

A: Yes.

Q: Who was that?

A: My wife.

Q: Would you please tell the Court and jury now what Mr. Demet said and what you said during that conversation?

A: Mr. Demet came in with the other police officers and they sat at the end of the bar toward the back. We exchanged greetings and he ordered a drink —what it was I don't know.

Mr. Demet asked me, "Do you have any problems? How is it going?" I told him, "In fact, yes, I do."

I told him about my parking problems outside; I had a 4:00 license and there was a 3:00 to 7:00 parking ordinance, alternate parking on each side of the street, and I was having a policeman cover it, well, usually on the weekends when we were real busy and it was always ten or twenty dollars, every time. It was on a Friday. I told Mr. Demet about a police officer who was covering it. It was a police sergeant then and every Friday and Saturday, without fail, he was there in the busy times. It was always, I was paying him ten or twenty dollars—not to Mr. Demet, but to this police sergeant.

Now I related to him about police officers coming in during the week, always in uniform, with regard to me being open after hours and there was no basis for this because I wasn't, at the time.

It was getting late and The Scene was getting busy, which we always did around 2:00 and Demet asked me, "Is there a place that is more quiet so we can talk?"

So we went into the back room. There is a kitchen in the back room and I went in the room, Mr. Demet and I, and pulled the door closed. . . . And the door was closed and Mr. Demet and I were in there and he said to me, "In order to avoid all this BS," he said, "why don't you pay so much a month?" I said to him then, I said, "Now what's the mutuals?"

He said, "Well, you tell us." I said, "Well, how about $50 a month?" He said, "Well, O.K."

So I called my wife, who was a waitress that night, and told her to bring me the $50 bill I had given her that I had taken out of the register for change. She brought it in. She gave it to me and I handed it to Mr. Demet. . . .

Q: Mr. King, why did you use the word "mutuals" in that conversation?

A: Well, frankly, I had given money to policemen before and that was the term always used.

Demopolous jumped out of his seat, objecting furiously to King's last answer because he had referred to payoffs to other policemen. Marovitz simply told the jury to disregard the statement. He also told Lapidus to reframe the question. Lapidus did so and King, who had obviously paid close attention to the exchange, now answered, "I had heard the word before in connection with police officers."

Demopolous objected again, but Marovitz let the answer stand. Demopolous was beside himself with frustration. The jury would obviously not disregard the fact that King had made reference to payoffs to other policemen and Demet's apparent understanding of the term "mutuals" had to be damaging.

Demopolous continued his flurry of objections when Lapidus asked King to tell the jury his state of mind during the conversation with Demet. Marovitz summarily overruled the objections, and King said, "My feeling was at the time that if I didn't pay, that I would jeopardize my liquor license and have more harassment." Demopolous was now sitting on the edge of his chair like an angry cat ready to strike. In contrast, Demet had not budged or changed his despondent look of resignation.

Lapidus then led King to later in December 1969, just before Christmas. King testified that Demet and three other officers came in one night. "We exchanged greetings. They had a drink. One of them brought up the question that a gift was given or going to be given to the commander. . . . Somebody said, 'What are you going to give?' or something to that effect. I said, 'Well—' I showed him a bottle, a bottle of Mextaxa, a ceramic bottle of Grand Mextaxa. And he said, 'Oh yes, that's what he likes.' Somebody said, 'Well, what about us?' I said, 'O.K. Stop around Christmas and I will have something for you.' "

During Christmas week Demet returned and took two cases of liquor and with King's help loaded them in the trunk of his car.

King described how between Christmas and New Year's he became increasingly frustrated because he felt that he was getting nothing for his accommodation of Demet and the vice squad. In fact, he had been arrested on one occasion, a problem he had assumed the monthly payments would avoid. King went to the Austin District station to complain. There he met Demet and several other vice officers. King took Demet aside and said, "What's going on? I am paying $50 a month and last night I was brought into the station, I was forced to pay $300 by a sergeant and a patrolman." Demet responded that he had not been aware of this incident, and took him in to see Thanasouras. But Thanasouras was on his way out and merely said he would take care of the problem.

King testified that he made only one more monthly payment to Demet. Demet was transferred to another district in February, although not for any alleged improper action. The heart of the government's case had been presented. The trial was just one day old.

The following morning Demopolous tried to establish in his cross-examination that Demet had not coerced King in any way. If the payments had been made, they were actually King's idea. Demet was simply too weak to refuse a handout.

Demopolous's defense was based on a loophole in the Hobbs Act which made extortion, but not bribery, a crime. His plan was to win acquittal by showing that King's payments to Demet were bribes offered freely and that King had not been afraid of Demet at any time.

Lapidus was amazed because he did not believe that the jury would ever buy this story or make a distinction between bribery and extortion. While Demet's coercion had hardly been blatant, there was little question that his uniform, power, and actions had posed a threat to King's business and liquor license. King had made it clear, from his experience with arrests for minor violations, that he knew a liquor license violation was a serious offense which could cause him to go out of business. Lapidus made a note to remind himself not to let the jury forget this crucial fact.

When King stepped off the stand late that morning, the government called Mrs. King, a good-looking, modestly dressed woman in her late thirties. She corroborated her husband's account of the initial payment to Demet and the gift of the two cases of liquor. Demopolous's cross-examination of her broke no new ground and he quickly excused her. Lapidus stood up and told Judge Marovitz that the government would now rest.

Everyone's attention turned to Demopolous, curious to see him pursue the defense about which he had only hinted during his cross-examination of the Kings.

There was no defense. A surprised Lapidus listened to Demopolous tell the judge that he would not call any witnesses. The jury was excused and Demopolous argued that the case should not be allowed to go to the jury because the evidence showed only a bribe. Furthermore, he said, King's testimony that he bought liquor which was manufactured out of state was insufficient to show an effect on interstate commerce. Marovitz denied his motion for a judgment of acquittal almost before Demopolous finished his argument. Demet's fate would be decided by the jury.

Because Demet had not taken the stand and no evidence was presented in his defense, there was little that Lapidus could tell the jury. By law, Lapidus could not comment on Demet's failure to testify, and the brevity of the case made it unnecessary to spend much time reviewing the evidence which the government had introduced. Instead, Lapidus concentrated on emphasizing that Demet's actions clearly constituted extortion and that he had callously enriched himself by abusing the power of his office.

Lapidus and Beigel had agreed that the key to these cases was convincing the jury that even the smallest misstep by an officer of the law who willingly used his authority to get money was criminal and contemptible. Whether it was $50 or $5,000, the crime was the same and just as serious. When Lapidus sat down he could only hope that he had gotten this across to the jury.

Demopolous's closing argument was a model of distraction and confusion. He spoke pointedly and quickly, alternately lecturing and pleading in a theatrical manner. But in the end all he really said was that, yes, Demet had received the money but there had been no coercion.

While the jury deliberated Lapidus was as nervous as Beigel had been during the weekend preceding the announcement of the Moore verdict. Before these cases had begun, Thompson, Beigel, and Davidson had agreed that winning convictions in half the cases would be a significant accomplishment. But now that Moore had been convicted, Lapidus did not want to be the first to lose.

A conviction was not guaranteed. The Demet trial had been short and Demopolous had taken an unexpected course by not bothering to have Demet deny that payments were made. Since there was no perjury count in this indictment, the jury had no leeway. Lapidus was concerned that some of the twelve jurors might not want to find Demet guilty on what could conceivably be considered a harmless, isolated aberration.

Thirty minutes after the jury retired the verdict was in. Despite the common myth among prosecutors that the quicker a jury reaches a verdict, the more likely it is for conviction, Lapidus rode the elevator to Marovitz's courtroom thinking that Demet might have been acquitted. It was difficult to believe that when only two witnesses who were related to one another had testified against the defendant the jurors would be so quick to convict. Thirty minutes of deliberation would allow only one ballot following a minimum of discussion.

Demopolous looked confident as the jury entered the courtroom. Demet still seemed detached from reality. Marovitz took the bench and asked the foreman if the jury had reached a verdict. The foreman replied that it had and handed the verdict form to the clerk, who gave it to Marovitz. The judge looked at it for much longer than it would take to read what it said. One reporter who had covered the trial had told Lapidus just before the jury returned that he was sure there would be a conviction. Now Lapidus, watching Marovitz, was not so sure. Marovitz handed the form back to the clerk. The clerk paused and then read, "We the jury find the defendant George Demet guilty on the indictment." Demopolous slumped and shook his head. Demet showed no reaction.

Although the trial of George Demet was over, both Beigel and Lapidus felt there was still one piece of unfinished business. They were concerned that the extortion of King might be viewed as an isolated example of greed which had only once gotten the better of Demet. Lapidus decided to put Marty Lindstrom on the stand at Demet's sentencing hearing to establish that Demet was no stranger to shakedowns.

Lindstrom was shocked when he found out he would have to testify after all. Still, he took the news with a certain amount of grace, saying, "If I have to, I guess I will." Lindstrom took the stand and, in a quivering voice, told Judge Marovitz how he had been approached by Frank Bychowski and another patrolman in 1966. (Bychowski had since taken leave from the department to become a police chief in a small Wisconsin town.) The two officers asked him if he would make monthly payments to avoid the trouble he had been having recently with arrests. Lindstrom agreed. Never one for concrete details, Lindstrom said that he believed he made between four and six monthly payments to Demet during the ensuing year.

Marovitz ordered the testimony stricken from the record, saying it was "too vague." He also refused to allow Lindstrom to testify about the conversation he had with Bychowski when the original solicitation was made, presumably because Demet was not present.

When the time for sentencing had arrived, Marovitz commended Demet for not taking the stand and lying. "It is to this officer's credit that he didn't compound the offense by committing perjury." Referring to standards of morality was one of Marovitz's favorite approaches to sentencing. He lectured Demet accordingly. "You've made the front page news and caused a lot of unhappiness to decent policeman. . . . These things just couldn't happen with proper supervision." Marovitz then praised Superintendent Conlisk as a man of "honor and integrity" and said that "apparently that honor and integrity hasn't seeped down to men of lower rank." Almost as an aside, he sentenced Demet to one year in prison. Unfortunately for Demet, it was not the end of his ordeal.

The Trial of Frank Gill and James Fahey

Stoyan Kovacevic and the story of his Chicago-Oak Liquors store had first come to the attention of the FBI in July 1971. Kovacevic, an informal contact of the FBI who periodically provided information about the activities of civic groups in the Serbian community, told an FBI agent detailed to the Internal Security Squad that he had paid $300 to the police to avoid arrest for selling beer to a minor. The agent had little experience with investigations of Hobbs Act violations and wrote a report without making clear when the payment had been made or to whom it had been given. The only police officer mentioned in the report was named Redden and he had apparently been involved only in the initial investigation of the tavern which had led to the shakedown and Kovacevic's later arrest. The only other person named in the report was "Dino" and his role in the shakedown, if any, was ambiguous.

In November 1971 Becker and another FBI agent went to see Kovacevic and his brother Boris at the store. The store was actually a combination retail outlet and bar with the bar being connected to the liquor store by a door at the back near the coolers.

In contrast to the ambiguity of the July report Kovacevic was very explicit about what had happened. He told Becker that, one day during the first week of July, he had been working behind the cash register when a young man came to the counter carrying a six-pack. Kovacevic sold him the beer and the young man left. His brother was stocking shelves in the back and did not see the young man enter or leave. Five minutes after the sale Kovacevic looked up to see the same young man and a uniformed police officer standing in front of him. Kovacevic did not ask the officer his name at that time, but told Becker that he found out it was Officer Redden a week later when he was taken to the police station by the same officer for another sale to a young girl. (Kovacevic had been furious about the second arrest because the girl had shown him several pieces of identification confirming she was over twenty-one. He thought the arrest had been trumped up and had taken special care to get the officer's name. Kovacevic told Becker that he was absolutely positive that it had been the same officer on both occasions.)

Redden asked Kovacevic if he had sold beer to the boy. He replied that he had. "Well, he's under age, you know," Redden said. "I'll have to call the station and get a lieutenant down here." Redden went to call the station, taking the boy with him to the patrol car.

If Redden had been a vice officer, he could have made the arrest himself. As a uniformed patrolman, however, unless he had witnessed commission of the crime, he was not supposed to arrest or conduct a solitary investigation. Rules required that a higher-ranking officer take over the investigation and determine what immediate action should be taken, including whether an arrest should be made. This procedure underscored the power of the vice officer who, although also a patrolman, was allowed to conduct investigations without resorting to the normal command hierarchy of the district. Therefore, unlike Walter Moore and George Demet, Redden had to call for higher-ranking assistance before police action could be taken against Stoyan Kovacevic.

Kovacevic told Becker that about ten minutes later two more police officers entered. At this point Kovacevic became a little vague. He recalled that one of the officers stayed in the store for a while, but could not remember if he said anything. He was certain that he directed all his comments to the other officer, a tall, light-complexioned man of about forty whom Kovacevic distinctly remembered being a lieutenant. He could not recall his name, however, and had never seen him before.

The lieutenant motioned Kovacevic to come out from behind the cash register. Kovacevic did as directed while Boris took care of several customers. Out of hearing range of the customers, the lieutenant, apparently with the other officer standing behind him, told Kovacevic that he would have to appear before the Liquor Commission. The two officers then abruptly left and Kovacevic went back to the counter and told Boris what had happened. Several minutes later the lieutenant returned alone and again motioned Kovacevic to join him in the middle of the store. By this time Kovacevic had had ample opportunity to begin worrying that his license might be in jeopardy.

Kovacevic asked the lieutenant what he should do. The lieutenant said, "What can you do?," a question which he interpreted as an invitation to offer money. Stoyan proposed $150. The lieutenant laughed and said he wanted $500. After some haggling Stoyan mentioned $300. The lieutenant appeared agreeable and left the store.

Shortly after the second conversation Boris, who after serving a few customers had gone to the back of the store, told Kovacevic that a man named Dino had approached him, saying he knew one of the officers involved and could take care of the problem. Kovacevic went back to the register and removed

$300, which he gave to his brother, who gave the money to Dino at the back of the store. Kovacevic never saw the lieutenant or the other officer again. Although he said it was possible that Redden had been present when the two officers had originally entered the store, he was sure he was not there when the critical second conversation with the lieutenant took place.

Becker was confused by the time sequence of these fast-moving events but Kovacevic was unable to remember precisely how long each of the conversations lasted or how much time had elapsed between the first and second conversation with the lieutenant. Becker was also puzzled by Dino. Kovacevic did not know his real name or where he lived. He was just someone he recalled seeing at the tavern several times. As to the officer who had accompanied the lieutenant and had not talked, Kovacevic could supply only a brief physical description and did not know his name or rank. Finally, Kovacevic admitted that he had only assumed that Dino had given the money to the officers.

Another agent talked to Kovacevic's brother, who corroborated this narrative, but was vague about the details. Becker also met with the bartender. He recalled seeing Dino talking to a sergeant while the police were there. He remembered Dino telling him that the owners were in trouble for selling liquor to a minor. He could not specifically retrace the movements of the sergeant, but said that the sergeant had not gone into the liquor store from the tavern after the conversation with Dino.

He was also not sure how many times the sergeant had entered and left the tavern during this time period. Finally, the bartender could not remember when Dino had left the tavern, although he did see him go into the liquor store following the conversation with the sergeant.

The bartender told Becker that Dino's name was Constantine Sanichas, and he had been a small-time bookie with no fixed address or regular employment. He told Becker that Dino was a chatty, harmless old man who liked to come in once a day for a beer and "shoot the breeze." He could usually be found at the Rex Restaurant, a coffee shop down the street, where he used to work.

These interviews led Beigel to request the arrest reports concerning Chicago-Oak Liquors. No report was located for this incident, but a report of the second investigation involving the sale to the girl was there. Becker and Beigel both agreed that further investigation was warranted.

Several days later Becker found Dino at the Rex. They sat down in a booth and talked. Dino said he knew "nothing about nothing" and denied that he had been at the store on the day in question. "Even if I was there," he said, "why should I tell you anything?" Becker handed him a subpoena for the grand jury.

A subpoena was also issued for Officer Redden. When he appeared before the grand jury he answered agreeably all questions which Beigel asked. He related what had occurred prior to the arrival of the two officers. He said that, while patroling down Chicago Avenue, he saw a young man come out of Chicago-Oak Liquors with what appeared to be a six-pack of beer. He saw him get in a car and followed him for a few blocks before curbing him. He asked for his license. Redden said he could not remember the boy's name, but distinctly recalled he was under twenty-one. He denied any knowledge about what had occurred after the lieutenant and sergeant, whom he had called, arrived on the scene. He conceded that he had not written any report of the incident, but said that after high-ranking officers were called to the scene, it was their responsibility to write the report if it was required. He did recall, however, that he was later told by either the lieutenant or the sergeant that no arrest had been made. He could not remember the reason. However, he did know their names, Lieutenant Frank Gill and Sergeant James Fahey.

Dino had nothing to tell the grand jury. He gave his name as Constantine Sanichas and took the Fifth on all other questions.

After learning the names of the lieutenant and the sergeant Beigel asked Kovacevic to come to the office to look at photographs. Remarkably, he immediately picked out Gill and Fahey from over thirty pictures. His brother was not as adept and could not recall enough about what the officers looked like to be sure about picking out their pictures.

Gill and Fahey were called before the grand jury to tell their versions about what had happened. Both appeared in early 1972 and testified. They denied asking for or receiving any money. Gill explained that he had decided not to make an arrest after the boy's father had come to the store. The father explained that he had sent the boy for the beer because he was recuperating from surgery and could not leave the house. Gill also said that he had examined the boy's driver's license and saw that he was only one month short of twenty-one. Gill explained that his experience with the courts had been that judges would always dismiss a case if the minor had turned twenty-one by the time of his appearance. Fahey corroborated Gill's story.

As to the lack of a report, the officers' explanation was that a card had been filled out on the incident, but a case report had not been written. These cards were routinely destroyed within a few months while case reports are retained for a longer time and sent to the Liquor Commission.

Fahey added one other piece of information. He recalled that the minor's last name was Powers and that he may have lived in Oak Park. Beigel, however, did not pay much attention to this. Powers was a common name, and everyone's narrative seemed to indicate that the boy, even if located, would not be able to add anything to the shakedown evidence. Becker also agreed that looking for the Powers boy probably would be a wild goose chase. To both of them the case seemed to depend once again on the credibility of the complainants. Since Kovacevic had given his story unequivocally and had selected the two officers from the photographs without any difficulty, the case seemed worth prosecuting.

The Kovacevics had no reason to lie. They had not been arrested. Since a case report had not been prepared, they had not appeared before the Liquor Commission on this incident. If they were mad at the police and had wanted to lie, the logical target would have been Redden. He had been responsible for the arrest following the second incident and for their appearance, as a result, before the Liquor Commission. Yet neither had accused Redden of attempting to extort money.

The most troublesome aspect of the case was the lack of evidence against Fahey. Neither Stoyan nor Boris Kovacevic had talked with him. During the first conversation, when Gill had not asked Stoyan Kovacevic for money, Fahey had stood behind Gill and said nothing. During Gill's second conversation with Kovacevic, Fahey had not even been present. If he had been involved, it appeared that only Dino could supply the missing pieces of the story. However, Dino had steadfastly refused to say anything. The only action that could be taken, therefore, was to indict Frank Gill and Dino Sanichas. Beigel hoped this would bring Dino to his senses and he would change his mind about talking.

If he did not, Beigel simply would have to persuade the jury that Gill's verbal shakedown plus the payment to Dino must have resulted in the money going to Gill. The problem with this approach was that it left Fahey as a possible defense witness who could support Gill without fear of contradiction. If he did, as his grand jury testimony indicated he would, the chances for conviction would be reduced.

The indictments against Gill and Dino were returned along with the rest of the March indictments. Gill surrendered voluntarily and Dino was arrested at a Marriott hotel where he had recently been hired as a security guard. Within several days Beigel received a telephone call from a young attorney who had been appointed to represent the indigent Dino. The lawyer said, "Let me come and meet with you. I'm sure we can work this out."

At the meeting the lawyer told Beigel that Dino was now ready to tell everything he knew if he would be granted immunity and dismissed from the indictment. This was just what Beigel had wanted, since he was worried about the case. Although it had seemed justified to indict Gill on the basis of the known facts, Beigel was still uncomfortable since the evidence did not add up and there were lingering doubts about what role Fahey had played. If Dino could furnish the missing parts of the story, these doubts could be resolved. Beigel agreed to dismiss Dino after the lawyer promised that Dino would provide valuable information.

Dino ambled into Beigel's office the next day, ecstatic. "I got nothing against you guys and I'll tell you what you want to know. I just never wanted any trouble."

Beigel and Becker spent three hours with Dino taking him through the events of that July day. Within a week the indictment was amended and James Fahey was now also charged with extortion and perjury.

Several weeks after the new indictment was returned Beigel met with Sherman Magidson, Gill's attorney, to give him a copy of Gill's grand jury testimony. Magidson was a good-looking, stocky man in his mid-thirties. He had been Thompson's classmate at Northwestern University Law School and during the past several years had achieved a wide reputation as one of the best criminal defense lawyers in Chicago. No one questioned his skill, his integrity, or his good judgment.

"Herb, you've made a big mistake," Magidson said. "In fact, a disastrous one. I have talked to Frank at length. I talked with Fahey. I have investigated this case thoroughly. Gill just did not do what he is charged with. He's not the kind of man who would get involved in an extortion, especially such a silly one as this. He's got a wonderful wife, ten children, and a clean police record. This case will ruin his career."

"What do you want me to do, Sherm?" Beigel said. "We believe we have the evidence. You can't or won't show me where I am wrong and I can't judge a man on his police record or wonderful family."

"If I thought he shook down that tavern owner, Herb, I'd advise him to come in here and tell you the truth and work out something. But he didn't do it. If a shakedown occurred, you have indicted the wrong man."

Beigel thought Magidson was referring to Redden, but did not want to discuss why Redden had not been indicted. He didn't know what Magidson was thinking and saw no reason to reveal his theory of why he believed Kovacevic was telling the truth. Now that he had Dino's cooperation, he was convinced more than ever of Gill's and Fahey's guilt.

Fahey's attorney, John Muldoon, took the same approach as Magidson. Muldoon was not a full-time criminal defense lawyer and admitted that "I'm not involved in criminal cases that much and obviously a case like this is a little strange. But Fahey was an officer for thirty-five years. He's retired now. Everybody in the department loved him. I don't know anyone who ever said anything bad about him. He's a widower and has no family. He could lose his pension. This case is destroying him."

Even a member of the press was critical. He telephoned Davidson after the indictment was returned and said he had known Gill for years and it was simply inconceivable that he could be corrupt. "This time you fellows have missed the boat. You're bringing down an honest, decent cop. I can't believe you are making such a terrible mistake."

The courtroom was more packed for the first day of the Gill-Fahey trial than it had been a week earlier for the Walter Moore trial. Thompson sat with Davidson in the first row. The press was present in full force, brought out by the verdict against Moore and the presence of higher-ranking defendants on trial. Also contributing to the excitement was the ongoing trial before Judge Marovitz. For the moment it appeared that the sole business of the federal courts was to hold trials involving policemen.

Frank Gill's wife and three of his children were at the back of the courtroom. Gill's wife was an attractive woman in her late thirties who carried herself with poise and self-assurance. Gill was dressed in a conservative business suit that seemed too big for his lanky build and made him look like he had recently lost weight. As he sat next to his attorney, he often turned around to glance at his wife, sending her a smile which she would return with a reassuring nod. If he was apprehensive, he managed to hide it.

James Fahey was alone. He had retired from the department before he was indicted and lived in a modest apartment. He was a widower and if he had many friends on the police force, they were not present. Unlike Gill, he looked neither poised nor confident. He said little to Muldoon and kept his left hand in his pocket. His white hair was short and neatly combed. He struck Beigel as a friendly neighborhood cop whom people respected and the kids loved. When Beigel went over to Magidson and Muldoon to discuss a few preliminary matters, Gill politely said hello. Fahey turned away and stared sadly at the jury box.

Because of the Moore trial, Beigel did not have sufficient time to prepare for the Gill-Fahey trial by himself. Beigel and Davidson had anticipated this problem and had explained the situation to Thompson. He recommended that Dan Webb, one of his Assistant U.S. Attorneys, become involved in the Gill-Fahey case.

He was young (twenty-eight), aggressive, and had not lost in sixteen previous trials. He grew up in a small town in rural southern Illinois and had held down several jobs to finance his law school education at Loyola in Chicago. Although he had never been involved in a corruption investigation, his other investigations had usually produced strong evidence and convictions. His youngish looks and folksy way of talking enabled him to establish an easy rapport with most juries.

Beigel and Webb were extremely concerned about the selection of the jury. Gill and his ten children and Fahey, with his grandfatherly appearance, would make it difficult for a jury to condemn them. The prosecutors hoped to keep housewives and mothers to a minimum. They felt that these jurors would be more likely to want to save Gill and Fahey if at all possible, if not for Gill's sake, then for his family; if not for Fahey, then in recognition of his kind demeanor and his thirty-five years of police service.

The jury Beigel and Webb wanted was a mixture of middle-class working men, career women, professionals, and academics. One housewife after another was called. At one point fifteen out of sixteen prospective jurors selected fell into this category. When the jury selection was finally concluded, ten of the twelve jurors were women and almost all of them were middle-aged housewives with families.

Webb delivered the opening statement. As he spoke, Beigel studied the jury. He saw nothing that gave him a clue as to whether it would accept the prosecution's contention that the two police officers on trial coldly shook down a tavern owner and employed the services of a transient ex-bookie to help them. Beigel only observed that they listened carefully to Webb's outline of the government's case. Otherwise, they were impassive, as were the judge, each of the defendants, the defense attorneys, and the gallery. The courtroom was like a landscape on which only Webb was moving.

Stoyan Kovacevic was the prosecution's first witness. Although his Serbian accent made it difficult to understand him, it also made the jurors pay close attention. Kovacevic told how he had sold the six-pack to the unidentified young man, and how Redden made his appearance with the boy and then called Gill and Fahey to the scene. Beigel asked Kovacevic if he saw the two officers in the courtroom. Without hesitation he pointed them out. He then described his two conversations with Gill, emphasizing Gill's laughing response to his initial offer of $150. A few jurors glanced occasionally at Gill during Kovacevic's testimony, almost as if they were having a difficult time making up their mind whether this decent-looking man with a fine family could have said the things that Kovacevic was swearing he had said in July 1971.

When Kovacevic finished his direct testimony, Magidson stood up to begin cross-examination. Kovacevic was in for a rough ride. Magidson was a top-notch courtroom examiner. Kovacevic was vulnerable, but it was not totally his fault. Beginning with the initial report prepared by the Internal Security Squad agent and continuing with the reports of later interviews conducted by Becker and his colleagues, some inconsistent statements had accumulated. The reports also omitted certain facts to which Kovacevic was testifying.

Magidson began by using the original interview to impeach Kovacevic's credibility. This interview report could be read as showing that Kovacevic had said he had paid the money himself even though his later statements and the testimony demonstrated that he had given the $300 to Boris, who had paid it to Dino to deliver to the officers. Magidson scrupulously pointed out where each part of Kovacevic's testimony differed from what was contained in the reports. Kovacevic, however, insisted that he consistently had told the same story when interviewed by the FBI. He tried to explain that he should not be blamed if the FBI agents had misunderstood him or failed to ask the right questions.

Magidson also intensively cross-examined Kovacevic about his second arrest by Officer Redden. He tried to force Kovacevic to admit that he was using the present case to get back at the police for unfair harassment. Kovacevic conceded that the second arrest had been his main reason for calling the FBI and telling what had happened in the Gill-Fahey incident a week earlier. This concession helped Magidson get his point across to the jury.

Muldoon did not spend much time cross-examining Kovacevic. Stoyan had never talked to Fahey and, by his own testimony, had given the money to Boris. Muldoon was interested only in establishing what everyone accepted, namely that Kovacevic was not a witness against his client. That is why everything depended on Dino.

When Stoyan Kovacevic left the stand, both Beigel and Webb thought that things were going as well as could be expected except for their disappointment about the jury selection. Court was adjourned and the two prosecutors returned to their offices to discuss an important development, one which could either make or break their case.

It had begun almost by accident. A week before the trial Beigel had received a call from Conlisk's liaison with the Strike Force. He explained that a Captain John Foley had been served with a subpoena by Gill's attorney and that, in accord with department policy, he was informing Beigel. Beigel assumed that Foley, a watch commander in the Austin District, had been subpoenaed to testify as a character witness. But he was taking no chances and asked if an interview might be arranged with Foley.

The next day Beigel and Webb greeted Foley in Beigel's office. Foley was somewhat perplexed by both the subpoena and the interview. "I don't know why I am being called since I don't know anything about the incident."

"Captain," Beigel said, "you are probably going to be asked questions regarding Gill's reputation. We assume that you will testify his reputation is good."

"That's right."

"What we want to know, Captain, is if you are sure there is nothing you can add to the evidence in this case."

"Well, to be perfectly honest with you gentlemen, the only thing I can remember is that Lieutenant Gill mentioned to me that he had investigated a sale by Chicago Oak-Liquors to a minor."

"When was this?" Beigel was suddenly more interested.

"Oh, I think it was that same afternoon. I don't remember the date. Anyway, Lieutenant Gill said that he had decided not to make an arrest. Naturally, as watch commander I asked him why and he said that the boy had just gone to buy some beer because his father was confined to the house. He also said something about the kid being almost twenty-one."

Beigel recalled that this was the same reason Gill had given in his grand jury testimony. He asked Foley, "Why? Is that a reason not to arrest?"

"Oh, I don't think it's a reason to skip an arrest because a minor had been sent by his father to buy the beer. The officer in charge of the investigation should still arrest the tavern owner and the boy. But when the boy is almost twenty-one, it doesn't pay to make the arrest. When it comes to court, he'll be twenty-one and judges routinely throw those cases out of court."

"One last question, Captain. Are there any Police Department records which would reflect either your discussion with Gill or this incident?"

"Well, we do keep a log where the investigating officer makes a notation even when there is no arrest. Gill would have probably filled one out in this case. But those logs are destroyed after a couple of months. We do that to avoid being buried under a mountain of paperwork."

When Foley left, Beigel said to Webb, "You know, Danny, I'm concerned about what Foley told us. Both Gill and Fahey gave the same stories about why they did not make an arrest. That's not so bad. But now we have another cop who is going to testify and corroborate Gill. He'll make it appear that everything Gill said is the truth."

Webb nodded in agreement. Then Beigel remembered that they had a last name for the minor. Beigel went to the file. Quickly he found it. "I had forgotten all about this. Fahey says he thought the last name was Powers and that he lived in Oak Park."

"Why should he give a name at all, if he isn't telling the truth?" Webb asked.

"Maybe because he thought we knew the boy's name already from Kovacevic or Redden. He couldn't make up a name. Besides, who knows if we can find the kid anyway. And he probably can't add anything. He wasn't part of the extortion. One more thing. By giving the name to the grand jury he stopped me from thinking it might be important."

"Who knows if it is?" Webb said.

Becker began the search for a boy named Powers, age twenty-one, who might live in Oak Park. Becker called every name in the phone book and came up empty-handed the first time around. When he made his report Becker said he had asked if there was a sick father in the family and everyone had said no. Beigel had another idea. "Look, why don't you just ask each person if they have a son of college age. After all, we don't know that the story about the invalid father is true."

The next day Becker came rushing into Beigel's office. "Herb, I found the kid. You were right, his father wasn't sick. His father is dead. He said he bought the beer for his friend's father, who was sick. He's a college student and he'll come downtown and talk to us."

Now, on the evening of the first day of the trial, Beigel and Webb reviewed what they had learned from Powers and contemplated what they should do. "We can't very well put him on as part of our case," Webb commented. "It might be ruled irrelevant before Gill testifies. Anyway, its impact would be lost."

"You're right, Danny, we'll just have to take our chances on being able to use him in rebuttal."

Beigel was still thinking about the Powers strategy when Webb began his examination of Boris Kovacevic. He was not nearly as effective a witness as his brother. He was confused about the sequence of events although he stated positively that Dino's approach occurred after Gill had finished his second conversation with Stoyan and walked outside. Boris also testified he had paid the $300 to Dino.

Magidson had not succeeded in unnerving Stoyan Kovacevic, but he had better luck with Boris. Magidson questioned him with great care about his statements to the FBI. Before long, Boris began to raise his voice and to interrupt Magidson's questions. Boris was confused, but this confusion partially saved him. His uncertainty counterbalanced his anger and allowed Webb to object and ask for clarifications of those questions which were troubling Boris. This gave Boris the time he needed to regain his composure. When Magidson finished it was obvious that Boris had not fared particularly well, but his testimony was only a small portion of the important evidence. The next witness, Constantine "Dino" Sanichas, would give the pivotal testimony.

Webb ushered Dino into the courtroom. Dino had spent the night at a downtown hotel courtesy of the Justice Department. Beigel and Webb were worried that he might not show up and an FBI agent stayed in an adjoining room. The prosecutors also wanted to make sure he did not get drunk and end up testifying with a hangover.

Dino was dressed in his best clothes—an oversized black suit with pleated pants and a single-buttoned jacket. He sported a yellow shirt and polka-dot tie. He looked as if he had been plucked from a rummage sale. As he shuffled uncomfortably toward the witness stand, he tugged nervously at his tie and looked at the floor.

Dino had been well prepared for the questions Webb would ask him. However, he was so tense that his responses sounded as if they had been memorized. It was true that he was giving the same story which he had told Biegel after being given immunity, but he had been more spontaneous then.

As Webb questioned him, he described how he often stopped at Chicago-Oak Liquors for a drink and was there on that afternoon in early July. He had been drinking a beer when he saw a police car drive up. He recalled seeing two officers on the sidewalk outside the entrance. He did not see where the first officer, whom he identified as Gill, went; but he saw Fahey enter the tavern. Dino said he knew Fahey from when he had worked at the Rex Restaurant. Since he was curious about what was happening, he started talking to him. Webb asked Dino, "Did you go to meet him or did he meet you?" Dino responded, "It was a dead heat."[2]

Dino's testimony implicated Fahey in the extortion scheme, the first time in the trial that Fahey had been linked to the crime. Dino said that Fahey had told him how the owners had been caught selling liquor to a minor and that it was going to cost them money to avoid trouble. Dino offered to talk to the Kovacevics and went into the liquor store to look for Stoyan and Boris. Fahey left the tavern.

As Dino entered through the connecting door, he saw Boris. Dino thought that $500 was the agreed-upon figure, but Boris told him that Gill had agreed to take $300. Dino and Boris talked for a minute and then Dino said, "I'll go talk to them." Dino testified that he then went back to the tavern and related his conversation with Boris to Fahey, who agreed to the $300 figure. He told Dino to meet him at the corner. Dino then returned to the liquor store and picked up the $300 from Boris.

2. Because of the unavailability of a complete transcript of this trial, Dino's testimony is paraphrased.

Dino described how he stopped to finish his drink before leaving the tavern, an exercise in nonchalance which contrasted markedly with the mechanical way in which he was handling Webb's questions. After a few minutes Dino finally left the tavern and walked to the corner. Shortly after he arrived Fahey drove up and Dino got into the car and gave him the $300. A few weeks later, when he saw Fahey again, Fahey gave him $40.

On cross-examination, both Magidson and Muldoon emphasized that Dino was testifying as a result of a grant of immunity. Dino was well prepared. He stated that he knew if he lied he could still be indicted for perjury. Both Webb and Beigel had spent a great deal of time impressing this upon Dino before the trial. Not only did they want him ready for this inevitable question, but they also wanted to make sure he would tell the truth. There was little else the defense could do on cross-examination. The evidence was clear that Dino hardly knew the Kovacevics and, if anything, felt friendly toward Fahey. Only the grant of immunity could give Dino a reason to concoct a story that corroborated the Kovacevics' version of the events.

To provide some corroboration for Dino's testimony, Beigel called the bartender. He stated that he recalled seeing Dino talk to Fahey in the bar that day. He admitted he did not overhear the conversation and could not trace completely the movements of Dino and the sergeant before and after the conversation. The testimony did support Dino's statement that Fahey had talked to him, a curious thing for Fahey to be doing during an investigation of an illegal sale.

The prosecutors rested their case. They had done everything possible to put the evidence before the jury, but they were still uneasy. Gill would make a persuasive witness and they prayed that their carefully planned strategy would work.

Muldoon put on Fahey's defense first. After several character witnesses appeared Fahey took the stand. He sat very rigid and kept his left hand in his pocket, as he had done throughout the trial. He spoke so softly that on several occasions Muldoon asked him to speak louder. He related the exact same version he had given to the grand jury, corroborating Gill and contradicting the testimony given by the Kovacevics and Dino.

On cross-examination Fahey admitted that he knew Dino. Fahey claimed, however, that he knew him only to say hello. Fahey said that when he had gone into the tavern to check things out, Dino had approached him to ask what was going on. At first, Fahey admitted only that he told Dino the owners were being investigated for the sale of liquor to a minor.

Beigel then asked Fahey if he had talked to Dino again. Fahey said that he had. "What was the conversation?" Beigel asked.

"Well, when Lieutenant Gill decided not to make an arrest he told me to inform the owners of that. So I went back into the tavern and saw Dino. I went up to Dino and said, 'You can tell the owners that they are getting off this time.' I then left."

Fahey's explanation of his second conversation with Dino would form an important part of the prosecution's argument to the jury.

Gill's defense was supported by a bevy of character witnesses, including a respected member of the department's high command, a priest, and, of course, Captain Foley. Magidson then called Gill to the stand. He walked to the witness box with the fluid but precise movements that characterized someone who was used to the courtroom. Magidson skillfully led Gill through his story. Everything Gill said was exactly what he had told the grand jury. In addition, Magidson asked Gill to give a résumé of his career, to describe the many awards and citations he had received during his more than twenty years of service without a blemish on his record, and to review his family life. The jury listened intently to Gill. Halfway through his testimony Beigel knew that if the jury were asked to reach a verdict now, it would be not guilty.

Webb handled the cross-examination. He asked question after question about why Gill had not arrested Kovacevic. Each time Gill repeated his story about the sick father and cited the boy's age as his reason for not making the arrest. As Webb continued relentlessly on this track, Beigel could see that Judge Austin was becoming annoyed, perhaps because he could not understand this line of cross-examination, which emphasized that part of Gill's testimony which was the most plausible. Austin began to frown and finally turned away in apparent disgust.

Within ten minutes Webb announced to a surprised courtroom that he had finished his cross-examination. Gill's story had not been dented. As he stepped down from the stand he was as confident as he had been when he had begun his testimony. Magidson announced, with equal confidence, that the defense rested. Austin looked at Beigel and Webb with frustration and dismay. "Any rebuttal?"

"Yes, Your Honor," Webb said. "We have one witness in rebuttal."

"Call him then." Austin could not conceal his impatience.

"Timothy Powers," Webb said slowly and dramatically.

Becker opened the door to the courtroom and led in Tim Powers. Beigel could see Magidson talking frantically to Gill.

Powers took the stand. Webb quickly got to the heart of the matter and asked him where he had been on the day in question. Powers said that he had been visiting a friend and that his friend had suggested that they go out and get some beer because his father was ill and could not do it himself. They drove to Chicago-Oak Liquors since it was not in Oak Park and they would be less likely to be tabbed as minors. Powers then testified how he went into the store to buy the beer and how Redden stopped him while he was driving away and brought him back. He also remembered Gill and Fahey arriving at the scene, but he did not overhear any conversations between the owners and the officers.

Q: Now, Mr. Powers, were you arrested that day?

A: No, I was not.

Q: Did either Lieutenant Gill or Sergeant Fahey tell you why you were not being arrested?

A: No.

Q: Do you know if any arrests were made at all?

A: No.

Q: Mr. Powers, do you recall if you showed a driver's license to the Lieutenant?

A: I did.

Q: Was it your license?

A: Yes.

Q: Was the information on it true and correct?

A: Yes.

Q: Did it correctly show your age?

A: Yes, it had my birthdate on it.

Q: And how old were you on that day?

A: I had just turned 19.

A loud gasp escaped from the lips of several jurors. Judge Austin, who had been leaning back in his chair with his eyes closed throughout the testimony, lunged forward. The gallery erupted in chatter. Webb said, "I have nothing further." The courtroom became suddenly silent. Austin said, "Mr. Magidson, cross-examination?"

Magidson stood up slowly. He betrayed no surprise, chagrin, or worry. Magidson knew that his only hope to defuse the impact of Powers's testimony was to treat it as if it had none. Magidson spent more than thirty minutes taking Powers through everything that had happened that day at the Chicago-Oak Liquors. His every movement, his every conversation, his every thought were the subject of Magidson's detailed questions. The only relevant information was Powers's age, but the wealth of detail which Magidson elicited was so overwhelming that this essential fact was being skillfully buried.

When Magidson had finished Beigel and Webb wondered whether the jury would remember the importance of his age. Muldoon did not want to do anything to disturb the cross-examination conducted by Magidson. He asked only a few questions and sat down. The case would soon be in the hands of the jury.

But first came the closing arguments. It was here that Webb and Beigel would have to hit as hard as they could. It would not be easy. While Powers's testimony would help avoid an easy and quick acquittal, it did not insure conviction.

Webb delivered the government's summation. As he finished he came to the nub not only of this case but of any case in which public officers are charged with wrongdoing and only testimonial evidence from the victims is presented.

"So you know right now that somebody lied and you have to face that fact. You are going to have to weigh the evidence and you are going to have to determine who lied in this case. Was it the defendant Gill, the defendant Fahey, or was it the government witnesses? You saw all three government witnesses testify. They have absolutely no motive to lie in this case. They are citizens who were involved and got involved in this extortion in the Chicago-Oak Liquors store in early July, 1971. They came forward and they told their story. . . .

"You have to ask yourself, were any of those witnesses motivated to lie? None of them has an interest in the outcome of this case. It doesn't make any difference what happens in this case. None of them will benefit at all. Whatever you do when you get back into the jury room, guilty or not guilty, has no effect at all on the lives of Boris Kovacevic, Stoyan Kovacevic, and Dino Sanichas.

"And since they have no motive to lie, they have no need to come in here and tell you a story about Gill and Fahey unless it is true. Because of that you know that when the witnesses took the stand they would tell the truth.

"Now, what I would like to do is examine the other side of the coin, because the defense went forward in this case and presented evidence. I want to tell you at the outset that the only evidence they presented which relates to the events in question was the testimony of Gill and Fahey. All of those other witnesses were character witnesses; they were not there. You've got to ask yourselves what did they add to your knowledge and your ability to make a determination of the facts.

"Your job is to find out what went on in the Chicago-Oak Liquors store in early July, 1971. What did those witnesses add? You've got to ask yourself that; the answer is nothing. They weren't there. If they weren't there, how could they add anything?

"You also know that both defendants have a very vital interest in the outcome of this case. Whatever happens they are the ones who are going to be affected the most. They have a reason to get on the stand and lie. You must keep that in mind because you have to weigh the credibility of the witnesses and determine who is telling the truth.

"We all know from human experience that people don't usually lie unless they have a reason. If the truth doesn't hurt, then the truth is told. It's when the truth has dire consequences that lies follow. . . ."

Webb proceeded to attack Fahey's testimony, particularly his statement that, after Gill had directed him to tell the owners that they would not be arrested, he went into the tavern and gave the message to Dino. "Now," said Webb, "if you were standing out in front of the liquor store and you were told to go in and tell the owners that they were not going to be arrested, you would go where you last saw them. You would walk in the liquor store because that is where the owners were. But Fahey can't say that because he has got to put himself in the tavern. Too many witnesses saw him there. So he says, 'I walked into that tavern.' The owners were never in the tavern. He never saw them in there. But he said, 'I walked in the tavern.' When he gets inside, does he do something reasonable? Does he tell the bartender as an employee. . . . No, he went over to where Dino is standing. He walked over to Dino, a patron, and he supposedly says to this patron to tell the owners that they are not going to be arrested. That is absolutely incredible. It shows that when a man lies he must come up with fantastic explanations."

Webb then shifted to Gill's defense.

"The same thing is true of the defendant, Gill, only more so. It was easier to prove him a liar. We have a logical argument that Fahey's story is incredible, but we have brought forward and proved to you that Frank Gill did lie in this case. . . . He has testified over fifty times, and he knows how to come off smooth. I wonder when you were sitting here and listening to his testimony how many of you believed him because he was very, very good. . . . I certainly didn't do much in my cross examination; I couldn't match my wits with that man. He was very good."

Webb next went into detail about the Powers testimony, emphasizing that Gill knew he would have to come up with a reasonable explanation as to why he did not make an arrest. He pointed out to the jury that Gill must have known that buying beer for a sick father is not a sufficient excuse and that is why he had to concoct the story that Powers was almost twenty-one.

Webb's argument was now drawing to a close.

"In the last few minutes I have been addressing my arguments to the credibility of witnesses. You are going to have to determine credibility. I hope that I have given you those arguments which are the most persuasive so that you will be able to arrive at the truth of what happened on that day in July, 1971. The Government expects you to reach the right determination.

"We have in this case two Chicago policemen who violated the trust imposed on them by the community, and each and every one of you is a member of that community. Gill and Fahey misused and abused their power. Instead of making the arrest, they decided to extort $300 from the owners of the Chicago-Oak Liquors store by using the power invested in them as Chicago police officers. Then they went before a federal grand jury and made false statements about their involvement. Because they did those things and because we have proved beyond a reasonable doubt that they did them, you can find the defendant Gill and the defendant Fahey guilty of the counts in which they are named in the indictment.

"Thank you very much."

It was now the turn of the defense. Although Muldoon argued first, everyone knew that his summation was not as important as Magidson's. Muldoon had followed Magidson's lead throughout the trial and there was no reason for him to change now. When Muldoon finished his remarks, all eyes turned toward Magidson. He glanced briefly at his notes and then stood to address the jury.

Magidson had a persuasive, mellifluous voice which overflowed with quiet sincerity. He began by telling a story about a coach's statements to his team before a crucial Yale-Harvard football game, impressing the team with the critical importance of what they would do that day, just as he hoped to persuade the jury of the significance of their actions. The jury relaxed, lulled by his calm yet impressive manner. Then, suddenly, Magidson began to sharpen his attack. He honed in on the differences between the testimony of the government witnesses as well as the inconsistencies between their testimony and the written FBI reports. He pointed out the anger of Boris Kovacevic to highlight his contention that it was the obvious desire of the Kovacevics to get back at the police. He deftly turned the government case into a vendetta by two tavern owners against decent cops who had devoted their entire adulthood to serving the community. "Yes, contrary to what Mr. Webb has told you, they did have a reason to lie and they did lie."

Over and over Magidson repeated this refrain. Expertly, he conceded the possibility that there might have been an extortion, leading the jury to what he hoped would be the conclusion that the extortion was the result of Dino acting on his own, with Officer Redden, or with Fahey, but certainly not with Gill. The owners were striking out at the highest-ranking officer they could find regardless of the truth and the horrible consequences which would befall a fine man.

When Magidson finally confronted Powers's testimony he had only one choice—to take an honest approach and hope that the jury would dismiss the testimony as inconclusive. He tried to convince the jury that the only reasonable explanation was confusion by Gill, that he had innocently misread the boy's birthdate on the license. Otherwise, why else would Gill testify as he had, knowing that the government could produce Powers to contradict him?

At the close of his hour-long argument Magidson returned to his story of the football coach and the critical importance of the jury's decision. "Don't shame this man on the basis of the evidence you've heard here today. Don't shame his family; don't destroy his career. . . . Ladies and gentlemen of the jury, you are about to do the most important thing in your lives. Never before have you done anything so important, never again will you do something so important. I think fifty years from now we will all be able to say the same thing."

Magidson walked slowly to his seat and sat down. Austin signaled Beigel to begin the prosecution's rebuttal argument. Beigel stood reluctantly. Magidson's argument had been almost overpoweringly effective.

Beigel first concentrated on destroying the value of the impressive character witnesses who had testified for Gill. Beigel emphasized that character witnesses can never know the truth about a man, and besides, the Powers testimony proved Gill had not told the truth.

Beigel then focused on whether the government witnesses had a motive to lie. He reemphasized what Webb had told the jury and again pointed out that inconsistencies do not mean that witnesses are not telling the truth.

He then turned to Magidson's seemingly effective argument that it was absurd to think an extortion would take place in the middle of the store.

"Mr. Magidson asked, 'Would they do this in the middle of the store when there are customers around? Would the lieutenant be so foolish as to do that?' Think about that for a moment. Why didn't the defendant Gill go straight to the counter? That's where Stoyan Kovacevic was. What was he doing walking through the middle of the store? The reason was because there was a line of customers waiting to pay for their purchases. The middle of the store was better than the counter. There is a difference between being seen and being heard. . . .

"Although customers were only a few feet away, they are not part of the conversation. A police officer is talking to the owner, ostensibly about the sale of liquor to a minor. They were not shouting at the top of their voices."

Beigel then tried to puncture Magidson's argument that the Kovacevics were out for revenge.

"Well, if that's [revenge] the case, he [Stoyan] missed the man who arrested him on the 12th of July and who was the one who started the problems the week before. If he was mad and wanted to lie, he would have certainly accused Officer Redden, whose name he knew, of being involved in this scheme. But he did not accuse Redden. Now certainly that one person who caused Kovacevic the most problems with his liquor license was Officer Redden. When he was forced to pay $300, he at least knew that because no arrest was going to be made, he would have no problem with the Liquor Commission. When he was arrested on July 12, he knew he was going to have a problem with the Liquor Commission. As Mr. Magidson said, whether he was ever convicted, he would have a problem. His revenge motive, if any existed at all, should have been directed against Redden, not Gill and Fahey who did what they told him they would do if he paid them money."

Beigel was now ready to remind the jury of the importance of Timothy Powers. Because Magidson had argued that Gill must have misread the license, Beigel pointed out to the jury that Powers's birthdate was in June 1952. According to Gill's testimony, Powers would have had to have been born in August 1950. The difference was too obvious for Gill to have been confused, Beigel told the jury.

As to Magidson's argument that it was the defendant who provided the name of the minor to the prosecution, Beigel said, "It would seem very unreasonable to you, wouldn't it, if in making this arrest, he never had any idea of the boy's name, especially when he was so clear about his various reasons for not making the arrest? He never thought we would be able to find the boy. Powers, Oak Park. It's not much to go on. But we found the boy."

Beigel had spoken to the jury for more than an hour. All arguments had been made and the evidence had been analyzed, dissected, and scrutinized from every angle. However, one of Magidson's arguments had still gone unanswered by Beigel and had to be met. "Mr. Magidson mentioned in his closing argument that you shouldn't shame Frank Gill. You won't shame Frank Gill by convicting him for the crime he committed. Frank Gill shamed himself the day he decided to get money from Stoyan Kovacevic. You won't shame his ten children by your verdict; Frank Gill shamed his children by taking $300 from these tavern owners. You won't ruin his career by your verdict. Frank Gill did that himself by abusing the trust given him by all of us."

Beigel sat down. Judge Austin turned to the jury and began reading the instructions. It was forty minutes before the jury left the courtroom to deliberate. On his way out of the courtroom, Beigel saw that Gill was still full of good cheer, talking happily with his wife and some of his children. Fahey wandered out into the hall alone, his left hand, as always, in his pocket.

Five hours later, at 6 P.M., there was still no verdict. Beigel and Webb went to the courtroom to see if anything was happening. The courtroom was locked. The jury was out eating dinner. Judge Austin had again used the sealed verdict procedure and had gone home. Beigel and Webb decided that they might as well do the same.

On their way out they passed by a dark corner of the corridor where a few chairs had been placed for people who were waiting to get in the courtroom. Sitting bent over on one of them, a silhouette against the city lights shining through the floor-to-ceiling windows, was James Fahey. The back of his right hand was pressed against his forehead. His left arm hung at his side, his hand clenched in a fist, apparently holding something. Beigel and Webb stopped, tempted to walk over to him and ask if he was all right. Embarrassed, they did not. They turned and hurried to the elevators, to go home to their families, leaving James Fahey to wait alone.

When Beigel and Webb arrived at work the next morning there was still no verdict. They learned that the jury had deliberated until 9 P.M. before retiring. At 11 A.M. Judge Austin informed all attorneys that if a verdict was not reached within a few hours, he would consider calling the jury back for an additional charge designed to encourage the jurors to reach agreement. Beigel thought about going to lunch, but changed his mind. He wasn't up to it. The industrious Webb was already thinking about another trial on an unrelated matter. Davidson paced the hallways telling everyone he was sure there would be a conviction.

At 12:30 Beigel's telephone rang. Judge Austin's marshal said, "The jury has reached a verdict. Be up here in fifteen minutes and bring Webb. I'm calling the defense lawyers."

Outside the courtroom Beigel and Webb saw several reporters who had been waiting there all morning, not wanting to take any chances on missing the verdict. Gill, Fahey, and their attorneys arrived shortly after Beigel and Webb and entered the courtroom, followed by the reporters. Gill's family had also come, but Fahey, as usual, was alone.

When the jury walked into the courtroom they looked, without exception, sad and defeated. Everyone's gaze was fixed at their feet. When they sat down they did not even look at the judge. Beigel noticed that a short, frail, middle-aged woman sitting at the end of the jury box was in tears. She held her hands to her face in an effort to hide her tears, but everyone could hear her sobs. Austin hardly glanced at the verdict form and gave it to the clerk to read. The clerk stood up, calm and deliberate. There was a tense silence in the courtroom, broken only by the juror's sniffles. He read the verdicts matter-of-factly. Fahey and Gill were guilty on all counts.

Magidson rose immediately. He asked if the clerk would poll the jury. Austin said, "Poll the jury, Mr. Clerk." The clerk asked, "Was this and is this your verdict?" One by one, the jurors replied in the affirmative. Then the clerk called out the name of the still-tearful juror. "Was this and is this your verdict?" She looked up, dropped her hands from her red eyes, and took a crumpled tissue out of her purse to wipe her eyes. She looked at Gill and Fahey and then back at the clerk. In a remarkably clear but hardly audible voice she said, "Yes." Judge Austin leaned over. "I'm sorry. I can't hear you." "Yes," she said louder, as her tears once again began to flow. The clerk continued the polling. All responses were the same.

The jury was excused. Frank Gill and James Fahey approached the bench for sentencing. Both Magidson and Muldoon made impassioned pleas for leniency, saying Gill and Fahey had suffered enough. Neither defendant spoke. Beigel repeated what he had said the previous week when Walter Moore had stood in the same place under the same circumstances. Austin turned to the defendants. Three years for Fahey and four years for Gill. Gill took the sentence stoically. His wife and children in the back of the courtroom remained seated. Fahey took his left hand out of his pocket. A string of rosary beads dangled from his fingers.

Chapter 6

The Conspiracy of Silence

"Your Honor, my client advises me he will again refuse to
testify."
"Is that your answer?"
"It is."
"I will give you one more opportunity. Will you testify?"
"No."

    —Colloquy between Court, John Cello, and Counsel,
      July 19, 1972

Following the convictions of Gill and Fahey, Beigel, Webb, Lapidus, and
Davidson joined Thompson for lunch at the Union League Club. Thompson
was elated by the unexpected total success of the first three trials. Davidson
was also excited, but for a different reason. For the first time he felt that the
investigation was truly on the verge of uncovering massive organized police
corruption in one of Chicago's most important districts.

Davidson told Thompson that the meeting with Roy Moore six weeks earlier
had accomplished its main purpose. Although Annes and Hill continued to
shoulder most of the responsibility for finding and interviewing tavern owners
suspected of belonging to either the vice or uniformed club, they also had
received help from several other agents. For the first time the Bureau had
recognized the investigation as a priority matter. And Annes had immersed
himself totally in finding tavern owners who would talk. Because of the ex-vice
officer's statement and Farrington's change of heart,[1] Annes was now convinced that corruption in the 18th District had been widespread for several
years. Despite the reservations he had about investigating policemen, he had

---

1. See Chapter 4.

plunged into his task with dedicated abandon, determined to find any evidence which existed as quickly as possible.

Annes was not the only impatient participant. Both Beigel and Davidson were weary. The investigation had required much of their time for more than a year and had resulted in the indictment of only nine officers. Interviewing a large number of tavern owners was time-consuming, and the Austin experience had demonstrated that this method would not necessarily produce better or more significant cases. The two prosecutors were convinced that the key to exposing organized corruption was to find a police officer who would cooperate.

This was easier said than done. In the Austin investigation neither Holder nor the other indicted officers would talk. The Austin investigation was temporarily at a standstill.

In the Rush Street investigation the situation was not much better. Although the ex-vice officer had given a full statement concerning organized collections by 18th District police officers, his knowledge did not cover recent years. Another cop who could give evidence about more current events would have to be persuaded to testify. Evidence had to be found against suspected bagmen. Then they could be given immunity with the hope that they would tell the truth about what they knew. The prosecutors could not count on this, however. The police appeared to be bound by a code of loyalty and silence more powerful than any weapon brandished by the government.

By the end of May several Rush Street tavern owners had agreed to talk about their payoffs to the police. These owners were financially secure and had retained lawyers to represent them. Since their attorneys were worried that their clients might commit perjury if called before the grand jury, they wanted to enter into agreements with the Justice Department which would assure them immunity if they told the truth.

Beigel and Davidson were more than happy to make this accommodation. They were not investigating tavern owners. Besides, a tavern owner who paid a police officer had not committed a federal offense. The prosecution would not be giving anything away by granting immunity, and the Rush Street owners had much to tell.

For example, tavern owner Frank Florio told Annes that in December 1970 he had been hired to manage Pokey's tavern, since the owner had full-time employment elsewhere. Pokey's was located near Chicago Avenue and Clark Street, a marginal area which bordered poor black neighborhoods to the west. Pokey's was a popular spot, employing several B-girls to work the bar and entertain the customers.

Within a month of Pokey's opening, Officer Eddie Rifkin came to the tavern and asked Florio if he wanted to join the "club" and avoid problems with the vice squad. Florio told Rifkin that he would have to talk with the owner. Rifkin said he would be back later. Florio called the owner that evening and told him that he thought it was probably a good idea to pay the money. Otherwise, said Florio, the vice squad would set Pokey's up for an arrest. The owner agreed. He told Florio to pay the officers. The owner put the required money in an envelope in the office safe for Florio to give to Rifkin when he next stopped by. Three days later Rifkin returned and Florio gave him the envelope. The payoffs continued regularly with Rifkin returning to the tavern during the first week of each month.

In June 1971 Officer Sal Mascolino came to Pokey's and spoke with Florio. The payments made to Rifkin were too low. The new price would be $200 per month. Florio told Mascolino that Pokey's was not doing enough business to afford such high payments. Mascolino said, "Take it or leave it."

Florio called the owner that night and told him about Mascolino's visit. The owner thought he had no choice if he wanted to avoid police harassment. He told Florio that he would agree to the higher monthly payments. Florio transmitted this message to Mascolino. For the next six months Mascolino picked up the envelope.

In January 1972 the unexpected occurred. One evening several officers, including a Sergeant Geraghty, raided Pokey's and arrested three B-girls for prostitution. Florio went to the district station the next day to complain. He told Geraghty that the vice squad should not be raiding Pokey's after so much money had been paid for protection. Geraghty told Florio that the vice squad no longer wanted Pokey's money.

During the next two months no one came to make a collection. Then, in March 1972, an officer came to the tavern and told Florio that Pokey's was back in the club, but it would now cost $250 a month. Florio talked with the owner, who agreed to "rejoin." A new officer showed up every month to receive the envelope. This arrangement did not last long. In June the bartender received a call from Geraghty, who said he wanted to see Florio at the district station the following day. Florio went to the station. Geraghty said that he was "getting too much heat from downtown" and there would be no more police protection for Pokey's.

This was the last time Florio talked to the police about money. It was not the last time he saw the police. Every few weeks Pokey's would be raided. It was not long before it had to close its doors.

The names of Rifkin, Mascolino, and Geraghty came up over and over as

Annes, Hill, and other agents made the rounds of 18th District bars. A pattern of collections by vice squad officers emerged, as did evidence that a club operated by uniformed officers also existed. Sergeant James White and Lieutenant James Murphy were most often named as the principal bagmen for this club.

One other officer who had played a prominent role in 18th District corruption was John "Skippy" Cello. His involvement as a collector dated back to 1966.

Robert Chartier and a partner operated the East Inn, a combination tavern and restaurant. The Inn opened in 1965 and had no problems with the police during the first year. In 1966 uninformed officers began to frequent the tavern and check patrons' identifications. Several months later Cello told Chartier that "things could be worked out." For $100 per month Cello gave Chartier his home phone number so that he could always call if a problem arose. This arrangement continued for two or three years as Cello or another officer would stop by the tavern each month for the payment. When Cello was transferred Rifkin took over the collections.

Tavern owners were not talking just because Annes was aggressive or because their lawyers were advising them to tell the truth. Rather, many tavern owners, impressed by the March indictments, were now inclined to believe that the "Feds" were on the move and would not stop until the tavern shakedown racket was exposed completely. The police were being investigated not only for extortion, but also for murder (the "hit squad"), discrimination, and brutality. The general crisis of confidence in the police leadership made it easier to locate cooperative witnesses.

One legend which could affect the progress of the investigation was still very much alive. Conlisk's predecessor, Orlando Wilson, had assumed the leadership of the department in 1960 following the notorious Summerdale scandal. Eight police officers had been indicted for conspiring to commit burglary and to fence the stolen goods. Mayor Daley established a blue ribbon commission to locate a new superintendent who would rehabilitate the tarnished image of the police. The commission decided that the best-qualified man for the job was Wilson, its chairman.

Wilson was a noted law enforcement expert with a nationwide reputation in police administration. His honesty and integrity were unquestioned. He started his new job with Mayor Daley's promise of a free hand and his own sincere desire to see the department reformed. His administration, which ended with his retirement in 1967, led most Chicagoans to boast that they had the finest police officers in the country and the most modern facilities to use in the fight against crime.

Despite the modernization of the department, Wilson failed to make any changes in the basic command structure. Names were simply changed. What had been known as "Captain's men" now became the vice squad, equally elite, equally low in rank, and equally corrupt. Politics still allowed an officer to use his connections. If the investigation revealed anything, it was that corruption had managed to live comfortably under Wilson's aegis.

But in June 1972 Wilson still had his reputation intact. Although there was a crisis of confidence in the police, the newspapers concentrated their attacks on Conlisk while wishing for a return of the days of Wilson. The *Tribune* took the lead in articulating this point of view.

We have grave reservations about the ability of his (Mayor Daley's) police superintendent, James B. Conlisk, Jr. to carry out the objectives he proposed—honest and rigorous law enforcement applied with justice that will gain the respect of an overwhelming majority of citizens. Supt. Conlisk has been superintendent since the departure of Orlando Wilson in 1967. He has had nearly five years to polish the image of law enforcement which Mr. Wilson brought to high luster in Chicago. Instead, the police department is confronted with a crisis in public repute so serious that a mayor is forced to call a public meeting to defend it.[2]

Thus, an ignorant and naive press had told its readers that police honesty had been badly served by Conlisk, fostering the belief that the problem was a crisis of men rather than of the system. There was no sign that the battle was being won to convince the citizens that more than cosmetic changes were needed.

The Brotherhood of Police

By June 1972 it had become obvious that two clubs had flourished in the 18th District for several years. Beigel and Davidson concluded that the time was ripe for a new session of the grand jury. Although they had gathered sufficient evidence to indict several officers, they decided that additional pressure should be put on recalcitrant tavern owners and police officers.

The grand jury was scheduled for the middle of June. Twenty officers from the 18th District were subpoenaed, including Cello, Mascolino, and Rifkin. Also subpoenaed was Captain Walter Maurovich, a controversial figure in the Police Department for the past twenty-six years.

Maurovich came from a family of policemen. His father had been a cop, as were his brother and wife. He had been a star athlete at the University of Chicago, was a law school graduate, and had even worked as an Assistant

2. *Chicago Tribune,* May 4, 1972.

State's Attorney. He had been at the Potsdam Conference with Truman as part of a special security detail and had received a Certificate of Merit award from the department for outstanding and conspicuous service in the investigation, solution, and prevention of crime.

When Wilson became superintendent in 1960, Maurovich was one officer who was not lacking in high praise from his peers. Wilson took a liking to this bright, tough, and articulate policeman and assigned him to a succession of sensitive posts, including the head of the IID, the organized crime unit, and the Vice Control Division. In 1964 Wilson, concerned with the problem of increasing vice in the troublesome 18th District, turned to Maurovich to solve the problem and appointed him commander.

Within a year and a half Maurovich had fallen out of Wilson's favor. It was not clear whether the disenchantment had been caused by Maurovich's failure to bring vice under control or by Wilson's suspicions about the extent of Maurovich's commitment to his appointed task. Whatever the reason, Wilson summarily replaced Maurovich in April 1966, saying publicly only that he was not satisfied with Maurovich's performance.

Maurovich's career slid gradually downhill after he left the 18th District. He served as watch commander in several other districts and reached his nadir in 1969, when he was censured by Conlisk in one of his rare acts of discipline of a high-ranking officer for misconduct in a corruption-related matter. He suspended Maurovich for ten days for failing to supervise properly four policemen implicated in an alleged shakedown in the Shakespeare District, where he was a watch commander.

Maurovich had been subpoenaed by the grand jury, not because of any specific evidence against him, but because of the information provided by the ex-vice officer who had related how the clubs had been in existence during Maurovich's command. Although the statute of limitations barred any prosecution for crimes that occurred in 1964 and 1965, the subpoenaing of Maurovich was the logical starting point. If, at this late date, anyone could shed light on how and why corruption had gained its present foothold in the 18th District, it was Maurovich.

Walter Maurovich resigned the day before his scheduled grand jury appearance, effectively preserving his pension and preventing the department from taking any action against him if he took the Fifth Amendment. Maurovich was fifty-six years old. His police career, without a real future since 1966, was now over. What he knew about corruption during those years would remain a secret.

Another subpoenaed officer followed in Maurovich's footsteps. Sergeant

William Simpson, who had served as vice coordinator during Maurovich's years in the 18th District and who was transferred along with Maurovich in April 1966, also resigned the day before his grand jury appearance.

The initial grand jury session lasted a week. Davidson handled the questioning. One or two tavern owners took the Fifth, several lied, and others decided to cooperate. The twenty subpoenaed officers, including Mascolino, Cello, and Rifkin, refused to cooperate.

This first session ended without producing much new information. While the return of indictments against Mascolino, Cello, and Rifkin was justified, Beigel and Davidson considered giving immunity to them. The use of the immunity procedure effectively eliminated the privilege against self-incrimination as a valid reason for refusing to answer questions since their testimony could not be used against them. An added benefit of immunity was that the witness could be indicted for perjury if he lied.[3] If, under this pressure, the officers told the truth, it was possible that not only would they implicate other members of the vice club, but they might also give evidence against higher-ranking officers.

The prosecutors also considered using the same tactic against members of the uniformed club. But since fewer tavern owners had come forward with substantial testimony, the cases were less developed. The uniformed club also appeared to be more loosely organized than the parallel vice operation and was therefore a less desirable candidate for a procedure which would, in effect, excuse its bagmen from prosecution in the hope that higher officers could be implicated.

There were other risks. Mascolino, Cello, and Rifkin were evidently the three principal bagmen of the vice club. If, in granting them immunity, evidence was obtained only against officers of the same or lower rank who did not make collections but only shared in the proceeds, the net result might be to convey the impression that the most culpable had been let off the hook in exchange for evidence and prosecution against those who were only on the periphery of the corruption.

Second, there was no guarantee that any of the officers immunized would implicate others, although they might tell the truth about their own activities. If this occurred, there could even be a problem in using the backup weapon of a perjury indictment.

3. Use immunity also preserved the possibility of prosecution as long as the immunized witnesses' testimony was not used. This right was rarely exercised since the purpose of immunity was not to put the witness in jail, but to obtain cooperation.

Third, no hard evidence had been obtained which established that noncollecting members of higher rank had received a monthly envelope containing their portion of the payoffs. If such evidence was obtained elsewhere, the granting of immunity to the collecting officers would have been unnecessary and they would go unpunished.

Beigel and Davidson finally decided that immunity was the best available option. If the Rush Street investigation dragged on, what little hold the Strike Force retained on the FBI would be lost and the entire inquiry would lose the impetus gained from the recent indictments. On the other hand, if the new plan worked, an immense amount of time and effort would be saved and a case could be built against the entire vice squad, including superior officers to whom money had been passed.

By mid-July Beigel and Davidson were ready to put their plan to the test. The first week of July had been spent interrogating another round of witnesses who also took the Fifth Amendment or denied any involvement in any kind of corruption. Among those subpoenaed was Clarence Braasch, the fourth-highest-ranking cop in the city, now Chief of Traffic but formerly a commander of the 18th District. In the grand jury he was aloof and authoritative, at the same time deftly showing the proper respect for the grand jurors. When asked if he had heard the term "club" used in connection with payoffs, he would admit only that he recalled seeing the term in a *Tribune* column written by Bob Wiedrich some time before. Otherwise, he stated, he knew nothing about alleged improper police activities in the 18th District when he had been in command.

Shortly before filing the immunity applications, Beigel and Davidson decided to limit the initial stage of their plan by excluding Rifkin. The interview reports of tavern owners prepared by the FBI suggested that Rifkin was merely a "pinchhitter" who had filled in when the regular bagmen were not making the rounds. Nothing would be lost at this time by not including Rifkin. He could always be granted immunity later if warranted.

On July 19 Beigel entered the courtroom of the Chief District Court Judge, Edward Robson, to present the applications for immunity of Cello and Mascolino. Alan Ackerman appeared for Cello, dressed nattily in a tight-fitting pair of pants and a Nehru jacket. Mascolino was also represented by an experienced criminal lawyer with an excellent reputation.

Judge Robson wasted no time in granting Beigel's request. The immunity orders were entered and Beigel turned to go back to the fifteenth floor, where the grand jury awaited the appearances of the two officers. As he turned, Ackerman stepped forward. "Your Honor," he said casually, "my client advises me he will again refuse to testify."

"Is that your answer?" Robson asked Cello, disbelievingly.

"It is," Cello said.

"I will give you one more opportunity. Will you testify?"

"No." Cello seemed very calm in the face of Robson's almost threatening manner.

"I will then enter an order that this man be taken into custody."

Although Beigel and Davidson knew that even with the grant of immunity the officers might still refuse to testify, they had not really expected this turn of events. Under the Organized Crime and Control Act of 1970, silence by an immunized witness could result in a jail term of up to the remaining life of the grand jury—in this case, nearly eighteen months. The Strike Force lawyers were aware that the code of silence and loyalty shared by police officers was strong, but they had not appreciated that its influence would reach a relatively low-ranking officer and that he would be so willing to accept the consequences of refusal to testify under immunity.

Cello's decision raised the possibility that Mascolino would choose the same course. But neither he nor his lawyer said anything. As Beigel led Mascolino downstairs to the grand jury, he noticed that Mascolino was sweating. Outside the grand jury room he looked about with despair. When Beigel motioned him to enter the grand jury room, he started to walk hesitantly, his arms hanging limply at his sides. Once inside, however, he calmed down, suggesting that he had finally made his decision. He did not answer a single question. Within five minutes he was back before Judge Robson. Together, Cello and Mascolino were taken to jail.

If Mascolino and Cello found life in jail uncomfortable, they did not complain. Days passed, then weeks. There was no sign that they were about to talk.

The prosecutors were also discouraged by the lack of progress in the investigation of the uniformed club. The key collectors were believed to be Lieutenant James Kinnally, Lieutenant James Murphy, and Sergeant James White. All had asserted their privilege against self-incrimination before the grand jury. On July 21 they were suspended by Conlisk, but it had no apparent effect. Davidson and Beigel discussed granting them immunity but after their experience with Cello and Mascolino, they decided against any further use of immunity for the foreseeable future.

It seemed that, if cases were to be made, they would have to come from the "conventional" method of indicting actual collectors based upon tavern-owner testimony. In March these indictments had been considered a real achievement by the Strike Force lawyers. Now they were no longer satisfied with a mere accumulation of charges and convictions against low-ranking officers. The police were succeeding in slowing the investigation by a conspiracy of silence as effective as that which had allowed them to collect, unchecked, substantial amounts of money from tavern owners and businessmen for so many years.

The few police officers who had on occasion talked to the FBI, the IRS, and to Beigel about corruption had given only general information. They were mostly informants or terrified officers who fearfully sneaked into the Federal Building on the condition that their identifies would be kept secret (as in the case of James Barley). Their statements were useless as evidence, although they obviously whetted the desire of the prosecutors to crack the organized pattern of corruption and silence. Once in a while these statements revealed in the officers an underlying attitude about law enforcement and corruption that offered insight into why corruption is able to flourish unimpeded in a police department for so long. Nothing brought this home more to Beigel and Davidson than a statement by an unidentified police officer who called Davidson on July 28, 1972, less than two weeks after Judge Robson had sent Cello and Mascolino to jail.

Davidson: Hello.
Officer: Yeah, who am I speaking to finally?
Davidson: My name is Sheldon Davidson.
Officer: Are you the fellow to talk to?
Davidson: I don't know.
Officer: I think you are. Mr. Davidson, you are very close to a lot of things in this town at the moment.
Davidson: Whom am I talking to?
Officer: Well, for general purposes, I'm Officer Sweeney, O.K.? . . .[4]
Davidson: You are a Chicago policeman?
Officer: Right. And I'm calling from a pay telephone. Boy, you're hitting it right on the head in this town. I gotta tell you that.
Davidson: Which district are you referring to, 18 or 15?
Officer: Eighteen.
Davidson: What do you think that we are not doing?
Officer: Well, you're not getting to the top yet. You had our boss in there and he was only in ten minutes and walked out.
Davidson: Who's your boss?
Officer: Braasch, at the time.
Davidson: Was Braasch on the take?
Officer: Well, let me just put it this way. You're hitting all around, but you're not there yet.

4. The officer refused to give his real name.

Davidson: Well, tell me what we're supposed to do. . . .

Officer: Right. Well, see now, you're not getting to Braasch. You're not getting—one other fellow you haven't got to at all, and well, the thing of it is, the way some of us look at it, you got Keep-It-All Murphy, Lieutenant Murphy—

Davidson: Keep-It-All Murphy?

Officer: Yeah (laughter).

Davidson: James Murphy?

Officer: Yeah (laughter).

Davidson: Why do you call him Keep-It-All Murphy?

Officer: Well, because he (laughter)—whenever there's a beef, he never shares. He's not a very sharing fellow. . . .

Davidson: Let me ask you this as a policeman. What's the reaction on the police force to the entire federal investigation?

Officer: We're glad you're here in a way.

Davidson: In a way?

Officer: Uh, yeah.

Davidson: What do you mean "in a way"?

Officer: You're gonna get rid of some of this stuff. Braasch is the most disliked fellow we've come across. Braasch is bad news. John Trinka is his father-in-law.

Davidson: Who is John Trinka?

Officer: Former Park District Special Services. He let out all the harbor permits. There was a big scandal on that a couple of years ago.

Davidson: Was everybody, when Braasch was there in 18, who was connected with vice—was everybody on the Vice Squad on the take?

Officer: I can't answer that. I don't know.

Davidson: What honest cops were there in 18 when Braasch was there? Guys that didn't take money?

Officer: Probably the only ones (laughter) that are there now. You're dealing with some rough people there, Mr. Davidson. . . .

Davidson: What do you think of Howard Miller collecting on the radio, or what's the feeling in the Police Department of him collecting money from listeners for a Police Defense Fund?

Officer: Well, he's always been well regarded.

Davidson: No, I mean, but do you think that's right that citizens should send in monies for those people under indictment?

Officer: Oh, yeah.

Davidson: You think so?

Officer: Sure, because the Police Department, uh, see, when all of a sudden it was whatever Daley decides, actually everybody on the Panther thing should have been suspended, but Daley decided he didn't want to suspend them. Any time you get indicted, you're supposed to get suspended, see. It didn't work that way. It's whatever the Mayor wants.

Davidson: All right. Let me ask you this. . . . Rifkin got a pile of dough and so did Braasch. Did Barry share in that money too?

Officer: Oh, Ed Barry,[5] absolutely, he's the kingpin, that's his (inaudible).

Davidson: Let me ask you this. What do you think Braasch's takedown on the year—give me a ballpark figure of what you think Captain Braasch took out of a year.

Officer: I don't think he kept it.

Davidson: You think some of it went downtown?

Officer: Well, one deputy just quit Area 6.

Davidson: Who?

Officer: The deputy chief, Linsky.

Davidson: What's his name?

Officer: Linsky. Bob Linsky.

Davidson: You think he was getting money?

Officer: I haven't the faintest idea.

Davidson: What do you think Braasch, Rifkin, . . . and other people—what do you think they did with the money? Think they spent it out of pocket? Do you think they've got it salted away?

Officer: It's gotta be salted somewhere.

Davidson: Where do you think?

Officer: I don't know. Eddie Rifkin is a pretty good liver. He lives pretty good. I—you know—you're asking me—

Davidson: Well, what's—yeah—what's the word on the street as to where a policeman could hide his money if he was dragging down an extra five or ten thousand a year?

Officer: Well, just like our old Secretary of State did, in shoe boxes.[6]

Davidson: (laughter) Well, somebody said they put them in bearer bonds—government securities.

Officer: That could very well be. That's a good safe place. But see, you hit on some and you miss some, and when Braasch walked out of there smiling, he was smiling, the fellows didn't take too well to that.

5. Ed Barry had also refused to answer questions before the grand jury.
6. This is a reference to the flamboyant, notorious Paul Powell, who was a powerful man in Illinois politics for many years. After his death thousands of dollars in apparent payoff money was found in shoe boxes.

Davidson: Let me ask you this. Does the Police Department—do the officers in the Police Department—feel that this is a political investigation?

Officer: Well, that's for sure.

Davidson: You think so?

Officer: They do. They do.

Davidson: Why do they think that?

Officer: Well, because Nixon wanted to embarrass Daley.

Davidson: You know that's a hundred percent wrong.

Officer: Well—

Davidson: You know that as a matter of fact. I'm telling you that.

Officer: Well, we hope so, but, you know, it just happens to be that way. A lot of them feel that way. But a lot of them are kinda glad they're getting rid of some of these political appointees. You know—as Braasch was. . . .

Davidson: There was a rumor that was going around that before a raid could go off in 18 that the vice had to call a number before the raid could go down.

Officer: Sounds reasonable.

Davidson: Do you know anything about that?

Officer: Sounds reasonable.

Davidson: And that the voice on the other end would either say yes or no, or give us a couple of hours so we can get our top people out.

Officer: It could very well be.

Davidson: You say very well could be or it sounds—

Officer: Sounds reasonable. You gotta remember. You got all the boys down in the Rush Street area.

Davidson: You know that to be a fact?

Officer: Absolutely. You're dealing with syndicate, see?

Davidson: Well—

Officer: There's too many—we have a lot of policemen—you must be aware we have policemen that are related to syndicate members.

Davidson: How is the. . . . And the price for making that phone call before a raid would go down, that money would be sent directly to the commander of the district?

Officer: I—see, you're out of my scope now.

Davidson: You're out of your scope. But you do know that phone calls had to be made?

Officer: Sure. We know that.

Davidson: Did you ever get any orders from downtown that you couldn't make a raid on a certain place?

Officer: Orders from Braasch.

Davidson: From Braasch?

Officer: Sure. . . .

Davidson: Is there anything else you can tell us that would help us in planning the next grand jury session which will probably be in late August or early September?

Officer: No, I wish I could, but that's about it. You're almost there, see. Don't stop if you can get it over with because otherwise it will linger on.

Davidson: Do you think the Police Department or the officers would be happy if Braasch were indicted?

Officer: I think so. I think that they would feel as though there wasn't always somebody low, you know, rank-wise.

Davidson: What'd you think of Frank Gill getting four years?

Officer: Most people thought—he had ten kids. That was the only thing they thought. He wasn't a nice guy. When I say nice guy it has more connotation, but you did the right thing. There's no regrets. It's just that everybody wants to see you move on to a different town. I'll be real frank with you.

Davidson: A different town?

Officer: Yeah (laughter). You know, like South America or some place. . . .

Davidson: Well, . . . if a Rifkin or a Mascolino testifies, don't you think they're going to bring down with them about 15 or 20 other guys?

Officer: Oh, I'm sure of it, but you know you've gotta use the right technique. Apparently you're not. If Mascolino and Cello won't talk. . . .

Davidson: Well, what do you suggest that we do?

Officer: Well—

Davidson: What would you do?

Officer: I'd look for the weakest character. . . .

Davidson: Is Braasch still on the take over in Traffic, or do you know?

Officer: (laughter) You gotta answer that in the cold light of day.

Davidson: Let me ask you this. There's been some allegations that lawyers have been serving as intermediaries, that the lawyers have taken care of the police on these liquor busts and paid off the police. Do you know of any lawyers that have been paying off the police?

Officer: You'd have to check your records for that. That's—now you're dealing—

Davidson: Do you know of any lawyers?

Officer: Sure I do.

Davidson: Could you give me their names?

Officer: I can't.

Davidson: Why?

Officer: Not ethical.

Davidson: I'm just as interested in making sure that crooked lawyers get out of the business as I am crooked cops.

Officer: Yeah, well we are too.

Davidson: Because the lawyers perpetuate it.

Officer: They act as very nice buffers.

Davidson: You mean between the victim and the police?

Officer: Sure. Because sometimes things go wrong. You know?

Davidson: How about judges?

Officer: Oh, now you're out of my area completely. . . .

Davidson: Do you think that the police are afraid that they themselves are going to be hurt by other policemen if they cooperate?

Officer: No, no—families, families.

Davidson: Do you think anybody is taking care of Mascolino and Cello insofar as money is concerned?

Officer: Well, their names would indicate to me that they're Italian.

Davidson: So what?

Office: Well, this is Chicago. . . .

Davidson: All right, I thank you very much for calling.

Officer: O.K.

Davidson: Thank you. Bye-bye.

Officer: Bye-bye.

Although this officer had talked about tavern shakedowns in the 18th District and had acknowledged that corruption was an integral part of life in the Police Department, he had been vague about details and, specifically, any connection between police corruption, organized crime, and politics. Shortly after the telephone call, however, Annes told Davidson about a lawyer with whom the FBI had periodic contact who was a potential fountain of knowledge about police corruption.

This lawyer had developed substantial connections during the 1960s with politicians and the agencies involved with liquor licensing. He was also intimately acquainted with the goings-on in the 18th District during the Maurovich and Braasch years. He did not want to talk to anyone about what he knew, least of all Davidson. He now considered himself removed from the dirty business of the police and politicians and no longer acted as an intermediary between tavern owners and businessmen who were looking for police protection. But Davidson was persistent and finally won the lawyer over. In several conversations during the summer of 1972 the lawyer told Davidson what he recalled about corruption in the 18th District.

Much of his knowledge coincided with previous information received by the Strike Force, particularly from the ex-police officer who had told in early 1971 about corruption in Summerdale. In the 18th District there were also strong ties between vice and organized crime, taverns and organized crime, and organized crime and city government. Other informers told the Strike Force and the FBI how police officers were actively engaged in illegal wiretapping, stolen auto parts rackets, prostitution, narcotics, gambling, and "juice." The Rush Street area was so volatile that not only were there the vice and uniformed clubs which dealt with quasi-legitimate taverns, but also a bigger, more secret club which protected organized crime operations. Informers described how, to protect against possible conflicts, officers were required to call special telephone numbers before conducting a raid. Clerks in City Hall were being paid off to obtain special license privileges, such as permitting drinks to be served until 4 A.M. Cops recommended lawyers and received kickbacks for their referrals. Police testimony was commonly changed in court to fix a case. All of this was carried out with the active participation of many lawyers, and ward committeemen, with the police acting as an arm of corrupt government and organized crime.

Unfortunately, little of this information could be used to make prosecutable cases. Either the statute of limitations had run out or witnesses willing to testify could not be found. If the investigation was to succeed, it was absolutely necessary that the highest-ranking officers involved be indicted. The failure of Cello and Mascolino to testify had been a big disappointment to the prosecutors. Their frustration was increasing as they found their progress stalled at the same time they were acquiring more and more information about general corruption which could not be used.

Austin and Elsewhere During the Summer of 1972

Although the Austin investigation had concentrated on interviews of tavern owners, the Strike Force lawyers saw no reason why immunity should not be given to certain Austin police officers, even at this late date. Because a major goal of the investigation was building cases against higher-ranking officers, such as Thanasouras, and because it was now abundantly clear that this would never be accomplished with the testimony of tavern owners alone, Beigel and Davidson decided to select two officers for immunity, both of whom might be able to testify against Thanasouras. The lawyers hoped that the officers selected would be more cooperative than Cello and Mascolino. Since indictments and convictions had already been returned against Austin District officers, immunity might turn out to be a more compelling weapon than in the Rush Street investigation, where it had been used against officers who had not been charged and who did not know whether the government had uncovered incriminating evidence against them.

Holder and Demet were chosen. Holder was thought to be a principal bagman for the $100-a-month club and Demet was reputed to be one of Thanasouras's closest friends. Interest in Demet had heightened during his trial when Louis King had testified that Demet had not been reluctant to bring "member" tavern owners directly to Thanasouras to air complaints. Perhaps Demet would tell what he knew about Thanasouras's involvement in corrupt activities. A recent informant had told an FBI agent that Demet's fondness for Thanasouras had waned. Facing jail, Demet might decide to avoid further trouble by testifying.

Holder's situation was entirely different. He impressed Beigel as a fatalist. His reaction to an immunity grant would probably be indifference. Still, it was worth a chance, although he had to be carefully handled. His history of reticence made Beigel and Davidson wary of giving away something for what was, at best, a gamble. Fortunately, the use immunity statute protected the prosecutor by not letting the witness completely off the hook. Granting use immunity to Holder would not require dismissal of the indictment against him. If he refused to testify or if he did not give the desired information, his pending indictment could still proceed to trial. Holder could also be indicted for perjury if he lied.

In Demet's case the government was risking nothing by granting immunity. He had already been convicted and there was little other evidence against him, and no plans to indict him for other offenses. If he testified and implicated others, much would be gained. If he remained silent, he could be imprisoned for the rest of the grand jury's term, a substantial penalty since this prison term would not be credited against the sentence he had already received from Judge Marovitz.

Holder and Demet were granted immunity on the same day as Cello and Mascolino. Holder was the first of the Austin pair to appear before the grand jury. Beigel had prepared carefully. He wanted to avoid any questions concerning those taverns which were related to Holder's indictment as added insurance against a claim that evidence to be used at his trial had been tainted by what he had said before the grand jury. Beigel also had to be deliberate in his interrogation because he did not want Holder to lie about what he knew.

Perjured testimony could destroy Holder's value as a witness if he later had a change of heart. It is difficult, if not impossible, to rehabilitate a witness's credibility once he has testified falsely under oath, especially pursuant to a grant of immunity. This is particularly true when the prosecution is seeking a conviction based solely on testimony of a witness without corroborating physical evidence.

Because of these concerns Beigel planned to lead Holder slowly through his involvement in tavern collections without getting into specifics until he knew whether Holder intended to be candid. Before Holder could be called into the grand jury room, Beigel received a hint of what might follow when Demopolous cornered him in the hallway and told him he was acting improperly.

Beigel was curious whether Demopolous was about to launch a new diversionary salvo and asked what Holder might be planning to do in the grand jury.

"I frankly don't know what he's going to do in the grand jury," Demopolous replied. "I've told him to tell the truth, but he's scared, naturally. He was convicted in state court, forced off the force, indicted here, and now you are after him again with immunity."

Beigel looked at Holder standing a few feet behind Demopolous. Holder nodded with a forced smile. Suddenly Beigel realized that if he called Holder before the grand jury and asked him anything significant, he would probably lie. Holder looked like a man who didn't want to go to jail. Holder's potential as a witness, even though not yet realized, was not worth risking. After a conference with Davidson, Beigel decided to postpone indefinitely any questioning. For the time being Holder would be able to avoid jail without testifying against his former colleagues.

Beigel led Demet into the grand jury room. Demet was a thoroughly beaten man. His broad shoulders drooped as he strained to avoid breaking into tears. He spoke so softly that the foreman, sitting immediately at his side, had difficulty hearing him. To test Demet's willingness to testify truthfully, Beigel first asked a series of questions about his collections from Martin Lindstrom. Although Demet had heard Lindstrom testify at his sentencing hearing before Judge Marovitz only five weeks before, he now claimed that his memory of his contacts with Lindstrom was hazy. Beigel pressed Demet for specific answers, reminding him that he could be indicted for perjury if he did not tell the truth. Demet would not be pinned down. Although he conceded reluctantly that perhaps he had made some collections from Marty's, he would not reveal what other officers were involved or describe the role of the vice coordinator, Frank Bychowski, who, according to Lindstrom, had arranged the monthly payments. When Beigel asked Demet if he had collected money from other taverns and for the names of other officers in Austin involved in shakedowns, Demet testified as if he were an amnesiac. Once again, Beigel reminded Demet of the consequences of perjury. Demet broke down in tears, speaking incoherently.

Beigel had no interest in intimidating Demet. It was clear that, for now, Demet would not implicate others. Beigel told Demet he was excused subject to recall. Demet, looking very relieved, stepped down from the witness stand and shuffled out of the grand jury room.

The failure to obtain either Demet's or Holder's cooperation was a severe blow. After the first three trials had ended with four officers convicted and sentenced to prison, Beigel and Davidson had been optimistic that the tide would turn and the long-hoped-for breakthrough would occur. Instead, the convictions had not even begun to crack the conspiracy of silence and, in some ways, it appeared stronger. Cello and Mascolino were in jail while Holder and Demet had failed to provide any valuable information. There seemed to be no choice but to continue with the canvassing of tavern owners, the return of more indictments, and the hope that, with time, the pressure on the police would increase to the point where they would start to come forward and willingly testify about corruption.

Although neither the Austin nor the Rush Street investigation led to indictments of higher-ranking officers during that summer, Becker continued to find non-police witnesses who were willing to testify about shakedowns in which they had been involved. But it was not easy. Even after the June convictions and all the publicity, it was not always possible to persuade witnesses to talk. They were either afraid of police retaliation or suspicious of an investigation, state or federal, which might disrupt the usual course of their relationship with law enforcement.

Despite the failure of the immunized witnesses to cooperate, interesting information peripheral to the main thrust of the investigation was constantly being found. One such enlightening aside was Lapidus and Beigel's investigation of the police practice of soliciting money from businessmen for either off-duty or on-duty patrol.

Throughout the country police departments must deal continually with police officers' desires to increase their earnings by moonlighting, often as security guards for private firms and businesses. The Chicago Police Department had always been permissive about off-duty employment, but it did have a rule that required police officers to obtain formal permission before taking on a second job. This rule was rarely followed or enforced.

During the summer Bill Hermann, who had continued to survey the Grand Crossing District after Robert Crowley's arrest in the hope of finding other businessmen who had paid money to the police, came across a group of store owners. The organization had been formed in 1970 as a result of the businessmen's concern that racial changes in the area would drive away good customers and leave them at the mercy of rowdy youths and gangs. The leader of the group had met an officer from the district at a community relations function and they had discussed how to help protect the worried store owners. The officer suggested that police be hired to patrol the street in their off-hours to guarantee adequate security for the businesses. The officer offered to organize a group of policemen who would be willing to provide this extra service. Later they arranged a monthly fee which was paid to an officer who would come each month to the leader's store to pick up an envelope containing a check in the required amount, payable to cash.

Although this new service was not within the bounds of traditional police moonlighting, it did not seem to Beigel and Lapidus that it was radically different from an officer being employed in his spare time as a security guard. Nevertheless, they decided to follow up because the scheme seemed a logical extension of the payments which Jack David had made to Sergeant Crowley to obtain more prompt police service for his bowling alley. As it turned out, further investigation and the subpoenaing of several officers to the grand jury failed to produce evidence of extortion, but it did lead Beigel and Lapidus to conclude that what the police were doing was hardly legitimate.

First, the officers were engaging in foot patrols in uniform, a function which police no longer performed routinely (police had largely given up foot patrol for the safer and more efficient patrol car runs). Second, the police were performing these "extra" services while on duty, with the knowledge of their superiors but without the official approval required for off-duty moonlighting. The whole operation appeared to be nothing more than a sophisticated version of the $100-a-month club.

Although the businessmen who subscribed to this service had been hoodwinked into believing that they were employing off-duty policemen as a glorified security force, they were only technically victimized, and more by their own fears than by the police. Many of these businessmen were too afraid to level with the investigators and identify all of the officers involved. The tavern owner who cashed the monthly checks for the officers absolutely declined to identify the officers for the grand jury. Beigel and Lapidus thought that, while it was conceivable that the payments were within the purview of the Hobbs Act, it was more sensible to turn the matter over to the State's Attorney's office. They gave what they had learned to an Assistant State's Attorney. Nothing happened.

Although the Grand Crossing investigation effectively ended here and no officer other than Crowley was ever prosecuted, the subtlety of the corruption discovered confirmed the relationship between police malfeasance and the public's tendency to believe that police are in the business of providing services as well as investigating crime. People feel a great need to form personal contacts with police officers with the expectation that somehow they will be better protected and better insulated from the ills of society or oppressive laws.

Although, at first glance, it may appear that a businessman paying money to the police for extra protection is worlds apart from a drug pusher paying for protection for his illegal trade, the truth may be that little distinguishes these activities. Both arise from the willingness of the public to view the police as a private security force. The police officer, who is taught from his first day on the job that his duties and responsibilities are important, that his work is dangerous, and that he must be able to make quick decisions and exercise great discretion, easily becomes accustomed to the idea, which the public by its behavior encourages, that he is all-powerful and uniquely able to control any situation.

When an officer goes into court the slightest twist of his testimony can make or break a case. How he reacts to a frightened suspect fleeing from the scene of a crime can mean the difference between that person's life or death. How he handles those situations which he confronts daily, but which never result in formal action, will dictate how he views the public and how the public sees him.

The police officer comes into constant contact with the upright and the downtrodden. It is not too surprising if he treats both the same. Used to the idea of exercising unfettered discretion and power, he often does as he sees fit and feels little need to ponder the consequences of what he has done. The temptation to be corrupted by one's own feeling of power is hardly an unexpected consequence.

The officers whom Beigel and Lapidus called before the grand jury in connection with the Grand Crossing investigation were no different in makeup and background from the officers who casually committed outright extortion. All had won awards for meritorious police service, could refer proudly to their unblemished records, and could look forward to steady advance in the department. The organizer of the "extra" service squad in Grand Crossing was a lieutenant in charge of day-to-day crime fighting in the area. What each of these officers, as well as many others, had done was to take advantage of peculiar or unsympathetic laws as well as changing social patterns in the areas for which they were responsible.

Officers paraded before the grand jury and lied easily about whether they had taken money or, in the case of Grand Crossing, sought to justify what they considered normal moonlighting. It began to seem that it was not the cop who was crooked so much as it was the system of law enforcement which placed a premium on reinforcing police discretion. The public, too, was guilty, with most people being concerned about what they could get for themselves.

By the beginning of August the excitement of the first convictions was waning. Although Annes and Hill were making some progress in convincing Rush Street tavern owners to cooperate, Cello and Mascolino continued to remain silent, apparently willing to pay the price of a jail term for what they believed was a higher morality. Their silence and the silence of other police officers threatened further investigation. No matter how many were willing to say that they had paid the police for favors and protection, a corruption investigation would never succeed if those corrupted would not offer evidence. When Beigel left in August on his first vacation since he had become involved in the investigation in January 1971, he wondered if, upon his return, he would be supervising the demise of the Strike Force's inquiry into police corruption in Chicago.

Chapter 7

The City Fathers React

Are there any of my deputy superintendents or other high-ranking administrative personnel or staff members who I can't trust?

> —Superintendent James B. Conlisk, Jr.,
> September 1972

Neither the public nor the press had any idea of the serious obstacles the Strike
Force faced. They saw only that there was a major crisis of police integrity.
By the time of the March indictments cries for significant changes in Police
Department leadership dominated the news. Opponents of Mayor Daley were
having a field day. Daley's refusal to take immediate action only added to the
pressure on Superintendent Conlisk to prove that he was capable of leading
the department through the storm of criticism.

The constant interest of the press was a key factor in the building pressure.
For example, hardly a week passed without Wiedrich of the *Tribune* making
a "new" disclosure about the investigation. He pursued his task with a ven-
geance on the front pages.

Of special note was Wiedrich's deviation from the standard *Tribune* position
that Conlisk was to blame for the present difficulties. Wiedrich pointed out that
"an examination of Wilson's seven year reign . . . revealed events far short of
revitalizing the Department into an incorruptible force."[1] Wiedrich reminded
his readers that less than a year after the Summerdale scandal and Wilson's
appointment as superintendent, a detective had been arrested and convicted
of receiving stolen property from a burglar who claimed to have a continuing
relationship with the police.

During subsequent years rumors had abounded of vice payments in several

1. *Chicago Tribune*, May 14, 1972.

149

districts. Several police officers were arrested for armed robbery, looting and stealing cars, and even shaking down visitors to lovers' lanes. Wiedrich also recalled that one police officer had been identified as an advisor to an armed robbery gang who "offered his wisdom in exchange for ten per cent of the loot."[2] Even Wilson did not escape unscathed. One of his special contingency funds had been found mysteriously short of $1,500. Finally, Wiedrich called special attention to how corrupt police officers kowtowed to no one in their nefarious pursuits, charging that a police guard was once caught stealing $16,000 in city funds from the city treasurer's office.

Neither Conlisk nor Daley could long ignore the growing crisis. Nevertheless, it was also apparent that city and Police Department leaders, although quick to react politically to the investigation, would not be as ready to act in a way which would either eliminate the roots of corruption or satisfy an almost vindictive press in its eagerness to force Conlisk's resignation.

From the beginning Conlisk had responded to stories about the expanding Strike Force investigation by ordering transfers, suspending officers who asserted their Fifth Amendment privilege before the grand jury, and issuing elegant but empty statements that he would not tolerate corruption in his department.

His father, James B. Conlisk, Sr., had been administrative assistant to the five police commissioners and superintendents who preceded Wilson, and one of the most powerful men ever to work in the department. He had also developed close ties with the Democratic politicians who ran Chicago and who liked to please their friends on the force by arranging promotions at the right time and assignments to important posts. In charge of the police budget, Conlisk, Sr., although only number two man, had consolidated his power and increased his authority until his name was synonymous with the Chicago Police Department.

The elder Conlisk was an early casualty of the Summerdale scandal. When Orlando Wilson became superintendent, he promptly removed Conlisk, saying, "I feel it is necessary that I have men of my own choosing to carry the changes into effect." Wilson got away with it, mostly because neither Mayor Daley nor any other political leader was prepared to challenge him so soon after the Summerdale scandal and after having gone to great lengths to assure everyone that Wilson would be totally independent.

At the same time, Wilson ignored Conlisk, Jr., who became a captain in 1964, after eighteen years of being assigned to a variety of administrative posts. Many astute observers believed that this quieter and more conservative version

2. *Ibid.*

of the older Conlisk was waiting patiently to become what his father had never managed—or perhaps wanted—superintendent of the Chicago Police Department.

The younger Conlisk was a friendly, accommodating man who stayed in the shadows after his father was deposed. He was a man after the Mayor's heart, priding himself on his ability to soothe wounds, bring enemies together, and generate respect. His family background also helped him to recognize the political realities of running a big-city police force. Wilson eventually promoted Conlisk to chief of traffic and then to deputy superintendent. By 1966 he was second in command and few had any doubt that, when Wilson retired, Conlisk would be appointed superintendent.

Conlisk did not change his ways after becoming superintendent in 1967. He tried to stay out of the spotlight. He held his meetings with the Mayor quietly. Conlisk was able to maintain this low profile partly because, when Wilson had retired, most experts considered the department the finest equipped and most modern in the nation. All Conlisk had to do was preserve this newfound respect and reputation.

Conlisk would not have the luck of his predecessor or the necessary independence to overcome the problems which would inevitably arise. Soon after he became superintendent rumblings started that the force was riddled with dishonest officers.

Early in his tenure he found himself at odds with a detective who had caught several officers stealing cars and tires and had accused the IID of being a "washing machine." Conlisk removed the head of the IID, saying, "I want the division to be a more aggressive department, to ferret out corruption and not just investigate complaints." The words sounded good, but the IID would never be effective as long as it was staffed with officers who were required to investigate other cops with whom they had worked in the past. The change in the IID command was typical of how Conlisk dealt with criticism.

In 1968 the press castigated Conlisk and his men for the way they had handled the disturbances at the Democratic Convention. A federal grand jury indicted several officers but all were acquitted. Conlisk emerged with his reputation intact. Daley defended him throughout and was so strong in his denunciation of the protesters that only a few wondered if Conlisk should be blamed for what happened in Grant Park or whether these events were a sign of more disturbing problems within the Chicago police force. For example, hardly anyone noticed when three policemen from the Summerdale District were indicted for theft and three others were found to be members of the Ku Klux Klan.

The national press condemned all Chicago for what happened at the Democratic Convention, which caused many Chicagoans to defend their police department. Even after the Walker Report blamed the police for what had happened at the convention, general public support gave Daley an excuse to avoid making changes in the department.

Despite the March 1972 indictments and the resulting transfers and demotions, Conlisk acted as if he did not need to worry unduly about the Strike Force investigation. Instead, he concentrated on the allegations that many officers had engaged in unnecessary force and brutality in making arrests. He established community relations panels in each district and instituted procedures whereby civilian review boards could investigate complaints of brutality. He appeared at public meetings with his top deputies to convince the citizens that the department was there to serve and protect and that necessary checks against abusive police action would be established.

While the Strike Force investigation continued, charges of brutality were supplemented by allegations that policemen were murdering drug pushers with whom they were involved and that a top police aide was connected with organized crime. Conlisk, beleaguered by the mounting criticism, grew defensive and detached. On one occasion he proclaimed, "Allegations in newspapers make us all very sad, but they are not proven. Every man is innocent until proven guilty; every man stands in the pure innocence of his birth."[3]

Mayor Daley did not relish scandal and criticism either. He resented any implication that he lacked the necessary desire to control corruption. After the March indictments and the publicity of the police brutality complaints, he said at a police awards ceremony, "We have no apology to make to anyone. We're all human. I don't know what I would do if someone called me a brute, a sadist, an s.o.b. I'm proud of the Chicago Police Department."[4] When the four officers were convicted for extortion in June, Daley parried suggestions that he force Conlisk to resign, saying he was "100 per cent behind" the superintendent.[5]

Daley was also not above righteous indignation, particularly when it could be used to avoid a direct response to an unpleasant question. When asked to comment on allegations of a police hit squad, he said angrily, "Has Conlisk done anything wrong? Is he involved in the alleged leaking of this information by the federal people which, in my opinion, is unbelievable, dastardly, foul, and deceitful. Would you like to be mentioned as a murderer without being indicted. . . . I'm not defending the policemen. If the policemen are wrong, they

3. *Ibid.,* July 2, 1972.
4. *Ibid.,* May 11, 1972.
5. *Chicago Sun-Times,* June 27, 1972.

should be off the force. But did Conlisk have anything to do with the murders?"[6]

Neither Conlisk nor Daley wanted to admit publicly that any changes they made were a direct result of either the Strike Force investigation or of other criticisms of the police. They usually did nothing immediately following a new disclosure, preferring to issue announcements of any changes when there was a relative lull in activity by the investigators.

Even then, they couched their statements in generalities which did not mention the investigation. For example, Conlisk announced on May 31, 1972, that fifteen police officers with the rank of lieutenant or higher would be shifted to new posts. Four were demoted (not in rank but in assignment), five were promoted, and six were transferred. One of the demoted was Captain Thurlow Simons, commander of the Grand Crossing District, which had recently been in the news because of the FBI's arrest of Sergeant Crowley. Captain John O'Shea, who was commander of the 18th District, was also demoted. Although his demotion suggested that Conlisk knew the Strike Force was investigating the 18th, he would say only that the changes were "made to strengthen the department."[7]

The shake-ups in command and transfers did not alleviate public concern about departmental integrity. Editorials continued to push for more substantial reform. When it became obvious that neither the federal investigation nor the inquiry into charges of police brutality would soon cease, Daley and Conlisk announced on June 8 the appointment of Marlin Johnson as president of the Chicago Police Board.

The Chicago Police Board, established by Mayor Daley in 1960, had limited powers. The board possessed the authority to set department policy through rules and regulations, to review and forward to the City Council's finance committee the annual budget, to approve or reject recommendations from the superintendent on disciplining officers, and to screen candidates on behalf of the Mayor when a new superintendent was to be selected. These powers seemed extensive, but the board was not independent. Its members were appointed by Daley. The board had no resources to initiate its own investigation and had to wait to hold hearings until the department presented a case for review. If an officer was exonerated by an initial police investigation, the matter was closed.

Johnson was a former FBI agent who had been in charge of the Chicago

6. *Ibid.*
7. *Chicago Daily News,* May 31, 1972.

office. He was generally regarded as tough, honest, and decisive. When calls for Conlisk's resignation had increased after the March indictments, rumors spread that Johnson would be the new superintendent. Johnson's appointment to the Police Board indicated that, for the present, Daley had decided to stick by Conlisk.

When asked about his plans, Johnson said he would consider creating an independent investigative unit of former FBI agents to root out corrupt policemen.[8] How he planned to do this was unclear since the board had little power and no money. Even if money was available to recruit these agents, it was doubtful that they would have easy success investigating corruption in view of the previously demonstrated difficulty of the Strike Force in putting together its cases.

It also remained to be seen whether the composition and attitude of the rest of the board would change. Johnson was replacing Morgan Murphy as president, although the retired Commonwealth Edison Company executive would still remain on the five-member board. Murphy agreed that Johnson could establish an independent investigative team, but felt that other substantive action was not required. He said, "I think we have a fine police department, but I think we have some bad apples. . . . It is a job of digging them out."[9] Other members included the president of Chicago's largest title insurance company, the president of a Teamsters Joint Council, and a minister.

No one could be certain how independent Johnson would be in his new post. He had been recommended by the outgoing president and was rumored to be on close terms with Conlisk. Without compensation, his commitment could be only part-time at best. Johnson retained his position in private industry as vice-president of the Canteen Corporation. Beigel remembered how he once had tried to impress upon Johnson the importance of testifying in a prosecution about which he possessed valuable knowledge. Johnson responded by demanding that the trial be scheduled around his appointments or he would not testify.

Johnson's appointment had no effect on police operations. If he ever established a unit of former FBI agents to do anything, no cases resulted from it. The revelations in late June about the police hit squad, the convictions of four police officers, and the continuing rumors that the Strike Force was expanding its investigation contributed to a fast retreat of Police Board news to the back pages, especially as weeks and months passed without Johnson taking any significant action.

8. *Ibid.,* June 2, 1972.
9. *Ibid.*

By July the Police Department's precarious position in the public eye was deteriorating faster than expressions of support from Daley or shuffling of personnel by Conlisk could counterbalance. Word spread that the Strike Force was intent on exposing widespread corruption in the 18th District. Two of Chicago's major daily newspapers called upon Daley to replace Conlisk by someone to be recommended by a new blue ribbon panel. One rumor suggested that Daley would call upon Wilson to recommend a man of high integrity who would be capable of cleaning up the current mess. This rumor ignored the fact that Wilson was in ill health and, according to his wife, did not know there was a scandal in Chicago.[10]

Despite rumors that Conlisk was about to resign, Daley gave no indication that he would abandon his superintendent. The Mayor was not content, however, to merely ride out a storm if he could find a way to demonstrate a "positive" attitude without totally giving in to the critics. With black leaders still critical because of the continuing charges of rank brutality, Daley decided, on August 3, to appoint Mitchell Ware a deputy superintendent.

Mitchell Ware was black, thirty-six years old, and a former head of the Illinois Bureau of Investigation. There was no better-known law enforcement officer in Illinois. In the five years since graduating from DePaul University Law School, he had successfully gained public attention by a series of controversial actions.

Ware entered law enforcement in 1960, working part-time as a state narcotics agent. He continued in this capacity while attending law school, except for a brief period when he worked temporarily as a television reporter in Chicago. After graduation he took a job as an attorney in the federal anti-poverty program, and then decided to return to his first love, narcotics investigation, accepting an appointment as director of the Illinois Division of Narcotics Control. Ware soon came to the attention of Governor Ogilve. The state legislature had created the Illinois Bureau of Investigation, and Ogilve appointed Ware its first chief. As head of the "little FBI" Ware was the highest-ranking black law enforcement officer in the state.

It was not long before Ware found himself the target of criticism. Some complained that the IBI was more concerned with headlines and spectacular raids than meaningful investigations. During one raid in April 1971 Ware had authorized television news cameramen to accompany IBI agents. Ware announced proudly that the raid had resulted in the seizure of more than $30,000 worth of cocaine. After a lab analysis Ware was forced to admit the seized

10. *Chicago Today,* June 22, 1972.

chemical was not cocaine, but stearic acid, a substance used in the manufacture of candles.

Ware liked to use the press as a forum for speaking out about the seriousness of the drug problem on college campuses. He publicized any investigation in this area even though many of them produced little in the way of drugs or indicted pushers. Ware's use of publicity finally led to a rebuke from Governor Ogilve.

In August a circuit court judge in Cook County appointed Ware a "friend of the court" in the investigation of whether State's Attorney Edward Hanrahan and several police officers had obstructed justice in their handling of the Black Panther raid which had resulted in the deaths of several Panther members. The Daley administration had not been happy with the special prosecutor who had been working toward the return of indictments against Hanrahan and the officers. Ware was given the assignment of determining whether the special prosecutor had improperly pressured the grand jury during its investigation.

Ware's decision to work for the court (and indirectly for Daley) was the last straw for Ogilve. He quickly let it be known that he did not believe this "friend of the court" role and the position of IBI director were compatible obligations. Ware resigned. Several weeks later the Illinois Supreme Court decided that the judge had overstepped his authority in using Ware. Now unemployed, Ware entered private law practice.

Ware had remarked on many occasions that he was not a politician and had no allegiance to either political party. His past actions seemed to support this candid self-assessment and future events reaffirmed it.

When Ware was appointed deputy superintendent, he assumed certain key responsibilities, including the running of the Bureau of Inspectional Services under which the IAD functioned. Ware replaced Michael Spiotto, who had been given the post only the previous January. Spiotto was being shifted to a nebulously defined assignment to assist Conlisk "in evaluating the total organization, operations, and procedures of the department."[11] Spiotto was a well-regarded administrator and his transfer was viewed as another example of how the department was feeling the pressure to do something spectacular to assure the public that it was intent on reform. Hiring an outsider, as had been done successfully with O. W. Wilson, might accomplish this. Conlisk, in an unusual display of candor, said on the occasion of Ware's appointment:

I have been deeply concerned about the criminal indictments and convictions of some police personnel. Nothing can be more harmful to the city and to the police department than the betrayal of trust on the part of officers who have sworn to uphold the law.

11. *Chicago Daily News,* August 4, 1972.

Accordingly, I have re-examined police operations and procedures. I believe an essential first step must be a reorganization of the Department's Bureau of Inspectional Services. . . .[12]

Ware's appointment drew favorable reaction from many who had been among the most vociferous in their criticism of the police. Congressman Ralph Metcalfe, who had earlier incurred the wrath of Mayor Daley by supporting those who made allegations of police brutality, thought Ware's appointment was "an obvious indication that Supt. Conlisk sees reforms are needed in the police department."[13] Metcalfe was also impressed that Conlisk had elevated a black to this sensitive position, commenting that Ware's leadership "should represent a new avenue of authority over police and open up new lines of communications between black and brown communities and police."[14]

After the initial excitement following Ware's appointment had died down, the question remained as to how Ware intended to handle the problem of police corruption. Obligatory statements from both Ware and Johnson that there would be a new spirit of cooperation between the department and the Police Board and that efforts would be made to give all complainants a fair hearing did not dispel concerns that nothing meaningful would soon be done.

Whatever Happened to Reform?

Ware telephoned Davidson late in August to set up a meeting to coordinate the investigation of police corruption. Davidson suspected that Ware was just looking for information, but he agreed to meet with him.

Ware arrived the following morning and greeted Davidson and Beigel. He was a good-looking, ruggedly built man, dressed in a modish suit and brightly colored shirt. He wasted no time in explaining why he had come.

"I need help. I've been trying to get organized in my new job so I can start taking some action against crooked cops. I figured the best way to do this is to set up my own unit with officers I pick myself. I can't take a chance on the IAD since they obviously did nothing about the tavern shakedowns. Unfortunately, I may have bit off more than I can chew. Conlisk isn't very happy about my idea of an independent unit."

"I would think you would have to expect that," Davidson said. "An independent group which only responds to you would keep Conlisk in the dark."

"I know that," Ware said. "That's one of the reasons I did it. I'm an outsider in that place, and if I'm going to be effective, I've got to have a free hand. That

12. *Ibid.*
13. *Chicago Today,* August 4, 1972.
14. *Ibid.*

was a condition of taking the job. But I still have to get along with Conlisk and it's too bad if he thinks I'm trying to undermine him, although he doesn't really have much choice with all the bad publicity he's been getting. But there are other problems too."

"Oh?"

"Would you believe that I can't find enough officers that I can trust? I went around to each district and asked for volunteers. I didn't get that many and most of the ones I talked to weren't so hot. I grilled them extensively. It's surprising how many of them are crooked or at least so tainted by a crooked department that they'd be ineffective in an investigative capacity."

Davidson laughed. "You'll get used to it."

"I also have to worry about spies. I've just started and I can't afford to have my men passing along all my plans to who knows who. You know, I think Conlisk really believes there isn't much corruption in the Chicago Police Department. I don't want him to get his information second hand. It will only make matters worse."

"It's hard to believe that Conlisk is that naive," Beigel interjected.

"Maybe," Ware said. "But he keeps insisting that there are just a few bad apples, and the morale of the department is being destroyed by your fishing expedition."

"What can we do?" Davidson asked.

"I need some quick action to convince Conlisk that I will be an independent force he can't ignore. I'd like to bust a few cops, catching them red-handed picking up money, and so on. Something that will catch the public eye and show the crooked cops in the department that I mean business."

"That's not easy to do," Beigel said. "We've arrested only one cop while he was taking money. If you spend all your time looking for a spectacular arrest, you won't reform anything. There's no way you can catch every crooked cop. There are too many and they are too well insulated by the command structure. You can die trying. Look at us."

"But I'm in a funny position. I have to establish my credibility." Ware stood up and began pacing. Suddenly he turned toward Davidson.

"Look, Shelly. What I would like from you and Herb are some tips. You guys must have more information than you can use. If you get word of something you can't follow up, let me know and I'll take over. We can work together on this and make a big impact."

"Right now we don't have anything specific."

"Something is bound to come up. We can help each other out."

"There is one thing," Beigel said.

"What's that?" Ware said, resuming his seat and taking a pad and pencil from the inside pocket of his jacket.

"We started a little digging a couple of months ago in the Grand Crossing District. We received information that cops were taking money from business-men for off-duty patrols which turned out not to be off-duty at all. But we met some resistance from our witnesses. We turned it over to the State's Attorney's office, but they've done nothing. Maybe you want to take a look at it."

"Are the payoffs still going on?"

"I don't think so," Beigel said. "If the cops hadn't stopped collecting before we looked into it, I'm sure the grand jury scared them out of their little sideline."

"Well, if it's not happening now, there's no point in me chasing after it. But thanks anyway. That is just the kind of information I need, only current, so I can make a bust. You have to remember I'm on tender ground with Conlisk. He doesn't like losing control and he thinks he has an honest police depart-ment. Would you be willing to meet with him to give him the facts of life and let him know that there is a real problem? If we can convince him that a lot of changes are needed, it'll make your work and mine easier."

Davidson looked at Beigel, who shrugged his shoulders. Davidson turned back to Ware. "Mitch, what exactly are you trying to do with your job?"

"I wish I knew. All I can think of now is to get some men together, arrest some crooked cops, and fly from there. But shit, I can't even get a decent crew together."

"If you can set the meeting up, we'll go. But Conlisk thinks our investigation is an effort to embarrass him. A meeting at your request is hardly going to change his mind."

"I'm sure he'll want to meet with you. He can't afford to ignore you. I'll be in touch." Ware shook Davidson's hand, smiled at Beigel, and walked jauntily out the door.

Ware called a few days later to say that he had arranged the meeting. He told Davidson that Conlisk was anxious to meet with the two Strike Force lawyers to receive an update on the investigation and where it was heading. Although Davidson believed that Conlisk was interested only in getting infor-mation, there was no point in rebuffing him.

On the appointed day Davidson and Beigel walked to police headquarters at 11th and State. Ware was not present. He had told Davidson that he did not want to interfere. Davidson did not understand why, but he did not press Ware for an explanation. Ware was clearly in a touchy situation.

Davidson and Beigel sat in a small railed waiting area for several minutes.

Finally a man appeared and motioned the two lawyers to follow him. He led them into a large room, past several desks, to an open door which led into a spacious rectangular office. The escort stood to one side and signaled Davidson and Beigel to enter.

Conlisk sat behind a large desk in the middle of the office just out of the line of sight from the entrance. He stood up and smiled, extending his hand. Beigel turned to shut the door. "Oh, that won't be necessary," Conlisk said politely. "There's nothing about our meeting that has to be kept secret."

Beigel, embarrassed, forgot to shake Conlisk's hand. Instead, he sat down in an old wooden chair next to Davidson and across from Conlisk. No one seemed to want to start the meeting. Beigel folded his hands uncomfortably on his lap while Davidson let his eyes wander around the office looking at the photographs, citations, and memorabilia on the walls.

Conlisk put a few papers which were in front of him to one side and looked at the two lawyers. He had a round, affable face. With the glasses he wore and his white hair, he seemed more like a fatherly college dean than a police superintendent. His relaxed attitude seemed inconsistent with the frantic way he had been reacting to his problems. Conlisk spoke first.

"I'm glad you could make it today, gentlemen. The last time we met, I believe, was quite a while ago at the Union League Club when your investigation was first starting. I trust that you have been able to receive all the information you have needed since then."

"Yes, thank you, Superintendent," Davidson said with exaggerated deference, almost mimicking Conlisk's excessive cordiality. "Your liaison man, Mr. Finston, has been quite helpful."

As slowly as the meeting had started, it now abruptly came to a stop. Conlisk seemed distracted, as if he was planning another meeting or thinking about one which had just ended. He opened the top drawer of his desk and took out a small white pad. Picking up a pencil, he moved to make a note. He reconsidered and put the pencil on top of the pad.

"I'm very anxious to know how you are coming in your investigation. Obviously, we at the department are very desirous of helping you uncover any illegal activity by members of the police force, but at the same time I'm sure you can understand if I say I wish it would soon be completed."

"We know how you feel, Superintendent," Davidson replied. "We don't like this job either. It is an unpleasant task, and we agree with you that it would be best if we could bring our investigation to a rapid close so that the police can get on with their job. We are all in the same business. But I am sure you realize that there is still much to do in our inquiry."

"Of course. Those officers who went to jail for not testifying. Terribly demoralizing to the men on the force. What do you think will happen there?"

"We don't know. Frankly, one of the difficulties in an investigation of this kind is the reluctance of a police officer to give evidence against a comrade."

"Yes, but it's understandable. Many officers, good and honest ones, are naturally disturbed by an outside investigation. That is why I am taking steps to encourage a more active internal investigation apparatus. I am confident Mitch Ware will be quite helpful in that area. I trust you will give him the help he needs and continue to keep me informed."

"We certainly will cooperate with you in every way," Davidson said.

Conlisk picked up the pencil again as if to emphasize the point he was about to make. "I want to tell you gentlemen," he said, "that I have deeply appreciated the advance notice you have given me of the formal actions which you have taken. It has helped me take the necessary corrective measures. But perhaps we could just spend a few moments on something that has been troubling me greatly."

"Of course," Davidson said.

Conlisk paused, looking away from Davidson and toward the open door and said in a barely audible whisper, "Are there any of my deputy superintendents or other high-ranking administrative personnel or staff members who I can't trust?" Davidson and Beigel, obviously surprised and not hiding it, glanced at each other.

"What I mean, gentlemen, is this. Naturally, I must be concerned about the integrity of my command and the honesty of my staff, especially since many of them came up from the ranks and some were not entirely of my own choosing."

Neither Davidson nor Beigel said anything, trying to collect their thoughts. Conlisk waited, holding the pencil above the pad, ready to write. Finally Beigel said, "Superintendent, obviously grand jury testimony is confidential and we can't give out information which is hearsay and might never lead to any charges being placed. I am sure you can appreciate the unfairness of such disclosures."

"Also," Davidson added, "we still have a long way to go in our investigation. Accusing high-ranking officers of wrongdoing would be premature at this stage."

"Yes, I can understand what you are saying. But, on the other hand, I need to know who I can trust. Perhaps I could run down a few names and ask you whether I can trust them."

Before Davidson or Beigel had a chance to respond, Conlisk began reading.

He sounded like a chaplain reciting a list of war dead. As he mentioned each name and the lawyers remained silent, Conlisk relaxed. On three names, out of the ten mentioned, Davidson responded, "His name has come up, but it is inconclusive." Conlisk did not react. He made no move to write anything on the pad.

Conlisk stood up and walked around his desk. The meeting was over. It had lasted fifteen minutes. There had been no talk of reform. There had been only a whispered exchange of "Who do you trust?" Davidson and Beigel walked out of Conlisk's office. It was the last time the Strike Force lawyers spoke with Conlisk.

Chapter 8

The Failing Brotherhood

If I had known that taking money from tavern owners was a
federal crime, I never would have done it.

> —Salvatore Mascolino,
> October 1972

The investigation was floundering. There was no indication that the long-sought-after breakthrough to higher-ranking officers was imminent. Six weeks had elapsed since Cello and Mascolino had been granted immunity and had refused to testify. They remained in Cook County Jail, still defiant. The police were winning the battle. They had been able to resist the grand jury and to defeat the judicial process.

Cello and Mascolino's stubborn resistance reflected the power of the police over the criminal justice system. And their decision to disregard the court's order to testify was in part an outgrowth of the police officer's belief in his ability to exercise discretion and power without fear of meaningful sanctions. If Cello, Mascolino, or any other officers were ever to testify willingly about corruption, it would take not the Strike Force lawyers, the grand jury, and the courts, but an event that would crack the conspiracy of silence. The control, confidence, and power of the police had to be broken.

A Waiting Game

In the second week of September Davidson and Beigel met with Webb, who had been recently invited to assist in the Rush Street investigation. It was at a standstill. The three lawyers knew they had to do something. But so far they were stymied. Webb had just completed reviewing all the files, and Beigel and Davidson hoped he could provide some fresh insights.

"I have to hand it to you, Shelly," Beigel said. "You could hit your head a hundred times against a stone wall, but you don't get discouraged. Still, you can't escape the facts. Face it, Cello and Mascolino have stuck it out in jail for two months now. We could wait until doomsday for them to talk."

Davidson shook his head in disagreement. "I can't believe that those two cops will be willing to spend at least another fifteen months in the can just to save their buddies. It doesn't make sense."

"It might not make sense," Webb interjected, "but there's no point in sitting around doing nothing and hoping they will talk."

"We can all agree on that," Davidson said. "That's why we're talking, to see what we do next."

"Why don't we return the indictments we have enough evidence for. We can indict Cello and Mascolino. Maybe they'll change their tune." Webb walked over to the file cabinets lined against the wall of the office and opened one of the drawers. "Look at this. Annes and Hill have come up with several tavern owners who will talk. There must be fifteen different files here with evidence against 18th District cops. Let's keep the pressure on."

"It might work," Beigel said. "But if we return indictments now against Cello and Mascolino and some of the other members of the vice squad, we'll be so bogged down in work that Annes and Hill will have to spend all their time helping us prepare for trial. Besides, I'm getting tired of cases against these lower-ranking officers. There always comes a time of diminishing returns, and we've just about reached it. In a couple of weeks I have to try a case against James Pacente. Another Stoyan Kovacevic case, just a couple of hundred dollars' extortion. There has to be a limit on how many of these cases we prosecute before we pack our bags and say we've made our point."

Davidson frowned. "The Pacente case is important. Every conviction helps demonstrate that our investigation is worth something. We have to keep going with indictments."

"Maybe we ought to just let the Eighteenth District investigation drift awhile and do something in Austin. We could recontact Thanasouras. He might be willing to talk now."

"That's not going to work either. We don't have any evidence against Thanasouras. Holder won't talk and Thanasouras knows it. I think that's why Thanasouras spun us around in March. Why should he react differently now?"

In March, at the time of the first indictments, an IRS agent had called Davidson about Thanasouras. He said that he had met with Thanasouras, who was worried about being indicted. But when Davidson and Beigel reviewed the report of the interview, it was obvious that Thanasouras was just fishing for a safe way out of his predicament.

Thanasouras had been full of gossip, but was vague. When pressed for details he had quickly changed the subject. He would not admit that he had engaged in any wrongdoing. The agent had even told Thanasouras that he knew that payoffs went to the top of the police command. But Thanasouras did not budge.

Actually, there was no hard evidence that the money went right to the top and it was only wishful thinking when Thanasouras was told that he would be confronted with evidence against him in the near future. Now, six months had elapsed without anything happening to Thanasouras. If Thanasouras had been unwilling to talk in March, he certainly would not now.

Webb finally suggested, "Why give up entirely on immunity? So we were unsuccessful with Cello and Mascolino. Let's try immunizing someone else. If we do nothing, Cello and Mascolino might think we've quit. On the other hand, if we immunize another cop they might decide to talk. After all, the next person we choose to immunize might agree to cooperate immediately."

"What about Eddie Rifkin," Beigel said. "We had planned to immunize him along with Cello and Mascolino. If Rifkin doesn't talk, at least it will show the cops we have no intention of throwing in the towel. And we have enough evidence against Rifkin to indict him for perjury if he lies before the grand jury."

"Okay," Davidson said. "Let's give it one more try."

Beigel completed the necessary forms and sent a memorandum to the Attorney General asking for his approval. On October 4 Beigel appeared in court to formally request an order which would compel Rifkin to testify. The order was granted and Beigel led Rifkin to the grand jury room.

Mascolino had been racked with fear when he appeared before the grand jury. When Rifkin entered the grand jury room he was snide and cocky, smiling as if he were about to make a particularly satisfying arrest.

Rifkin was a model of righteous indignation. He opened with a tirade on the unfairness and unconstitutionality of the proceeding. He defiantly told the grand jury, "I have made up my mind to spend eighteen months in jail never having been accused of a crime. . . . Immunity means nothing to me at this point." He then refused to answer any questions except to give his name and address. He even declined to say whether he had been employed by the Chicago Police Department or assigned to the 18th District. Some of the grand jurors tried to persuade him to testify. But Rifkin remained firm and accused the jurors of subjecting him to a miscarriage of justice. When he saw that his comments were not having any effect, he sneered at them, "Don't sit so smugly. It could happen to you."

Rifkin joined Cello and Mascolino in jail. "Now what?" Beigel said to

Davidson when he returned to the Strike Force office from court.

"We ought to proceed on those officers against whom we have evidence. We can indict five or six cops. Murphy and Kinnally are lieutenants and White is a sergeant. The indictments of uniformed officers will tell Cello, Mascolino, and Rifkin that we have gathered evidence on an Eighteenth District club."

Beigel began preparation of the indictment. Although several tavern owners were ready to testify that they had belonged to the uniformed club and had paid money to the officers, nearly all agreed that there had been no particular pressure to make the payoffs. They had paid voluntarily because they wanted protection and freedom from arrest. In attempting to draft an indictment Beigel realized that the evidence did not meet the traditional test of the Hobbs Act, which referred to fear and coercion. The defense would argue that the payments were bribes, and it would receive additional support if some of the tavern owners testified that they had approached the officers to join the club because of the benefits of membership.

Beigel thought he saw a solution to this problem in that section of the Hobbs Act which seemed to indicate that any taking of money by a public official was extortion, whether or not state law labeled it a bribe. Before he could resolve this question completely, however, he had to put aside the uniformed club indictment to prepare for the trial of James Pacente.

Stoyan Kovacevic had paid Pacente in May 1971. Pacente was Victor Vrdolyak's vice coordinator and had met Kovacevic while conducting the routine investigation of his qualifications to hold a liquor license. Pacente demanded $200 and Kovacevic, worried about getting his license, paid the $200 by a check made out to cash. His accountant turned over the check to Beigel. Unfortunately, Stoyan was the only witness to the alleged extortion. Boris had not been present when the check was given to Pacente.

The $200 check was endorsed and cashed by Frank Velillari, who owned a bar within walking distance of Pacente's home. The FBI had a more than passing interest in Velillari, since he was rumored to be an acquaintance of a well-known Chicago hoodlum currently under indictment in a mail-fraud case. The connection seemed more than a coincidence when the lawyer retained by Pacente turned out to be the same lawyer who was representing the alleged hoodlum in the mail-fraud trial.

Beigel suspected that Pacente had cashed the check at Velillari's tavern, but he could not prove it. Both Beigel and the FBI had talked to Velillari and, although he acknowledged endorsing the check, he first denied that Pacente could have cashed it. He then said he was not sure. In a later interview he claimed that another police officer who lived in the neighborhood had cashed the check. This officer was now dead, fatally injured in a fire which he had allegedly set as a syndicate "torch" job.

Although Velillari would not offer any evidence against Pacente and might even damage the case, Beigel felt it was absolutely necessary to put him on the stand. To corroborate Kovacevic it was essential to convince the jury that it was more than coincidence that the check turned up at a tavern near Pacente's home, even if there was no evidence that Pacente had cashed the check himself. At worst, Beigel concluded, he could argue that Pacente had given the check to the dead officer, with whom it was known he had socialized, who in turn cashed it at Velillari's tavern.

At the trial Pacente's defense was designed to raise doubts about the validity of Kovacevic's identification as well as to suggest that if Kovacevic was shaken down it had been by the dead cop. Pacente's attorney attempted to buttress his theory about the "other man" by introducing evidence that Pacente had a mustache at the time of the alleged extortion. He called Pacente, his wife, his barber, and a close friend to the stand. Although this array of witnesses seemed to justify a conclusion that there was a reasonable doubt of Pacente's guilt, it was also clear that the witnesses were hardly free of bias. In addition, Beigel extracted from Pacente an admission that no other Austin District vice officer lived in the vicinity of Velillari's tavern.

Pacente's attorney made two critical errors. First, he could not find anyone who was not a friend or relative of Pacente to testify that he had a mustache. Second, although the attorney called several character witnesses, none was asked about the mustache, a curious failure to seize a perfect opportunity to buttress the defense.

The jury deliberated for twelve hours. During that time several newspaper-men telephoned Beigel to express amazement that he would prosecute an obviously innocent man. Although Beigel thought that it was very possible that Pacente would be acquitted, he did not agree that Pacente was innocent. He had seen Kovacevic select Pacente's photograph from more than thirty.

The jury returned a guilty verdict. Pacente and his lawyer were stunned. Pacente sat at his counsel's table muttering, "I can't believe this thing, I can't believe this thing." He remained there for ten minutes after the courtroom had emptied. His attorney had rushed out into the hall.

Beigel was left alone in the courtroom with Pacente and his wife. He finished gathering his papers, not turning to look at the wife, tears streaming down her face. As Beigel walked toward the door, Pacente's lawyer appeared. "Well, you ruined my consecutive win streak in federal court. I guess I'll just have to start a new one." Beigel turned around and saw Pacente and his wife sitting together. Pacente was still muttering to himself. His wife was resting her head on his shoulder. Beigel walked past the attorney and out into the hall.

A Tale of Three Cops

Although the Pacente trial had produced headlines for several days, renewing public attention in the Strike Force investigation, Beigel did not feel the same elation he had experienced after the first three trials in June. He could not get his mind off Cello, Mascolino, and Rifkin, who were still in jail, silent as ever and symbols of the investigation's failure to move beyond isolated cases of extortion. The Pacente case had been only an interlude in the waiting game which the police were clearly winning. How much longer the Strike Force could continue the game, Beigel did not know and was afraid to guess.

A few days after Pacente's conviction Beigel was sitting in his office reviewing the latest batch of 302 reports about 18th District tavern owners. His mind was not on his work. Instead, he was weighing the pros and cons of leaving the Justice Department to take a job offered by a Chicago law firm. Like many other young lawyers, Beigel had entered the Justice Department to gain experience in trial work, but had never intended to make it his career. He had delayed making a final decision about the offer because he did not want to leave without finishing important work. It would be difficult for Davidson to carry the day-to-day burdens of the investigations and still function as Strike Force chief. But Webb was now deeply involved in the Rush Street investigation and could take over there.

The latest trial had been a disappointment to Beigel. He was no longer excited about winning a difficult corruption case. For him, it was a sign of the dulling effect caused by spending too much time on one investigation, no matter how important. Beigel worried that, after nearly two years, his effectiveness was diminishing. Perhaps it would be better to give the investigation to someone else. After all, there had never been a real breakthrough. Another lawyer might have better luck.

Beigel was so deep in thought that he did not notice Davidson standing at the door. "Those reports can't be that dull," Davidson teased.

"What do you mean?"

"You look like you are about to fall asleep."

"Actually, I was thinking about taking that job I've been offered."

"Forget it for now. We've got more important things to do."

"Such as?"

"Don't be dense. We may have finally made it."

"Made what?"

"I just got a call from Cello's lawyer. He says that Cello and Mascolino want to meet with us."

At 3 P.M. Cello and Mascolino were shown into Davidson's office. Their lawyers followed a few minutes later. As Davidson and Beigel took them to meet their clients, Alan Ackerman, Cello's lawyer, stopped outside the door. "Before we go in, I'd like to talk with you."

Ackerman, Beigel, and Davidson remained in the hall. "Shelly, you know that I'm Cello's lawyer, but he does what he wants to do. He's no dummy and he didn't spend three months in jail for nothing. He wants out of jail. Who wouldn't? It's got to be pretty bad for a cop. But he's not the kind of guy to do any favors."

"What's that supposed to mean?" Beigel asked.

"Very simply this. He is prepared to go before the grand jury and answer questions if the contempt citation will be dismissed."

"He could have done that three months ago."

Ackerman smiled. "He knows that." Ackerman looked around the corridor and noticed the secretaries staring. "Is there another office we can use?"

Beigel pointed to his office. "We can go there." The three lawyers walked into the office.

"I'll give it to you straight," Ackerman said. "I think Cello and Mascolino are ready to give you fellows everything they know, but there is a price."

"We're ready," Davidson said with a sigh. "What do they want?"

"Don't get anxious, Shelly," Ackerman said.

"Nobody is anxious. We wanted their cooperation. We still do. If they tell the truth, they won't be prosecuted."

"They want more than that."

"What?"

"Their police careers are over. When they testify they can chalk off as friends the cops they worked with all these years. Now they need protection and new jobs."

"You know the standard policy," Davidson said. "If they legitimately need protection, we will provide what we can. We'll also help them find jobs if they need help. But we can't guarantee anything."

"I know you can't make guarantees. But when you go in there and talk to them just let them know you have their interests at heart. At this point they need a friendly face."

"I'm curious about something," Beigel said. "Why the sudden change? I thought they were going to protect their fellow cops until doomsday."

"They did too, but not anymore."

"Do you know why?"

"They can tell you themselves."

The three lawyers went to Davidson's office. Cello and Mascolino were sitting on the couch with their hands folded in their laps. Davidson and Beigel approached them. "I'm Sheldon Davidson and this is Herb Beigel. We have just had a conference with one of your lawyers and I'm assuming that what he told us goes for the both of you." Davidson paused to see if there was any objection from Mascolino's lawyer. There was none.

"Alan tells us you want to cooperate. All we want is the truth. If you give it to us, you have nothing to worry about. You'll get out of jail. If you feel you will be in danger and your fear is reasonable, we will protect you. We will also try and find you new jobs. But we can't give you any guarantees except that the truth will keep you from being prosecuted. We always lay all our cards on the table and we expect that you will do the same."

"I would like to say something if I may," Mascolino said. Beigel looked at him more closely. He had been nervous when he had appeared before the grand jury and Judge Robson in July. Now he seemed depressed and defeated. His eyes were red and he looked fatigued and distraught.

"What is it?" Beigel said.

"I'm not down here for any noble reason. I didn't want to talk; it didn't seem right to me. I'm not sure Skippy even wants to now. But we're here and we've decided to tell you everything. My wife has been writing me every day for the last month asking when I'm going to get out of jail, telling me she's got no money to buy food and she can't get along without me. That wasn't so bad. I expected it. Skippy and I were willing to stick it out, hoping the families would understand what we were doing. But it's different now. I want to tell you why."

"It isn't necessary," Davidson said.

"Just the same. It's worth getting it out so you know the shit you're dealing with. I got a letter from my wife the day before yesterday. Here it is. Take a look at it." Mascolino fished a crumpled piece of paper out of his pants pocket and handed it to Davidson. "She says she can't go on and is thinking of committing suicide unless I get out. And I gotta get out now."

"What about you?" Beigel asked Cello. "Why are you here?"

"There is something else," Cello said. He appeared much more self-possessed than Mascolino. "A raffle was set up to raise some money to support our families while we were in jail. It was supposed to be enough to keep us going. Except, our families never saw any of it. The cops who set it up ripped it off! The goddamn scum. I can't believe it. Can you believe it?"

Davidson looked at Beigel, who was standing by the door trying to figure out if what he was hearing could possibly be true. "I can sympathize with what you've gone through," Davidson said. "But Herb and I are here to do a job and now so are you. You level with us and tell what you know and your worries will be over. Put the other stuff behind you. We still have a long way to go. But you'll be out of jail."

Mascolino stared at the floor. "We'll be out of jail, but I doubt if our worries will be over. Will we have to testify at a trial?"

"You never know, but you have to be ready for it."

Cello stood up. "You guys have done a number on us, but we're ready to spill out guts. We just want to get it over with."

"You spent three months in jail," Beigel said. "You're out now. How fast things go depends on you and what you say. But don't rush it."

"From now on," Cello said, "you call the shots."

They agreed to meet the next day. The two officers would be released from jail. The marshal entered Davidson's office and motioned for the two officers to accompany him. "I'll see you tomorrow," Cello said.

"And many days after that," Beigel said.

"I guess we'll just have to get used to it," Mascolino said with a smile. The tension broke.

After the officers and lawyers had left, Beigel looked at Davidson. "Would you ever have thought this is how it would happen?"

"I always knew they would finally break."

"Sure. But don't you see? The very people Cello and Mascolino were protecting did them in. Now Cello and Mascolino are going to tell us about them. The conspiracy went up in smoke because of a raffle." Beigel shook his head. "Two years and it took a raffle to get them to come over."

Mascolino and Cello were interviewed simultaneously so that the debriefing process could proceed as quickly as possible. Beigel and Davidson did not want to take unnecessary chances and were anxious to guard against the possibility that the two officers would change their minds about cooperating. They also decided to wait before approaching Rifkin. Depending on what Cello and Mascolino said, Rifkin's testimony might not be needed. In any event he would stay in jail until the lawyers made up their minds what to do with him.

It soon became clear that although Cello and Mascolino could reveal in fascinating detail the mechanics of corruption in the 18th District, they had been too far removed from the center of power to offer anything but hints about the involvement of the district commanders under whom they served. Nevertheless, Beigel was satisfied. The corruption was definitely there and it was large, even though elusive.

Cello had joined the Police Department in 1956. From the beginning he was assigned to the 35th District, which later was consolidated with another district to become the 18th.

"In the beginning, I was a patrolman assigned to do the normal work that a patrolman does. I worked the beat, and I also worked in a squad car. . . . At that time I had no personal involvement with police corruption. The information I received from other policemen on the street was that a bag man was picking up money from various bars and taverns in the Eighteenth District and taking the money directly to the Commander of the district. Supposedly, the Captain would then split up this money among people who at that time were called the Captain's Men. These Captain's Men later became what was known as the vice squad in later years."[1]

O. W. Wilson became superintendent in 1960. The commander at that time was John McDermott, and Cello said that the word in the department was that he was honest. In 1964 McDermott left the district and was replaced by Walter Maurovich. About five or six months prior to Maurovich's appointment Cello received his first vice squad assignment.

"When I first came on the vice squad at that time, I had a conversation with Sam Farmer.[2] He told me at that time that money was being collected from various bars and taverns in the Eighteenth District. He told me that a package was made up from that money that was being collected and that as a member of the vice squad I would be getting approximately $300 a month. Farmer told me which bars and taverns were paying into this club and that I was to stay away from these places."

Cello recalled that Farmer mentioned that at least nineteen taverns belonged to the club at this time. Cello also remembered participating in a few of the collections with Farmer and Mascolino. During those five or six months prior to Maurovich's takeover of the district Cello received $300 each month. He believed that Farmer was delivering money to the vice coordinator but he never saw the payments made. Cello also named six officers who at one time or another he saw receive shares of the package.

When Maurovich became commander a new vice coordinator was appointed and Cello was removed from the vice squad. His name was William

---

1. All quotes are taken directly from the written statement of Cello.
2. The name of this officer has been changed.

Simpson. (He resigned along with Maurovich before appearing before the grand jury.) Cello was reassigned to the night crime car. Although no longer on the vice squad, Cello had made many friends in the district and was invited to attend a meeting with several vice officers including Simpson.

"At that time Simpson said that we would have to get the club going like it was under McDermott. He said he would like to know ahead of time which bar owners were going to be in the club so that he could review it and let the vice squad know if they were o.k. to be in the club. Simpson said we were not to pressure the bar owners and we were not to promise them anything. He told us that we should tell the bar owners that if anything came up and we could help them with it, we would."

Although Cello was no longer on the vice squad, two of the vice officers asked him to pick up the money from some of the taverns. Everyone trusted Cello. Simpson agreed.

Cello said he collected money from more than fifteen taverns during Maurovich's tenure, although many more belonged to the club. Cello could not remember the names of all the taverns, but he detailed the club's operation during the Maurovich years, including a description of a fight that broke out because some vice squad members believed that the collectors were "skimming money off the top of the package for their own use." Nevertheless, members of the vice squad consistently received about $250 a month as their share of the package.

When Maurovich was transferred to another district in 1966 he was replaced by Commander James C. Holzman. Within a month almost all of the officers who had served on the vice squad were also transferred. Cello remained on crime car assignment with his new partner, Sal Mascolino.

Holzman had a reputation for honesty. Cello said that, after Holzman took charge,

"He told all of the men . . . that he wanted all bars and taverns in the Eighteenth District watched very closely. He said we should keep such a close watch on them that many of them would close up and leave the district. He emphasized that no one should take any money from any bar owner or anyone else, and if any police officer was caught doing the same he would immediately be fired. . . ."[3]

3. This lecture may have been the result of Wilson's dissatisfaction with Maurovich's failure to clean up vice and reduce the high crime rate in the district. In any event, Holzman was wrong about one thing. If an officer was caught taking money, he could not be immediately fired. A hearing was required before the Police Board, assuming charges were ever filed.

Despite Holzman's statement, Cello said, a certain amount of corruption continued as usual. Although there was no club, there were persistent

"rumors . . . that Holzman's own vice officers were raping the district by shaking down the bar owners for large sums of money every time they found a violation. The word on the street was that Holzman's vice men were taking $2,000 and $3,000 a crack whenever they could get a bar owner who was in trouble and was willing to pay off."

Although the club had been temporarily disbanded, Cello remained semi-active in corruption. He was approached by a bookmaker who offered him money if he would inform him when any raids were planned. Cello agreed and collected a monthly fee for providing this service.

Holzman was the commander of the 18th District for only six months, shortly thereafter resigning from the department. The Strike Force later received information that Holzman had left because of his failure to receive support from his superiors at police headquarters. Reportedly he was so discouraged with his Chicago experience that when he retired from the department he moved to Seattle.

Holzman was replaced by Clarence E. Braasch, one of the department's most respected young leaders. Braasch brought with him a new vice coordinator and old friend, Robert Fischer.

"Shortly after Fischer became vice coordinator . . . there was a meeting held in the vice office of the Eighteenth District police station. Present at that time were myself, Sal Mascolino, Edward Rifkin, Lowell Napier, and Robert Fischer. Fischer said that we should get the club going again in the Eighteenth District. He stated that Mascolino and Napier would work nights and I and Edward Rifkin would work days. He stated that Mascolino and Napier would collect from bars at night and I and Rifkin could collect from bars in the daytime."

Some of the men then compiled a list of those bars which might be recruited for membership in the club.

"Within a few days after this meeting I had another meeting with Fischer in the 18th District police station and Fischer brought back the list to me. Some of the bars that were on the list were marked out. At this meeting, besides myself and Fischer [were] Napier, Sal Mascolino and Edward Rifkin. . . . At that meeting Fischer said he had crossed out some of the bars because they were troublesome or they were too new and nobody knew anything about them. Fischer also said that there were some places that were doing something for somebody else. He told us that we were to watch out for these places and not create any trouble for them [and] we were not to collect any money from them. . . . Many of these bars . . . were certain strip joints that we all suspected were paying money directly to the Commander of the District. It was always the word among police officers that this was called the "Big Club" and the money went directly to the Commander of the District with some of the money then going downtown to high ranking police officers."

After several months Fischer was promoted to lieutenant and transferred. He was replaced by Sergeant Edward Barry, who continued to supervise the club as Fischer had except for a third scheme. In addition to the "little club" and helping out with the "big club," he also collected from card games in the district. For his help Cello received from $150 to $200 a month. This represented only 50 percent of the proceeds, with the other half going to a person unknown to Cello.

From the beginning there was discrimination in sharing the club's proceeds. Each vice officer usually received $250 a month. However, because of the risk they took in making collections, Cello and Mascolino each got $500 a month. Rifkin also received $500 a month. If any money was left over, it went to the vice coordinator.

Cello named eleven officers to whom he personally distributed monthly shares while Braasch was commander. Although the organizers of the club were not particularly concerned that they would be exposed, they took certain precautionary measures which quickly became standard procedure.

"When Braasch became the District Commander and Fischer became the Vice Coordinator, the following rules were laid down by Fischer. The first month that an individual was assigned to the vice squad he would get no share of the package for that month. For the second month that he was assigned to the vice squad, he would get a ½ share of the package. . . . The reason we had this gap of one month before any member of the vice squad was to share in the package was so that members of the vice squad could check out the guy to make sure that he was not too aggressive and that he would not cause any problems if we cut him into the package."

After Cello was promoted to sergeant in 1970 he was transferred out of the 18th District, a routine move following a promotion. As had other departing vice squad members, he received a payment for the first month after he was gone, a form of severance pay. From Cello's own statement it could be estimated that, during the six years he was actively involved in the club, he received between $15,000 and $25,000 tax-free. The total take of the club was several hundred thousand dollars.

Webb, who had interviewed Cello, had little problem extracting the information in detail and in chronological order. Beigel, who was talking to Mascolino, had a different experience. Mascolino had a bad memory and a great deal of difficulty in organizing his thoughts. He was constantly in a state of nervous agitation, repeatedly interrupting the questioning to talk about his family and how sorry he was to have gotten himself in the current mess. He admitted taking money from almost the first day he joined the 18th District vice squad in 1960. Until 1972, almost without pause, he had participated in the club's activities.

It took several sessions spread over two weeks to obtain an outline of what Mascolino knew. Mascolino was not happy with the grilling, but was consoled by being out of jail and home with his family, knowing that as long as he told the truth he would not be indicted.

One day, toward the end of the grueling series of interviews, Mascolino asked for a break. "I have trouble going on like this for too long at one time. It all runs together in my mind. I can't keep anything straight."

"What do you mean?" Beigel asked.

"For years I took money from bars. I didn't think it was any big deal. It certainly wasn't anything new, although I suppose if I had thought about it maybe I'd have decided it was wrong."

"You didn't think there was anything wrong with what you were doing?"

"Not really. I don't know. Maybe. But we weren't protecting murderers. There are guys on the force who did that and take money from drug pushers and the Mob. But I wasn't one of them. We were just making an extra buck. If I had known that taking money from tavern owners was a federal crime, I never would have done it."

In the middle of the interviews with Cello and Mascolino the lawyers received word that Eddie Rifkin wanted out of jail. His lawyer told Davidson that Rifkin wanted the same deal as Cello and Mascolino. Davidson met with Beigel and Webb to discuss what to do.

"You realize, Danny," Beigel said, "that our information indicates that Rifkin probably won't have anything new to offer. He was just another collector. It's doubtful he can give us any evidence against Braasch. From what Cello and Mascolino have told us, we'll probably have to get Barry to talk before we go that high. Besides, Rifkin is a smart-ass. He's bound to make a bad witness. You saw him in the grand jury. We just don't need him."

"I'm sure you're right, Herb, but it will look bad if we don't give Rifkin the same deal as Cello and Mascolino."

"I think Dan's right," Davidson said. "As much as I hate doing it, we'll have to let Rifkin off the hook if he cooperates. We could still indict him, but there's really no point. With or without him, we still have a case against several officers. Rifkin wants to join the bandwagon. We might as well let him."

"I guess so," Beigel said. "I just hope he makes a decent witness and can be helpful."

Rifkin could not give any evidence against Braasch, but he corroborated Cello and Mascolino, and further implicated Fischer and Barry, making it more likely than ever that Braasch had played a role in the planning, and possibly the carrying out, of the little club.

Rifkin had entered the department in May 1966. Shortly after completing training he was assigned to the 18th District, where he joined the vice squad. He started during the last part of Holzman's brief stewardship and then served under Braasch for the entire length of his command.

After Fischer became vice coordinator Rifkin attended a meeting with him, Napier, and Cello. They asked Fischer if something could be arranged for the men on the vice squad and he replied that it was okay with him. Fischer instructed them to prepare a list and he would clear it with Braasch. Rifkin and Cello prepared the list and then met with Mascolino in the parking lot of the Lincoln Park Zoo, where they gave him a copy for his approval.

Of particular interest was Rifkin's description of what happened after Braasch was promoted to deputy superintendent in 1970. The new commander was John O'Shea, and he soon replaced Barry with his own vice coordinator, Sergeant Geraghty. Rifkin met with Geraghty, who asked that he continue to make collections. Geraghty added that Rifkin no longer would receive his premium of $500 a month, but now would receive $250 just like everyone else. Rifkin protested but Geraghty said "that's the way it's going to be."

Although Rifkin was not happy with Geraghty, he continued to make collections for the next several months until he was transferred to the Traffic Division in October 1971. Rifkin named twelve taverns from which he collected regularly and said that he recalled distributing money to eleven vice officers, some of whom had not been named by either Cello or Mascolino.

By the middle of November the Strike Force had obtained a complete picture of the vice club's operations. The specific information they now had made it easier to convince the tavern owners to cooperate. In a short time Annes and Hill signed up more than fifty tavern owners who would testify that they had been members of the vice club during the eight years when four different police commanders were in charge of the 18th District. The picture of the tavern shakedowns emerged as a perfectly set mosaic of greed and dedication to the job of protection for hire.

With the cooperation of Cello, Mascolino, and Rifkin, sufficient evidence existed to indict about twenty officers. Although some officers could not be charged because of the statute of limitations, the indictment would be of unprecedented size. The vice club had been responsible for taking hundreds of thousands of dollars from businesses as well as diverting an unknown amount of police time from the normal duties of fighting crime and enforcing the law. The main focus of its energies had been directed toward keeping the club working smoothly and efficiently. Not once during the interviews did Cello, Mascolino, or Rifkin mention police work.

The uniformed club appeared relatively self-contained. With the cooperation of many tavern owners, Beigel, Davidson, and Webb now had strong cases against several officers, including Lieutenant James "Keep-It-All" Murphy.[4] At this point it seemed best to indict them along with the vice club officers. If any officer wanted to cooperate, there would be plenty of time before trial. For the time being they decided that use immunity had been used enough.

Although the lawyers were confident that Braasch had been deeply involved in corruption, it was not clear if they could prove it. They did not know if Braasch had received any money from the vice or uniformed club or the exact nature of the "big club" and how it was handled. If Braasch was not getting money from the "little club," why did he allow it to continue, risking at least embarrassment if it was exposed? The answer to this last question, Beigel felt, would be the key to indicting Braasch, now the fourth-highest-ranking officer in the department.

With Cello, Mascolino, and Rifkin fully debriefed, Beigel felt better about making a decision to leave the investigation. It finally looked as if it was headed in the right direction. He had always wanted to enter private practice, and he now felt he could make the move without jeopardizing the investigation.

"Why are you doing this?" Davidson asked Beigel incredulously when he told him about his decision to leave.

"If I really believed I was needed, I would stay. But Webb knows what he's doing. He has a good relationship with Cello, Mascolino, and Rifkin and it won't be hard to find someone to take over the Austin investigation. Besides, Becker will be able to brief whoever gets the assignment."

"Even if that's true, don't you want to see your investigation through to the end?"

_____

4. See Chapter 6.

"It's not my investigation. It has a life of its own. The conspiracy of silence is broken. The FBI obstinance isn't a factor anymore and the investigation will follow its own course no matter who runs it. You could investigate corruption for an entire lifetime. I've done it for two years. It's time for someone else."

On his last day of work Beigel moved his files to Webb's office. Davidson walked in. "Look at all these files. Beigel, you're crazy. This is the biggest investigation of police corruption ever and you're letting Webb have it all."

"Shelly," Beigel said with a smile, "the day you can tell me that this or any other investigation has stopped corruption, I'll say it was truly big. Until then, it's just hard work and the kind of thing that few people outside this office were ever interested in doing. At least I'm not the only one here who was crazy enough to want to do it."

Beigel left the department quietly. The following week he was walking down the hall on the twenty-fifth floor of the Civic Center to appear at his first civil contested hearing, dealing with a suit to foreclose a mechanic's lien on a parcel of real estate. Outside the courtroom door he saw Jim Demopolous.

"Herb Beigel," Demopolous said with a big grin. "How are you doing?"

"Okay."

"Sure, sure," Demopolous said as if he knew differently. "Herb, I have to ask you something." Demopolous grabbed Beigel by the arm and pulled him over to the other side of the corridor away from the lawyers standing around the door. "I understand you left the Strike Force. Did they squeeze you out?"

"What are you talking about?"

"You know what I mean. That police investigation. It's real explosive. They didn't want it to go on any more. Right?"

"I don't know who 'they' is, but you have it all wrong. I just wanted to do something else. That's all there is to it. As far as I know the investigation is going on in a big way."

"Okay. I understand. You can't talk about it. Say, how about a cup of coffee?"

"Jim, I have a court appearance to make. Some other time."

Beigel walked back toward the courtroom thinking about what Demopolous had said. It was strange. As he opened the door, he noticed Demopolous still standing where he had left him, leaning against the wall, looking worried. Beigel had the strange feeling that Demopolous had been upset to learn that the police investigation was continuing. Crazy, Beigel said to himself. Why should Demopolous care? Beigel walked into the courtroom trying to put police corruption out of his mind. He had to concentrate on the intricacies of mechanic's lien law. He suddenly realized that, for the first time in two years, he was in a courtroom where he did not see a familiar face.

Chapter 9

Silence Is No Longer Golden

Around June of 1970, I saw Braasch after he was promoted to Chief of the Traffic Division. We had lunch at Ricardo's and I asked him if he was surprised or disappointed when he was promoted out of the 18th District. Braasch said no, as he felt that the problems had been piling up and the pile would probably topple soon, and a guy could probably fall with it if he wasn't careful.

—Statement of Robert Fischer,
January 23, 1973

After Beigel left the Strike Force the job of bringing the 18th District investigation to a successful conclusion went to Dan Webb. Another young lawyer, Farrell Griffin, was assigned to work with him. Davidson remained in charge, with Thompson's guiding hand in the background.

Beigel's departure and the rapid developments in the 18th District investigation made it difficult for Davidson and Thompson to continue the police corruption inquiry as an integrated effort. Because of the excitement generated by the cooperation of Cello, Mascolino, and Rifkin and because of the loss of Beigel's full-time involvement, the work in Austin was quickly forgotten.

Inserra, too, was caught up in what had been learned about the 18th and found little time to worry about Austin and the dedicated Becker. Annes and Hill now had his ear because of their quick success. Although the cooperation of Cello, Mascolino, and Rifkin did not occur because of any action by Annes and Hill, Inserra was impressed by results. Becker was left without support from his own office.

Becker also found it difficult to find a sympathetic and knowledgeable ear in the Strike Force. Aside from the Gill-Fahey trial, Webb had never been

180

involved in the Austin investigation and was now too busy with the 18th District vice and uniformed clubs to devote time to a "separate" matter. Davidson, who knew the most about the Austin investigation, was also thinking of retiring to private practice and eager to see the 18th District investigation wrapped up. In this jumbled state of affairs it was not surprising that Becker was ignored.

Becker, however, was not easily discouraged or put off. But the indictment against Holder had been transferred from assistant to assistant, each of whom was reluctant to try a police corruption case. The witnesses were difficult to handle, the evidence was usually marginal, and the chances for conviction were never more than fifty-fifty.

One of these reluctant assistants had thought he might score a quick coup by getting Holder to cooperate. He called Holder down to his office. Acting mean and hard, he abrasively told Holder that he would not see the light of day for years if he failed to cooperate. His efforts were a dismal failure. Holder was so upset by this show of force that Becker feared Holder would never talk, no matter what happened.

Becker still felt that Holder held the key to Thanasouras, and he also had several new ideas he wanted to discuss with a knowledgeable prosecutor. He had thought about trying to find more evidence against the previous vice coordinator, Frank Bychowski, who was now "retired" and living peacefully in a small Wisconsin town where he was the police chief. Perhaps it might be worthwhile to consider granting him immunity, especially if the government possessed sufficient evidence to indict him for perjury if he lied. More pressure on Demet, who already had immunity, might make him talk.

Becker, nearing the limit of his frustration, called Beigel at the beginning of December and asked to meet with him. As soon as they sat down for lunch in a coffee shop across from the Federal Building, Becker anxiously explained what had happened to the Austin investigation since Beigel had left (only two weeks before).

"Tom, what do you expect?" Beigel said. "The big thing now is the Rush Street investigation. You can hardly expect Inserra to push Austin when he sees a big indictment coming down in the 18th District. Inserra is going to lend his support to whoever he believes will get the quickest results."

"I know that. But Austin is where we started. It doesn't deserve to be abandoned. If only there was a way to get Holder to talk."

"We tried everything. All you can hope for is that he will change his mind once he is convicted."

"I suppose. But that could be a long wait. The judge who has the case keeps putting it off. I don't know when it will go to trial. I'm beginning to think that if I wait for Holder to turn, I will be burying the investigation for good."

"What about Demet or Bychowski?"

"Demet is so wedded to Thanasouras that I don't want to approach him before I know where I am going. We have very little against Bychowski. You always told me it's a mistake to give immunity when you don't have the evidence."

It was clear that Becker was upset. "I know how you feel," Beigel said, "but wait a little and see what develops. In the meantime try and dig up more evidence against some of the other vice cops. Maybe somebody like Charley Eckenborg."

"The longer I keep looking around, the more cases we'll lose because of the statute of limitations."

"Worry about Thanasouras. At this point you still have time. He was commander until early 1970. We're still in 1972."

"So I have time, but for what? Everything is passing me by. No one cares about Austin anymore."

Beigel lit a cigarette and tried to think what he could say to make Becker feel better. But there was nothing. Still, Becker had spent too much time and worked too hard to be left without something to hold on to.

"Tom, why don't you wait and do more planning? If indictments are returned soon, everyone will have a pretty good idea what Cello, Mascolino, and Rifkin are going to say. If those cases get pushed to trial, which they probably will, and if there are convictions, Holder, Demet, and Bychowski will come running to save their skins."

"That's quite a few ifs."

"They represent the road to Thanasouras. You have to be patient."

"I guess that's what I'll have to be. But I can't say I'll like it."

"Who would?"

Silence Is No Longer Golden

While Becker was expressing his frustration Davidson and Webb were reviewing the statements of Cello, Mascolino, and Rifkin. They were satisfied. Organized, detailed, and consistent with one another, the statements exposed completely vice club operations in the 18th District. They were also disturbing. Nowhere was there any clear indication how officers above the level of vice coordinator might be involved. Strong cases could be made against most of the officers who had served on the vice squad as well as Fischer and Barry, the vice coordinators who had served under Braasch. Clarence Braasch, however, was not directly implicated. Hearsay, inference, and common sense indicated that he had been involved deeply in corruption. (The same could be said about Maurovich, but Maurovich was out of reach because of the statute of limitations.) Braasch was a tantalizing target, but he could not be charged solely on the basis of inference and intuition.

Webb and Davidson were disappointed that Cello, Mascolino, and Rifkin were unable to give direct evidence against Braasch, but they were not surprised. None of them had been close to Braasch and were too far removed in rank to have been confidants. Others would have to provide the testimony.

Davidson decided to discuss the problem with Cello. "Skippy, in your discussions with Webb were you able to give him any ideas about how we could get to Braasch?"

"Braasch had plenty of meetings with the vice coordinators, but they were always behind closed doors."

"All right, then. Let us assume we have to go to a vice coordinator to get testimony. Who should we approach?"

"I think you ought to contact Bobbie Fischer."

"Fischer? I thought that he was only in the district for a couple of months."

"That's right. But he was involved in the club even after he left. And I think he continued to have meetings with Braasch. Don't be fooled because he was transferred to another district. He was tight with Braasch."

"Do you think he would talk to us?"

"He might. He was a pretty tough man around the station, though. And another thing. If he was involved in the big club, he may have collected from the syndicate joints. He has to worry about what would happen if he testifies. Still, I would talk to him. What can you lose."

Davidson went to Webb's office. "Dan, Cello said that if we want to go after Braasch, we should contact Fischer."

"Who?"

"That was my reaction too. He was only in the district for a little while. But Cello said he was involved even after he left."

"It would be fantastic if Fischer would talk. Has he been before the grand jury?"

"No. We never knew who he was or that he might be important. I don't even know if he's still on the force."

"Let's get a subpoena prepared for him, then."

"If we subpoena him, he'll get a lawyer and take the Fifth before the grand jury."

"We can immunize him."

"And have him spend time in Cook County Jail like those other three guys, delaying things. There has to be a better way."

"I'm open for suggestions."

Davidson sat down across from Webb and continued, "I remember a few years ago we had a similar problem. We wanted a witness bad, but we didn't want to call him before the grand jury. We thought about conveniently running into him on the street and having a casual conversation. Then we thought about going to his house. We finally did."

"What happened?"

"Nothing. It was a big bust. We got nowhere."

"It doesn't sound like a very good idea."

"Maybe that isn't. But I still think we ought to find a way to approach him informally before giving him a subpoena."

Davidson returned to his office. He looked at Cello's statement on his desk. It was clear, Davidson thought, that Braasch was involved. It was also obvious that any large indictment without Braasch would look strange, especially with the principal collectors testifying against cops who simply took their share each month. Suddenly he had an idea. Mitchell Ware had offered to help in the investigation. Now there was a way to use him.

After talking with Webb, Davidson telephoned Ware and told him he wanted to see Fischer.

"Who is Fischer?" Ware asked.

"He's a lieutenant, but I don't know where he is assigned."

"Why do you want to see him?"

"If it's okay with you, Mitch, I would prefer not to go into it now. I would consider it a big help if you would contact him and bring him to my office."

"What am I supposed to tell him?"

"Don't tell him anything. You outrank him. He'll go with you. Pick him up one day and drive over here."

"It sure sounds mysterious."

"Not for long."

Several days later Ware called Davidson. He was going to meet Fischer that afternoon at two and would immediately bring him to the Strike Force office. Davidson went to see Webb.

"Dan, Fischer is coming this afternoon. Because you don't know Ware, let me handle this meeting alone. If Fischer decides to talk, I'll call you in."

At 2:30 Ware arrived with Fischer. Fischer was tall and lanky and looked to be in his late thirties. He spoke quietly and measured his words in a way which conveyed the impression that he was always telling the truth. He was articulate and thoughtful, responding to questions only after stopping to think them over. If Fischer would cooperate, thought Davidson, he would make an excellent witness.

Davidson had formed this basic impression after hearing him describe how long he had been a police officer, how he liked his job, and the kind of police work he did. Fischer also looked bewildered, not understanding why he had been brought to the Federal Building on such short notice. Finally he said, "Mr. Davidson, why am I here? Deputy Superintendent Ware picked me up, did not explain anything, and brought me to this office."

"Before I explain why I wanted to see you, Lieutenant Fischer, I want to emphasize that this is a strictly off-the-record conversation."

"I don't understand." Fischer was clearly apprehensive.

"We are investigating allegations that there was a vice squad club in the 18th District during the time you were there which solicited money from tavern owners. I want to talk to you about it."

"I don't know anything."

"We have evidence which indicates differently, but please understand that we want your cooperation. We are looking for your help. We are not out to crucify you."

"I haven't done anything wrong."

"Lieutenant Fischer, do you have a lawyer?"

"No. I don't believe I need one."

"Lieutenant, I will be frank with you. I would not tell you that we have evidence which convinces us that you were deeply involved with setting up this vice club if we did not have it. We know that you received a list of proposed taverns from several of the vice cops in late 1966 and that you took it to Braasch for his approval."

Fischer grimaced when Davidson mentioned Braasch, but said nothing. Ware stood up. "I can tell you, Bob," Ware said, "that I have known Shelly Davidson for a number of years and when he says he has evidence, he has it. He wouldn't lie to you."

Ware walked around Fischer to the back of the desk where Davidson was sitting. He leaned over and whispered into Davidson's ear. "Shelly, do you mean it? Do you really have evidence that this cop was involved? You have evidence that he was on the take?"

Davidson couldn't believe that Ware was now whispering this question after he had just finished telling Fischer that Davidson would not lie. Fischer was sitting quietly. Davidson turned to Ware and said in a voice that Fischer could hear, "That's exactly right, Mitch."

Ware shook his head and returned to his chair. "Lieutenant, I think you should be honest with Shelly."

"Deputy Superintendent, I have done nothing wrong. I don't know anything about any club." Although Fischer's voice was clear and he seemed outwardly calm, Davidson knew that Fischer must be a bundle of nerves inside.

"Lieutenant, are you worried about your position as a police officer?" Davidson asked.

"Nothing I did in the Eighteenth District gives me any concern."

Ware walked over to Fischer. "Bob, don't worry. I promise you that if you level with Shelly, no one will trick-bag you. What I am saying is that if you are open and honest, it won't jeopardize your job as a police officer."

Davidson was shocked. How could Ware possibly tell an officer who had been involved in organized shakedowns that he did not have to be afraid he would lose his job if he told everything he knew, including an admission of his role in the corruption?

Davidson glanced at Fischer. Fischer had not reacted to Ware's statement, although it was obviously unbelievable. Davidson couldn't blame him for not reacting. It was the logical way to hide from what was facing him.

"We have the evidence, Lieutenant. Believe me, we do. I would not have asked you down here if we didn't."

"I told you I have done nothing wrong."

"Let me outline a little more of what we know." As Davidson related what Cello, Mascolino, and Rifkin had described about the operations of the vice club while Fischer was vice coordinator, Fischer continued to sit calmly. When Davidson began to list some of the bars he thought he detected a flicker of worry in Fischer's eyes.

Ware again approached Davidson and whispered in his ear. "Shelly, are you kidding? Was he really involved?" Davidson, annoyed at Ware's interruption, simply said, "Yes." Ware again shook his head disbelievingly and walked to the back of the room.

Davidson turned back to Fischer. "You see, we know you were up to your ears in it. And if you don't cooperate, we will have no choice but to issue you a subpoena."

Fischer leaned forward. "Why do you have to do that?"

"It's very simple. We believe you have important evidence about the club and about Commander Braasch. It is something the grand jury is investigating and they are entitled to hear from you."

"It would cause me a serious problem."

"What do you mean?"

"My job."

"You have to understand our position. We want your cooperation. But you are obviously not ready to give it to us. We have no alternative."

"It puts me in a terrible bind."

Fischer was now scared, but Davidson wasn't sure whether he was worried about losing his job or afraid to tell what he knew. Perhaps, thought Davidson, he could use Fischer's concern about a grand jury subpoena to convince him to talk.

"Why don't we do this, Lieutenant," Davidson said. "We don't want to hurt you, but we have a job to do. We think you are a key witness and we simply can't let you go without getting your testimony. However, I would be willing to do one thing. I have tried to tell you that we know how you were involved. Now it's obvious you believe me, but you are unsure about what to do. I think you should talk to someone. Get yourself a lawyer. Discuss it with him. I will put off the subpoena for a week. After you have spoken with a lawyer, call me. If your position is still the same, you will have to appear before the grand jury. If you change your mind and want to help us, we can take it from there."

"Remember, Bob," Ware interjected, "that you don't have to worry about your job if you tell the truth." Fischer quickly turned in the direction of Ware and glared. But all he said was, "I understand, Deputy Superintendent."

"Do you understand what I'm saying?" Davidson said. "I will wait a week."

"I understand."

The meeting had lasted forty-five minutes. After Fischer and Ware left, Davidson went to report to Webb.

Webb was not surprised by what had occurred. "I didn't think he would talk, Shelly. We'll just have to call him before the grand jury."

"I don't know. He struck me as someone who is really in a turmoil and, most of all, afraid."

"More afraid than the other cops?"

"I think so. Remember, he may have collected from syndicate operations. He might be worried about his safety if he talks."

"Well, I guess we'll find out in a week."

Several days later Davidson was still wondering about the Fischer meeting when the phone rang. He picked it up. "Shelly, this is Tom Maloney."

"Tom, how are you?"

"Fine. Do you have a minute?"

"Sure, what's on your mind?" Davidson could not imagine what Maloney, who was one of the more experienced criminal defense attorneys in Chicago, wanted. At the present time he had nothing pending with the Strike Force.

"The other day, a Lieutenant Robert Fischer came in to see me. He said he had met with you in connection with the police investigation and those shakedowns of tavern owners. From what he tells me, you were pretty frank about some of the evidence you have collected against him and others. You really startled him."

"I was trying to impress upon him the importance of telling the truth."

"I don't think he understood your motives, at least not completely. But that's neither here nor there. Actually, the reason I called is to see whether there's any possibility of working something out."

"We're willing if he is."

"How about if I come by to see you later today. I'll bring him along."

"Fine." Davidson had difficulty concealing his excitement.

Maloney arrived at 3:30 and left Fischer in the reception area while he went back to Davidson's office. Davidson had told Webb about Maloney's call and they had agreed to offer Fischer use immunity if he cooperated fully.

As soon as he walked in the door, Maloney, who never wasted any time, began talking. "Shelly, this is what Bob wants to do. He will tell you everything. Frankly, I don't know what it all involves. I did not go into it with him in great detail. I do know enough to realize he needs immunity from prosecution and some assurance that if he ever has to testify or it becomes known that he talked, you will give him the necessary protection. From what he has told me, I think he will need protection. The man is petrified."

"I can't judge the extent of the danger he might be in until I hear what he has to say. If he needs help, we will give it to him. The important thing now is that he is ready to give us help, and not hold back. For that, we will give him immunity, but only use immunity. That is Justice Department policy— no more transactional immunity. If he tells the truth, he won't be prosecuted by us."

"I understand. Let me go outside and talk to him."

Five minutes later Maloney returned with Fischer and a woman in her early thirties. Fischer looked calm, but the woman was shaking and appeared to be on the verge of tears. "Shelly," Maloney said, "you've met Bob Fischer and this is his wife. She wanted to meet you."

Mrs. Fischer stepped forward and took Davidson's hand. "It's very nice to meet you. Bob is worried about all of this, and so am I. I hope you will help us."

"Mrs. Fischer, if your husband cooperates and tells us what he knows, we will do everything possible to make things easier for him and for you."

"Shelly," Maloney said, looking at Fischer, "I have explained what we arranged. He understands, but he would like to ask you a few questions."

"All right." Davidson noticed that Fischer was carrying a small black notebook.

"Mr. Davidson, I apologize about the other day. But you must understand that it took me by surprise. I didn't know what to think. Ware never told me what was going on. He's an outsider to most of us on the force and doesn't understand the current situation. I hope you do."

"I think I do."

"Frankly, I'm in a very difficult position. Talking to you is bound to cost me my job, no matter what Ware says. I don't believe him. No one is going to make an exception for me. But to tell you the truth, I'm more worried about my safety. I hope there's some way this can be kept under wraps."

"I want to be honest with you. In all likelihood it is not going to be possible to keep what you tell us a secret. We want to return indictments, and if we do, you have to recognize that it is likely you will have to testify at a trial."

"If that happens, I'll have to leave town. Believe me, I won't be able to stay here."

Webb walked over toward Fischer. "Lieutenant, we can keep it quiet up to a point. If you cooperate fully, we might be able to put you in the grand jury for just a couple of questions and have your immunity handled in chambers. That way, no one will know you have cooperated for at least a little while."

"Whatever you can manage, I would appreciate."

Fischer's wife went home and Maloney returned to his office. Davidson and Webb began the tedious task of coaxing Fischer to release what he had kept secret so long, his knowledge about corruption in the 18th District.

During the next few days Fischer provided the most detailed statement to date about corruption in the 18th District. The little black notebook he had brought to the first meeting with Maloney and Davidson listed all the members of the "big club." Not only did it help Fischer recall the specifics of what had happened several years earlier, but it also provided the missing links which tied Braasch to the vice club and revealed the extent of the relationship between the police and organized crime.

After the first several meetings Webb took over Fischer's debriefing. At times Fischer was reluctant to answer questions and occasionally he was evasive. Eventually he gave the wanted details. Fischer's memory for details was extraordinary. He not only recalled all events, but was able to piece together conversations and provide the smallest detail, including what individuals were wearing at a given time. His impressive memory and sincere manner would make him a credible witness and would enable Webb to find corroborating evidence more easily.

In addition to showing how Braasch had been involved, Fischer gave a detailed statement concerning his own involvement in the planning and organization of the vice club. He described the procedures which he had implemented to avoid embarrassing mix-ups between the vice club and the big club. Although Braasch had apparently never received a single cent from the proceeds of the vice club, he had knowingly participated in establishing and maintaining it to avoid complaints from lower-ranking officers that he was getting all the money and they were getting nothing. The scheme worked even though the amounts Braasch received from his own activities far exceeded what any vice officer could collect.

Webb could not help but be curious why Fischer had decided to cooperate in the investigation. Of all the officers who had talked, Webb considered Fischer to be the most sensitive and the least likely to break the long-established police tradition of not turning in a fellow officer. Fischer had been friendly with Braasch. Now, however, his testimony would not only aid in the prosecution of the vice officers who served under him, but could lead to the downfall of Braasch, a police officer who had built a successful career and who was often mentioned as a possible successor to Conlisk.

For a long while Webb and Davidson assumed that Fischer just did not want to be indicted and was afraid of jail. While Fischer was tough on the outside, he was very vulnerable on the inside. He did not look like he could survive in prison or withstand the rigors of a trial. His wife also reflected this concern. On more than one occasion she lamented about how poorly things had gone. However, there was an additional reason for Fischer's cooperation. It was betrayal.

Confronted with the possibility that he would suffer alone for the major corruption in the 18th District, Fischer had decided he could no longer protect a man who long ago had deserted him. During one debriefing session, he could not hold back his feelings any longer. More animated than ever before he poured out all the pent up frustrations and fears, "I always did what Braasch asked me to do," he began. "When I was promoted to Lieutenant, he asked me to stay on and make the collections. It was a big risk. But he said he needed me and I believed him. I looked up to the man. I thought things could stay the same. But I learned that Braasch was only interested in himself. I guess I always knew it deep inside. Braasch had always been a son of a bitch and difficult to get to know. But I didn't wake up to the truth until he screwed me. He told me that Barry was reaching out for more money and that there was pressure from the syndicate to reduce the payments. He said I would have to take less. I believed him. Then I found out that the syndicate had agreed to restore the original payments and that Braasch had instructed Barry to pressure them to do it. Barry wasn't reaching. Braasch just wanted me out. He used me until he decided he could trust Barry. Then I was dumped."

"He was really that kind of guy?" Webb said.

"I don't know. But Braasch was aloof, no question about it, 'though I never dreamed he would stoop to playing me off against Barry. I liked and respected him. He did it to me for no reason. We had a meeting in the Forest Preserve. I'll never forget it. I told him I was having trouble with the payoff. You know what Braasch said? He said he was considering dropping the whole thing. Nothing could have been further from the truth. I found that out soon enough. Not that it mattered. He didn't need me. Maybe he did think about stopping. But I don't think he did until he was promoted and your investigation started. The money was too good. But I faced up to the fact that I had fooled myself into thinking that there was some mutual respect between us. There never was. It was a one-sided relationship. I realized then that I didn't owe him a damn thing."

"Is that why you decided to testify?"

"You know, I don't like outsiders meddling in police affairs. I always thought we could take care of ourselves. I didn't like the way Ware acted, telling me that if I confessed I could stay on the force. What bullshit. I never did trust him. I didn't trust you at first, either. Your investigation doesn't do anybody a damn bit of good. But it doesn't matter. We got caught and that's it. I've had it, and I'll have to go somewhere else. I never dreamed I would testify against another police officer. But I guess that's what it's come to."

The Indictments

With Fischer on the side of the government, it was now time to draft the indictments. Davidson and Webb knew that the traditional concept of extortion was insufficient, and therefore decided to adopt the novel legal theory that extortion under the Hobbs Act did not require actual coercion or threats when a public official took money. In their theory, if a public official received a payoff it implied that it was the office which acted as the inducement or threat. The indictment against Braasch would be based on the taking of money under "color of official right." Although this approach had never been taken before, Webb and Davidson felt that it was the only feasible way to present the Braasch case and that the court would uphold it.

On December 22 Webb met Beigel for lunch at Berghof's, a German restaurant next door to the Federal Building and the scene of many previous lunches between the two. Webb was carrying a large manila envelope. He opened it and pulled out a thick sheaf of papers stapled together. "Here it is, Herb. The vice club indictment."

Beigel looked at the front page and read: "United States v. Braasch et al. And it is some et al." Beigel ran his fingers down the list of names. "Twenty-four defendants."

"All the vice officers against whom we had evidence and could indict without running into a statute of limitations problem. Also, Barry and Geraghty, two vice coordinators."

"How did you handle Fischer?"

"We gave him use immunity in chambers and put him into the grand jury for just a few questions so as not to prematurely alert anyone that he's cooperating. He's scared. He's going to need protection and we wanted to give him time to get used to the idea. His wife is also worried."

"Do you mind if I read the indictment?"

"Go ahead. I want you to. I want to go over something with you."

Beigel read through the indictment. Immediately he noticed the section which charged the defendants with conspiracy to commit extortion under the Hobbs Act. There was no allegation of coercion, force, or threats. "I see you have used the color of official right theory."

"What do you think? Will it stand up? I'm worried about it."

"You really don't have much choice, Dan. Too many of the club members paid voluntarily and you have no 'victims' to testify about the big club. I think we have the right Court of Appeals for this kind of theory if the case ever goes up. The developing trend around the country is also in your favor."

"Well, as you say, I have no choice. There is one other problem. I think my idea is okay, but I would like your feelings. We don't have any evidence that Braasch got any money from the vice club. All he did was approve or disapprove the club members. I'd like to go with the theory that Braasch was responsible for the vice club, not because he wanted money from it, but because he figured he had to satisfy the vice men if his big club was going to run smoothly. The vice coordinator would do only what his title implied, coordinate between the vice club and the big club."

"I guess your only witness against Braasch is Fischer. I think that's a bigger problem than whether Braasch received any of the money from the vice club. You're going to have a trial with a bunch of defendants, and God knows how many witnesses, all but one of whom can't say a thing against Braasch. Even if Fischer makes a credible witness, and I haven't met him, the jury is liable to lose track of the real gist of the case. You may have a three-month trial and all it'll come down to is Fischer against Braasch."

"I realize that's a problem, but we have to go ahead with the evidence we have. We can't invent any."

"Just keep one thing in mind. When the case goes to trial, be sure you tie in at every opportunity the vice club to the big club. Even though the payoffs by the big club aren't really a part of the case, make sure you get it in. Just the sheer amount of dollars should keep the focus on Braasch."

The indictment was returned on December 29, 1972. On the same day another indictment was returned against the seven cops who had managed the uniformed club. The defendants included Murphy, Kinnally, and White. Although this was a significant indictment (Murphy and Kinnally were lieutenants), it attracted little public attention because of the immensity of the Braasch case. Fifty-three taverns were named in conjunction with fifteen counts of extortion and perjury against twenty-four police officers, including Braasch, Barry, and Geraghty.

Although the prosecutors knew they could not prove that Braasch had ever received money from the vice club, a perjury charge was lodged against him (Count XV) as a result of his grand jury testimony that he had never been told by another Chicago police officer of the vice club's existence. The charge further stated that he had learned about it from Fischer, thereby revealing to everyone that he was the witness upon whom the government was relying to make its case against Braasch.

One vice officer against whom there had been sufficient evidence was not indicted or named as a co-conspirator. Charles DuShane had been in the district for just three months and had received his share of the vice club proceeds only during that time. Webb was worried that, by parading to the stand his accomplice witnesses, Cello, Mascolino, Rifkin, and Fischer, it would appear that the case was one in which the real brains behind the operation were being let off the hook to go after the little guys who did nothing but pick up their envelopes each month. To alleviate this problem, Webb wanted to have as a witness the least culpable vice officer he could find. DuShane was the natural choice.

DuShane was also valuable as a witness because he had had enough exposure to the vice club during his three months in the 18th District to confirm the syndicate connections to the police. For example, DuShane told Annes: "I recall another time when I was riding with Steve Munson[1] and he told me that the Commander wanted him to call the syndicate gambling boss, Bill Gold, before we made any arrests of bookmakers in the district. Munson stopped at

1. His name has been changed.

the telephone booth at Belden and Clark and made a phone call. Five minutes later, the phone rang and Munson talked with someone he later told me was Bill Gold. Munson said he liked to use this phone booth because if there were any problems, you could talk to someone at the bar across the street." The name of Bill Gold was to come up time and time again before the Braasch case was over.

The indictments of thirty-one officers shocked Chicagoans as they prepared to enjoy New Year's Day 1973. It was now apparent that corruption in the department had not been limited to isolated shakedowns by individual "bad" cops. The earlier statements of Conlisk and Daley that the police were in fine shape were no longer credible. The newspapers again demanded Conlisk's resignation, but the city fathers were not quite ready to give up. There still had to be a trial and neither they nor Webb and his associates were ready to assume that the outcome was a foregone conclusion.

The return of the indictments did not signal a lull in activity. The following day Webb received a call from Lowell Napier's lawyer. He had originally been considered for immunity, but when Cello, Mascolino, and Rifkin talked there was no need to approach him. Now he too wanted to make a deal. Since little distinguished him from the other three "accomplice witnesses," Webb felt it was only fair to give him consideration if he entered a plea of guilty.

Napier became a government witness and further corroborated the evidence previously accumulated regarding the planning and operation of the vice club. His testimony supported the hypothesis that the vice club could not have continued without the express approval of the district commander. Napier was "tough-looking" and had, one officer told Webb, been picked to collect money from taverns because he looked the "meanest."

On the same day Webb was surprised by a telephone call concerning Lieutenant James Murphy, who had been indicted as a member of the uniformed club. He also wanted to give in and cooperate. Murphy was the "Keep-It-All" Murphy referred to in the anonymous telephone call which Davidson had received in July.[2] No one had ever thought that this hardened cop who had a reputation for being selfish would decide to give up so easily. But he did. He pled guilty and agreed to testify in the vice club trial.

Only three months earlier no police officer had agreed to cooperate with the investigation. Now seven police officers were ready to testify against other

2. See Chapter 6.

officers. An amazing about-face had taken place, but it had not been accomplished by any specific action of the prosecutors. Instead, it had been the result of the prosecutors' perseverance and the deterioration of the loyalty which had bound one officer to another so closely that it seemed unbreakable. The code had been finally repealed and the conspiracy of silence broken.

Chapter 10

The Apple Orchard

"Look, this is Braasch's apple orchard. If you are going to pick apples, you are going to pick them his way."

—Robert Fischer to Edward Rifkin,
November 1966

Seven attorneys filed appearances on behalf of the defendants in the Braasch indictment. All were experienced criminal lawyers who had tried countless federal cases. David Schippers, a former Justice Department prosecutor who had worked with Davidson on several cases against organized-crime figures, represented Edward Barry and five other police officers. Eugene Pincham, considered by many to be the foremost black trial lawyer in Chicago, represented eight defendants. Harry Busch, a veteran of the criminal defense scene, and Pat Tuitt, a clever young criminal lawyer, filed joint appearances on behalf of four others. The colorful and exuberant Marty Gerber represented Geraghty. The star of the defense team, however, was George Cotsirilos, one of Chicago's most distinguished trial lawyers. He represented one defendant, Clarence Braasch.

The trial was assigned to William J. Bauer, who had been U.S. Attorney when Beigel had first begun the investigation in December 1970 and who had assisted the Strike Force lawyers in obtaining from Conlisk the much-needed photographs and personnel information of Austin District officers. Since Bauer had been the U.S. Attorney during the early part of the investigation, Webb worried that Bauer's actions at the Braasch trial would be questioned more than those of another judge who had had no connection with the prosecution. Although he had become a judge before the Strike Force had begun its work in the 18th District, it was still possible that it would be claimed he was biased against the defendants. Webb anticipated that some of the defendants would

196

file motions challenging Bauer's right to handle the case.

None were filed. Perhaps Bauer's solid reputation as a fair judge dissuaded the defendants from attacking his impartiality. They might even have believed that Bauer's prior association with the prosecution would cause him to bend over backward in his rulings at trial to avoid any suggestion that he favored the government's case.

Preparing the Braasch case for trial was, at best, tedious. Webb had two assistants, Farrell Griffin and James Holderman, but the work was still overwhelming. Not only was it necessary to prepare carefully the police witnesses so that they would be able to relate clearly their long and detailed stories to the jury, but the owners of the fifty-three taverns named in the indictment also had to be interviewed and reinterviewed.

During his preparation Webb often wondered whether his plan to call all of the tavern owners to the stand should be changed. Much of their testimony would be against other government witnesses, namely Cello, Mascolino, Rifkin, and Napier. They could provide no evidence against Braasch or Barry. All of the defendants, and particularly Barry and Braasch, would argue that the prosecution was engaging in overkill to obscure the basic weakness of its case. Webb was aware of this danger, but still believed that he had to call the tavern owners to testify. His whole case depended on the jury accepting the premise that the vice club had been so large and so organized that the commander must have known about it. If the jury did not make this inference, it would certainly not be prepared to believe Fischer's testimony that Braasch not only knew about the vice club's existence, but also approved its continuation.

The Case Against the Police

On a hot summer day at the end of July 1973, Judge Bauer called his crowded courtroom to order and asked if the government and the defendants were ready to proceed in the trial of *United States* v. *Braasch, et al.* The seven defense lawyers crowded around the judge's podium and stated they were ready. On the left side of the courtroom, at the prosecution's table, stood Dan Webb, Farrell Griffin, and James Holderman. They also acknowledged they were ready to begin.

As Bauer outlined the procedures he would follow, Webb looked around and saw that the scene was no different from that at the other police corruption trials. Familiar courtroom watchers, newspaper and television representatives, and ordinary citizens who had come to see their police on trial were present in force. A definite tension was in the air.

The jury selection did not pose any significant problems, although it was laborious because the number of defendants increased the preemptory challenges available to the lawyers. Jury selection lasted a week, but in the end there was nothing to distinguish these jurors from others who had served in previous police corruption cases. Relatives and friends of police officers and tavern owners were excluded. The jury was a standard mix of men and women, city dwellers and suburbanites, blue- and white-collar workers.

The defendants, knowing they were in for a long haul, watched the opening proceedings with detached equanimity. They were plainly and neatly attired, making it difficult for Webb, who felt as if he knew each defendant personally, to distinguish one from another. One defendant, however, stood out. Braasch, sitting next to his attorney, displayed an almost charismatic self-confidence. He was a tall, lean, silver-haired man who conveyed the authority of a leader. His conservative brown suit and glasses gave him the look of a college administrator. He never reacted to anything the lawyers and the judge said. When he would occasionally lean over to confer with Cotsirilos, he acted as if he were advising an inexperienced police cadet. Although Webb knew that Braasch's testimony was weeks away, he could not help thinking ahead to the crucial part of the trial. But he dared not hope that, as had happened in the case against Frank Gill a year ago, a witness would magically appear to destroy the confidence and credibility of this experienced and respected police officer.

During the early days of testimony Webb was pleasantly surprised. The jury did not seem bored with the testimony of the tavern owners. The spectacle of one owner after another testifying that he had paid money to the police had an almost hypnotic effect on the jury. Perhaps it was because, unlike those who had lived day and night with the investigation, they found it hard to accept that so much corruption had existed. The jurors' interest reassured Webb that the decision to call all of the tavern owners had been correct.

Although the jury was fascinated by the testimony of the tavern owners, the defense attorneys, as expected, acted as if one witness were no different from the next. Occasionally they energetically cross-examined a tavern owner, especially when the testimony was vague or sketchy. Most of the time, however, they asked few questions, which concerned largely the grant of immunity to the witness. Webb was puzzled by this kind of cross-examination. The defense was engaging in the very process which it would argue the government had used—the construction of a smoke screen to conceal the weakness of the case.

Typically, a tavern owner would testify that he had paid Mascolino or Cello or Rifkin and the defense attorney would establish what there was no argument about—that the witness had not paid other vice officers. Webb knew that the jury might be reluctant to convict a vice officer who did nothing more than collect his share each month from the bagman, especially when the bagman had been given immunity from prosecution. However, he hoped that if the jury believed that Barry and Braasch were guilty, they would convict all those who had received money, whatever their feelings about Cello, Mascolino, Rifkin, and Fischer escaping any punishment.

As the days passed a certain routine developed. The participants took their places in the courtroom each day as if guided by the hand of a stage manager. One person stayed out of the mainstream. Braasch made a point of disassociating himself from the rest of the defendants. While the others sat on folding chairs lined along one wall, Braasch sat with his attorney at the counsel's table. During recesses, when the defendants would congregate in several groups in the hall, amiably conversing with one another, Braasch would invariably either remain in the courtroom or pace the halls alone. Even though he was standing trial with twenty-two fellow police officers, he managed to remain aloof, almost as if he considered it his badge of honor.

Since he had spent considerably more time with Cello than Mascolino, Webb decided that Griffin would question Mascolino on the stand while he would handle Cello. Although Mascolino had been in a continuous state of readiness since the return of the indictments, the period of time which he would have to cover on the stand was so large that there could never be too much preparation. To ensure that Mascolino would be thoroughly ready to testify, the prosecutors decided to put him on the stand on a Monday. That way, Griffin would have a full weekend for a last-minute dry run. The lawyers decided to use this system for each of the police witnesses.

Mascolino began his testimony with the kind of general personal background which Griffin hoped the jury would appreciate. He had been married for seventeen years, had three children, and was presently working as a security guard. He described how he had been subpoenaed before the grand jury a year before and the events that led to his imprisonment. He told how he had been granted immunity, how he had then refused to testify, and how he had been sent to jail for contempt of court. He then related how he appeared again before the grand jury and testified. He finished this phase of his testimony in less than ten minutes. It could give the jury only the barest inkling of what had gone into his decision to testify against the defendants on trial.

The gradual unfolding of Mascolino's story and his description of the 18th District vice squad during the early sixties provided a compelling backdrop for the events which were the subject of the trial. Countless police officers had been involved in one way or another with illegal police activity. Had the statute of limitations period not expired, it was obvious that more officers than those presently on trial could have been indicted for the same abuses. Extortion was, as the prosecutors would argue, a way of life in the 18th District.

Mascolino's testimony also documented the remarkable continuity of corruption which had existed in the vice squad. Although each vice coordinator handled the organization and planning of the club differently, the net effect was the same. Large sums of money were collected by a few vice officers and distributed among all vice officers, with the vice coordinator receiving the largest share. Only during the brief command of Holzman did there appear to have been no formal package. Even then, collections were made on a large, if sporadic, basis.

After Mascolino completed his narration of what had occurred under the commanders who had preceded Braasch, Griffin directed his attention to late 1966, just after Braasch had been promoted to commander.

Q: (Griffin) Now, sir, I want to direct your attention back to the fall of 1966, when you first joined the vice squad under the District Command of Clarence Braasch. In that fall, sir, did you have occasion to have a meeting with certain other vice officers in that district?

A: (Mascolino) Yes, I did.

Q: When did that meeting take place?

A: In October of 1966.

Q: And where did that meeting take place?

A: In the south parking lot of Lincoln Park Zoo.

Q: Who was present at that meeting?

A: Rifkin, Cello and myself.

Q: Sir, will you describe to the ladies and gentlemen of the jury what occurred at that meeting and will you please relate what each of you said at that meeting?

A: I arrived first at that meeting. A few moments later, Officers Rifkin and Cello arrived. At that time, Officer Rifkin presented me with a list of taverns, approximately 20 taverns. He stated that we were about to start up a club for the vice men. With this, he told me to look over the list and decide if I wanted to add any more taverns on or if I wanted to take any more taverns off. Cello then stated that he and Rifkin would pick up from half of these taverns on the day shift and Napier and myself would pick up from half of these taverns on the night shift. At this time, I looked over the list and I didn't add any taverns on and I didn't take any taverns off. With this, I gave the list back to Rifkin.

The conspiracy had begun. Mascolino, Cello, and then Rifkin would testify that it had continued throughout 1967, 1968, and 1969, and into 1970 and

1971 under Vice Coordinator Geraghty and Commander John O'Shea, who replaced Braasch after his promotion.

Mascolino described in detail how the vice club had enlisted taverns into membership and how first Fischer and then Barry were in charge of approving the collection of money from these taverns. Mascolino identified many of the defendants, testifying that he had seen them receive shares of the package. He also mentioned several taverns whose owners had already testified or would later testify. His thorough recounting of the club's operations along with the testimony of the other cooperating officers would set the stage for the climactic moment of the prosecution's case, the testimony of Robert Fischer.

During his testimony Mascolino described a strange incident which seemed at the time to have little significance. In May 1967 Lowell Napier had telephoned Mascolino, upset that he had been suddenly transferred to another district. He threatened to go to the newspapers and the FBI with the story of the vice club. Mascolino finally persuaded him to change his mind, but Napier wanted Mascolino to ask Barry for $400 which he believed was due him for the current month. Mascolino did as Napier asked and Barry agreed to give Napier the money.

By August, Mascolino was in charge of dividing the money due many of the other vice squad club members. He put the money in envelopes and made sure that each participating officer received his proper share. Mascolino also gave money to Barry to deliver to Cello and Rifkin for distribution to officers on the day shift. In the meantime Barry retained the authority to approve any new taverns added to the list. Sergeant Geraghty adopted essentially the same procedure when he became the vice coordinator in 1970.

Cello and Rifkin followed Mascolino to the stand and corroborated much of what he had said. Although many bars had been involved and considerable amounts of money had changed hands, the story was straightforward and easy to understand. The evidence presented by the tavern owners also supported the testimony of the three officers. By the end of the trial's third week the prosecutors felt that they had accomplished the first part of their plan—to convince the jury of the club's existence and to document its scope during the eleven-year period from 1961 to 1972 with a special emphasis on the Braasch regime. They were now ready to enter the second stage of their presentation.

At 10:30 A.M. on August 27 Webb announced that his first witness would be Lowell Eldon Napier. Although Webb was confident that Napier's testimony would provide the first definite indication that there was much more on trial than a vice club made up of patrolmen, he could not be certain that the judge would allow certain portions of his testimony to be heard by the jury. Defense counsel would surely object to many of his questions.

Napier first joined the Police Department in 1962. Four years later he was assigned to the 18th District. He served there as a vice officer from May 1966 until May 1967, when he was reassigned to another district.

When Napier arrived, Holzman was the commander. Supporting the earlier testimony that there had been no formal club in the district at that time, Napier related that during his first three months in the 18th District he neither received nor distributed any money on a regular basis.

As Mascolino, Cello, and Rifkin had already testified, things changed considerably when Braasch became commander. Napier outlined how the club began and how he and Mascolino had participated in the preparation of the list of taverns which were to be solicited for club membership. Napier then described a conversation with Cello, Rifkin, and Fischer at the beginning of October, a little more than a month after Braasch had become commander.

"I told Sergeant Fischer that I had spoken with Bill Gold and that he had told me that he was giving the monthly gambling package to Commander Braasch. I further asked Sergeant Fischer if Commander Braasch intended to send some of the money downstairs to the vice men and he stated that Commander Braasch was going to keep all of the gambling and he knew of no intention that Commander Braasch had of giving any of it to the vice men."

Napier was the first witness to refer to a gambling package which represented Braasch's private kitty. This clearly hearsay testimony—insofar as Braasch was concerned—was designed not only to preview the Fischer testimony but to provide a context for a conversation between Napier and Braasch which Napier was about to relate.

The defense attorneys objected vigorously to this line of questioning. They were all upset by Napier's reference to Bill Gold. Schippers made an immediate motion for a mistrial and Cotsirilos added that Gold was dead and it was therefore impossible to rebut anything Napier said about him.

This objection was directed, of course, at the very heart of Webb's trial plan. If evidence about the "big club" and gambling payoffs could not be admitted, Webb knew it would be difficult to convince the jury that Braasch had a motive to actively approve of the "little club," from which he did not receive any money. Webb explained to Judge Bauer that the government's theory was that "they [Fischer and Braasch] had a meeting and decided that if they were getting the gambling money, they had to allow the vice men to have something for themselves." Bauer asked Webb to assure him that there would be testimony directly on this point. Webb did so. Bauer also realized that Napier had already mentioned Gold and gambling money. The cat was out of the bag, or as Judge Bauer put it, "The fat is in the fire."

Napier continued his testimony about the October meeting during which Fischer agreed to obtain Braasch's approval for a "little club," which would collect money from taverns, payoff money which, Fischer told Napier and the other officers present, Braasch had no interest in taking for himself. Fischer returned later and said that he had Braasch's approval. The vice club was born.

Napier also confirmed the testimony of the other witnesses about the operations of the "little club," including the preparation of the list and Fischer's statement that Braasch would have the final say on whether a particular tavern would be permitted to join the club. As bars were added and dropped, different lists were prepared. Several meetings with Fischer took place and, at each of them, Fischer repeated that approval had to be given by Braasch because of the existence of payoffs from gambling and syndicate operations.

Napier remained on the vice squad after Fischer was promoted to lieutenant and Barry took over as vice coordinator. For the first month the club continued as usual and Napier handled his normal duties as the night-shift officer in charge of distributing the package. Then Napier suffered a setback which ironically led to an incriminating comment by Braasch, suggesting that he had knowledge of what his vice officers were doing. The incident began with a conversation between Napier and Barry.

Q: (Webb) Would you relate the conversation, indicating what the defendant Barry said and what you said?

A: (Napier) Yes. Sergeant Barry told me that Commander Braasch had seen my car parked on Rush Street with a sign in the window that said, "18th District Vice Officer"—and that he had become very disturbed about it and Commander Braasch wanted me to get the sign out of the window. At that time I stated to Sergeant Barry that the reason for the sign being in the window of my car was that—it was necessary for me to use my car almost every night [and I] was receiving parking tickets at the rate of fifty or sixty dollars a month and I could not afford to pay that many tickets. Sergeant Barry stated at this time if you want to argue about it, maybe you had best talk to the Commander and he switched me over on the phone to the Commander's office.

Q: Would you relate the conversation that took place?

A: Yes, sir. I told him [Braasch] who I was and told him that Sergeant Barry had called me and told me that he had seen my car parked on Rush Street with the sign in the window and I went ahead to explain the reason I did have the sign in the window. . . . At this time, Commander Braasch said, "You are making plenty of money," and slammed down the telephone.

On May 18, 1967, Napier received word that he had been transferred to the 6th District. Napier acknowledged that he had been upset by the transfer and had told Mascolino that "it might be a good idea just to call up a couple of newspapers and put the club out of business altogether." Later, Napier and Mascolino agreed that Barry ought to allow him his $400 share for that month.

Napier identified the bars from which he collected money and amplified on the club's operations by pointing out that Barry had decided to change Fischer's system by taking sole responsibility for the distribution of the monthly envelopes. Napier identified several of the officers on trial as club members whom he had seen receive their monthly allotment.

After Napier completed his direct testimony attention turned to the cross-examination. Several defense attorneys pointed out that Napier would not be sentenced until after the trial and that his cooperation would be taken into account by the sentencing judge. Attempts were made to paint Napier as a mean, selfish officer who had a reputation for harassment of taverns and callous disregard for anyone but himself. At one point he was asked if he had been known as the "18th District Terror." He admitted that he had been given that informal title.

The main burden of attacking Napier's credibility fell on Cotsirilos, whose client had been named for the first time by a government witness as a participant in an incriminating conversation. Cotsirilos knew that Napier's testimony was trivial compared to what Fischer would say, but he also recognized that it was important to conduct an effective cross-examination so that the jury would not be predisposed to accept everything these vice officers were claiming.

In Lowell Napier, Cotsirilos had a challenging target. Napier knew how to handle himself in difficult situations. If there was any officer whom tavern owners actually feared, it was this man.

Cotsirilos first attempted to show that Napier had been thoroughly corrupt for a long time. He succeeded but he also gave Napier the opportunity to further testify that organized corruption was not the exclusive property of the 18th District.

Q: (Cotsirilos) How soon after you went on the police department did you take any money from a tavern owner, or in any improper way. . . .

A: (Napier) About a year after I became a policeman, I was called in by my commanding officer and he stated that I was going to be transferred out of the

First District unless I started taking money and splitting it with my partners because they were refusing to work with me. . . .

Cotsirilos next switched to the main line of his attack.

Q: (Cotsirilos) On direct examination, you talked about a telephone conversation with Lieutenant Barry and then a subsequent conversation with Commander Braasch. Do you recall that, sir?

A: (Napier) Yes.

Q: How soon after that conversation were you transferred out?

A: Maybe two or three weeks.

Q: You did not mean to leave the impression with this Court and this jury that because of that telephone conversation with Commander Braasch, that is the reason you were transferred out?

A: Sir, I do not know the reason I was transferred. I was never told . . .

Q: Have you ever been told that on the 18th day of May . . . that Joe Morang, a newspaper reporter, told Captain Braasch that he had better get rid of you, because you were on the take and shaking down taverns. . . .

A: By nobody, sir.

Q: Have you ever been told by Mascolino or anyone on the police department or elsewhere, that in addition to the fact that Captain Braasch was told that you were on the take by Joe Morang, that Captain Braasch found out that you were seeing a stripper named Sheer Folly?

Mr. Webb: Objection, Your Honor.

The Court: Sustained.

Q: Did you ever have an affair and see this woman privately in a room in her apartment, in a hotel, or any place like that? Yes or no?

Mr. Webb: Objection.

The Court: Mr. Webb, in view of the present condition of the record, I will rmit the question and the answer.

A: Did I ever see er in a private room? Yes.

Napier shifted in his seat, showing discomfort for the first time. Webb could now see the first line of Braasch's defense. Braasch would testify that Napier was upset because he was being transferred out of the district as a result of his illicit activities and now Napier was committing perjury in a perverted attempt to obtain revenge. Although this argument had superficial appeal, Webb already saw its basic flaw, just waiting to be exposed and used against Braasch. However, he would have to wait for Braasch to testify and fall into the trap which his own attorney had set for him.

Cotsirilos continued with his attempt to weaken Napier's claim that he had told Braasch he displayed a sign on his car to avoid tickets and that Braasch had replied with a snide reference to the amount of money he was making. Again, Cotsirilos expertly made his point to the jury.

Q: (Cotsirilos) Mr. Napier, are you aware of a procedure known as a request for a nonsuit of a citation, sir?
A: (Napier) Yes, sir.
Q: What is that?
A: That is a ticket can be nonsuited by that method.
Q: How long were you a police officer?
A: Approximately about ten and a half years.
Q: Would you explain how a ticket is nonsuited by that method?
A: I never saw one nonsuited, sir.
Q: Would you explain how a ticket is nonsuited by that method?
A: I don't know.
Q: Well, isn't it a fact, sir, that when a police officer gets a ticket in conjunction with his official duties, that he can make a request of his commanding officer to have that or to have the commanding officer have that ticket nonsuited; is that correct?
A: He can make that request.
Q: When you got any of those tickets, did you ever go to Commander Braasch and ask him—fill out such a form [request for nonsuit] and ask him to request that the ticket be nonsuited?
A: No, sir.

Although Cotsirilos had hit hard at what he believed were Napier's true motives in testifying, he did not want to conclude his cross-examination without referring to Napier's statements about gambling payoffs. Cotsirilos brought out that Napier had received $1,200 from Bill Gold during the one-month period between the time Holzman left and Braasch arrived. It was the only time Napier had spoken with Gold, and Napier admitted to Cotsirilos that he had no personal knowledge of gambling payoffs while Braasch was commander.

Webb rose to question Napier again. He proceeded immediately to the traffic ticket question. Napier testified that he had twice asked Fischer to nonsuit tickets and on the second occasion was told that Braasch "would not do so in the future." Although this explained why Napier complained to Braasch about later parking tickets, it did not justify completely why Napier had fielded Cotsirilos's questions as if he were totally ignorant of the nonsuit procedure.

Webb simply had to trust that the jury would accept Napier's testimony at face value and chalk off his earlier evasiveness as the result of the natural resistance which any man like Napier would present when challenged by an adversary.

Finally, Webb used Cotsirilos's cross-examination about Gold as an opportunity to have Napier relate to the jury what Gold had said to him during their only meeting a month before Braasch came into the district. Napier said that Gold had told him "he had a gambling package, a package of money for us to lay off of the bookies in the 18th District." Napier did not follow up on this invitation since, after Braasch became commander a month later, he had his own ideas about who should receive the benefits of this lucrative proposal.

The trial was beginning to pick up steam. But there were still many tavern owners who had to testify. Despite the preview of what was to come, Webb was not about to diverge from his plan to intersperse the tavern owners with the accomplice witnesses. It would be ten days before Robert Fischer would take the stand.

On Sunday, September 9, Webb and Fischer were relaxing, drinking coffee in the fifteenth-floor grand jury room where Webb was preparing him for his first appearance the next day. It was early evening and near the end of a long day during which Webb carefully had "walked" Fischer through his entire testimony. Fischer appeared in control of himself, calm and reconciled. In his gut, however, the fear that plagued him since the day he first had met with Davidson nine months ago was bothering him. Testifying about Braasch did not scare him. Rather, he was about to do what few had done before. He would testify about the relationship between organized crime and the police. And he would name names.

Webb looked across his desk at Fischer, who had been sitting quietly since the coffee had been brought in. "How do you feel, Bob?" Webb asked.

"I feel all right."

"I know you're worried about tomorrow. But then it will be over."

"I'll probably never stop worrying."

Although Fischer did not casually talk about his feelings, it was obvious to Webb that he was absolutely terrified. No wonder. He was haunted by the possible consequences of talking openly about organized crime. More than a shattered seventeen-year police career was involved. He knew that he could never again live in Chicago. Fischer had not been able to overcome the feeling that he had been trapped in a labyrinth of poor options. It was as if he was now more in prison than if he had never cooperated and gone to jail.

Although Fischer was scared, Webb believed that Fischer would tell his story, truthfully and well. During the past nine months Webb had come to respect Fischer's intelligence and his sense of honor. The case against Clarence Braasch rested on this one man. As Webb watched Fischer finish his coffee, he knew that there could not be a better man in this case to carry that burden. If anyone on the stand giving evidence against the honored and respected Braasch would be believed, it would be Robert Fischer.

When Fischer took the stand the following morning Webb felt the excitement swell in the courtroom. This was the moment that the spectators, the media, and the jury had been expecting for six weeks. The clerk administered the oath and Fischer sat down in the witness box. He stared directly at Webb.

Q: (Webb) Sir, would you please state your full name and spell your last name for the benefit of the court reporter?

A: (Fischer) Robert W. Fischer, F-i-s-c-h-e-r.

Fischer sat, bent over awkwardly. He was so nervous that he had reached over with his right hand to grab his pants to keep from shaking.

Webb gradually led Fischer into the main portion of his testimony. Fischer concentrated on each question, trying to recall as many details as possible before responding.

First, Fischer testified about the beginning of the vice club. He recalled how he had been approached by Rifkin during the fall of 1966 in the corridor just outside the vice office.

". . . Rifkin said that things had been tough for the bar owners under the previous district commander, who was Holzman, and that some of the vice men had talked to him, Rifkin, about getting something going on a monthly basis. He described this as a system whereby the vice men would go around the different bars in the district and collect money and distribute it among themselves, and Rifkin asked me how I felt the man downstairs would feel about that, referring to Braasch. So I told Rifkin, 'Well, I will find out, Eddie. I will ask him.' And I asked Rifkin, 'What will your obligations be because certainly I will be asked that question?' and Rifkin said, 'Well, we just won't harass the bars and we won't make petty arrests.' He says, 'When you talk to him, tell him that this is going on in other districts too, and it might be nice if we had it going on here.'

Fischer then described how he went to Braasch and related what Rifkin had said.

Q: (Webb) What happened then, sir?

A: (Fischer) Well, Braasch asks me—he says, "Do you know what bars they are going to collect from?" I says, "No, I don't." He says, "Well, don't you think you ought to get a list? Don't you think you ought to find out?" I says, "All right, I will tell them that."

Q: What, if anything, did Braasch say after you first explained this club to him?

A: Well, he said, "I guess it is not a bad idea if these guys want to make a buck for themselves." He said, "We got our own thing going, haven't we?" I says, "Yes." And he says, "Besides, I have had complaints from others and," he says, "specifically a Lieutenant Murphy; that we would get the places lined up for ourselves and nobody else can seem to touch them."

The list was prepared and the vice club was organized. Later Rifkin asked Fischer if Braasch wanted anything from the club. Fischer returned to Braasch and told him what Rifkin had said.

"I told Braasch that I told Rifkin that I would talk to you about it and I suggested that you felt the same way about it for this reason. That if there is ever any complaint on these places and there has to be an arrest made, why, if we weren't taking money from it, why we could tell them to go out and make the arrest. But if were taking money from the thing, we would be in kind of an awkward situation. . . . So I suggested that we don't participate, partake in any money in this and besides we got our own thing going and let's not get hungry."

Braasch agreed. During the next few months the club's operation was refined. Because bars were constantly being added, Braasch insisted that a new list be prepared each month for his approval. Fischer testified how he picked up the lists and submitted them to Braasch. On one occasion a tavern appeared on the list which was a member of the "big club." Braasch became angry with Fischer. Fischer, embarrassed, told Rifkin he had better be careful. "Look," he said to Rifkin, "this is Braasch's apple orchard. If you are going to pick apples, you are going to pick them his way."

When Barry became vice coordinator, Fischer testified, Braasch told him to fill Barry in on the vice club, but not to disclose the details of the "big club" or the gambling payoffs. Fischer described how he met with Barry several times to bring him up to date.

During the next several months Barry gradually assumed control and made sure that the vice officers did not overstep the bounds of their authority in collecting money from taverns. Fischer had completed his testimony about the vice club.

Q: (Webb) Now, Mr. Fischer, earlier in your testimony you referred to a conversation with Napier and Rifkin, in which you told them not to take money or harass what you called ten bars, which you named for them. Was there a slang term used by police officers in the 18th District to refer to those ten bars?

A: (Fischer) Yes, sir.

Q: What was the slang term used to refer to those ten bars?

A: The "big club" or the "big ten."

Q: Would you tell the Court and jury briefly what the "big ten" or "big club" was?

Mr. Cotsirilos: Objection, Your Honor.

The Court: You may answer the question.

A: (Fischer) It referred to ten bars on or about the Rush Street area, for which I was receiving money from a man by the name of Bill Gold.

In the middle of October 1966 Fischer had received a phone call from Bill Gold. After listening to what Gold had to say, he immediately went to Braasch's office.

"I told Braasch that Gold . . . said to me that he had some business that may be of interest to me and my boss, Braasch, and that if I wanted to discuss this business further that I should call him back at five minutes before the hour and let him know. If I didn't, we should discuss it no further. I should simply forget the whole matter. . . . And Braasch thought about it for a few seconds and said, 'Well, make the meeting; be a listener. Don't do any talking, just be a listener.'

Twenty minutes later Fischer called Gold from a telephone booth on the lower level of the nearby Lawson YMCA. A meeting was arranged. The next day Fischer went to Alexander's Restaurant, far away from the 18th District on the southeast side of Chicago. Gold was a short, pudgy man who dressed well and who stood out in a crowd because of what Fischer described as his "peculiar-shaped head." They spoke privately over lunch.

Webb did not ask Fischer to relate his first conversation with Gold since Braasch was not present and had not yet been implicated directly in the "big club" or the gambling payoffs. There would have been objections which probably would have been sustained. Webb had another way of having the conversation admitted, since Fischer had gone back to Braasch and reported carefully what had been said. Fischer related what he had told Braasch. Braasch instructed Fischer to continue with plans to institute a lucrative payoff system.

Another meeting between Fischer and Gold was arranged.

Fischer described this meeting to the jury (Braasch was now implicated) and his description followed closely his previous written statement to the FBI. It is that statement which the jury, in effect, heard Fischer now tell from the stand.

"During the lunch [the first meeting], Gold said that he normally likes to be introduced to someone, but that he could not find anyone who knew me, so he had to work it like this. He then began to ask me questions as to whom I knew in the syndicate. I thought he was trying to find a common associate so that he could trust me, so I lied and said that I knew Ralph Pierce, who I knew was the gambling boss of the South Side of Chicago. This seemed to relax Gold, and he began to talk more freely. He stated that his people would like to get things going again in the 18th District because things had been slow under Holzman. He then asked me if I was acquainted with Braasch's father-in-law, John Trinka.[1] Gold then went on to say that he felt he could talk to my boss, meaning Braasch, through me as he did not think it would be a good idea to meet directly with Braasch. Gold then took a napkin from the table and wrote the figure $3,600 on it. He then asked if my boss would like it. I replied I did not know and would have to ask him. I then asked what the money was for. Gold said it would be paid each month to protect bookmaking in the 18th District. Gold said the money was to make sure that the Chicago Police Department did not hurt them. Gold said that $1,500 would be paid each month separately for ten spots in the 18th District, meaning nightclubs, that belonged to Gold's people. Gold said that it was a buck and a half, meaning $150, for each club each month. . . . Gold and I then moved to the bar where we continued our conversation. Gold explained that the Commander could take either the gambling package or the gambling and the clubs, but not the club package alone. . . . I wanted to get the whole program down from Gold to avoid having to run back and forth between him and Braasch working out details. I then asked him to be more specific as to what they expected. Gold replied that as an example, if a horse book had to go down, meaning being arrested, he wanted a call first. I said that this would not be good as Braasch would probably want a list of the books to be protected. Gold replied he did not want to give a list of the books. I then asked for a list of the ten nightclubs that were to be protected, and he said that I could have a list when he was sure that he had an agreement with Braasch.

1. A politically connected park district official.

"Gold then took something out of his left coat pocket and slipped it into my right coat pocket. When I reached for my pocket, Gold said not to look at it until after he left, and he would leave first. Gold then walked out of the restaurant, and I then walked to the men's washroom and reached into my righthand pocket and found four $100 bills. I then left the restaurant and took the IC train to the Randolph Street terminal and went in to see Commander Braasch at the station.

"The next day I went to the Lawson YMCA and again used the public phones in the basement. . . . I told Gold that the boss said it was O.K. Gold said we should get together and talk about it some more. . . . The following day I . . . went to Alexander's, and at approximately 11:00 A.M. met Bill Gold there. We had lunch in a booth and during the course of the lunch, Bill Gold pulled a piece of crumpled paper from his pocket and read off of it the names of ten nightclubs in the 18th District. . . . Gold said again that he wanted to be called whenever we would raid a gambling spot. I again refused to go along with this, saying the boss didn't like it. I felt that if we were to call Gold, we would in effect be identifying other independent bookmakers that Gold's syndicate bosses would pressure into joining the outfit. Gold insisted that this was the way that it used to be done under Commander Maurovich. Gold said that the packages would be paid as follows: between the first and ninth of every month, and probably closer to the ninth, Gold would call and give me a street address and time. I was to ignore the street name and the number would be a hotel room number at the Dearborn Hotel, located at Dearborn near Maple. I would come to the room the next day at that time and receive the money. Gold then asked if I had told Braasch how much money was involved. I said I had, and Gold laughed and asked how Braasch liked that amount. I said he thought it was fine and Gold then said that we've got to be careful about snoops. Gold told me that when we met, it would be a good idea to take the elevator a few floors past his room floor and walk back down the stairs to see if I was being followed.

"Gold then said that Braasch would have to take care of the captains and lieutenants in the 18th District out of his $3,600. Gold also told me from now on that when I call his number to identify myself as Mr. Walton and leave a message for Mrs. Scott. I then left the meeting with Gold and returned to the 18th District and went in to see Braasch."

Fischer next testified how, after he had returned, he and Braasch had gone to the Germania Inn on the northern end of the 18th District for a quiet lunch. Fischer laid out for Braasch what Gold had proposed. Braasch was agreeable except that he did not want to pay the lieutenants. "What I want to do," Braasch said, "is get together a package of $500 for the captains." Braasch also mentioned Barry. "Edward Barry and I have been friends for a long time and I would like to do something for him. I would like to give him $100 a month, even though he is not working vice." As for the rest of the money, "Let's split it."

Braasch did not realize how unhappy his scheme would make the lieutenants. Fischer testified that, the next month, Gold told him that some of the lieutenants had been by a store called Shirts Unlimited[2] and were complaining. Gold said he would increase the package by $450 to cover the lieutenants. Gold gave Fischer an envelope containing the first monthly payment, totaling $5,550.

Fischer returned to the station and told Braasch what had happened and that he had picked up the money. Braasch instructed Fischer to put his and Barry's share in one envelope and the captains' in another and "then give it to me." In addition, $400 was to be given to Rifkin and Cello, whom Gold knew from the days when Holzman was commander. After the split was made Braasch and Fischer each received $2,200.

Fischer continued to handle the division of the monthly payments and also spoke to the lieutenants about what they would get. (These lieutenants included Kinnally and Murphy, who were charged in the uniformed club indictment.) Fischer had kept a record of how he organized the split of the money and explained to the jury what he did each month. Webb had organized the records for admission into evidence. For the first time, a written record of police corruption was available.

By January 1967 the total package had swelled to $6,660, $5,180 of which was split equally between Braasch and Fischer. Throughout this time Fischer had dealt exclusively with Gold. Then, in February, he met a man named Glitta, who said he would handle that month's distribution because Gold was out of town. Fischer never saw Gold again. He died of a heart attack later that month. Glitta permanently took over his job.

The distribution and collection system, which Fischer had established, continued in its basic form until the first week of February 1969. Even though Fischer had long ago been promoted to lieutenant and assigned to another district, Braasch had asked Fischer to continue his duties. Barry now would get a flat fee of $1,000 a month, leaving $400 a month for Fischer. Fischer

2. Shirts Unlimited was operated by Caesar DiVarco and Joe Arnold, who, newspaper reports had stated, were connected with organized crime on a fairly high level.

asked for $500 and Braasch agreed. During this period of time Fischer picked up the money. It continued to increase, ultimately resulting in a net payment to Braasch of $3,660 a month. Each month Fischer delivered the money to Braasch at his home.

The acuity of Fischer's memory was impressive. Not only did Fischer describe what had occurred each month, but he also identified the locations of all meetings, their approximate dates and times, and what those individuals present were wearing. Throughout his testimony the jurors hardly moved, transfixed by his story.

In late January 1969 the operation ran into a snag. Fischer received a telephone call from Glitta, who said that his bosses wanted to knock the payments down by $500. Fischer told Braasch what Glitta had said. Braasch replied angrily, "I think I will just put the whole thing down. I want to think about it. I'll let you know."

Fischer contacted Glitta and told him Braasch was threatening to cancel the entire arrangement. "Well, that is up to him," Glitta said. "These people are insistent."

Several days later Fischer met Braasch in the bitter cold at the foot of the toboggan slides in the Dan Ryan Woods. Fischer said that since he had not heard from him, he didn't know what to do. Braasch replied, "I am going to put the whole thing down. Just don't bother to see your friend Glitta any more."

The pickup was not made that month. In the middle of February Glitta called Fischer and told him things which made Fischer wonder what was happening. Fischer called Braasch immediately and said he wanted to talk. Fischer again went to Braasch's home.

Q: (Webb) Please relate that conversation, indicating what you said to the defendant Braasch and what Braasch said to you.

A: (Fischer) I told Braasch that I had received a phone call from Glitta and he asked me a question, "What is going on?" I told Braasch, I says, "I don't know the answer." I said, "Maybe you can answer it for me, what is going on?" Glitta had told me that a Sergeant Edward Barry was reaching out, was reaching out to talk to him about the package and Glitta wanted to know, was Barry authorized to talk about this package.

So I asked the question of Braasch. . . . And Braasch said, "Well, those people wanted to knock it down $500," and he says, "Ed Barry volunteered to try to get it boosted back up." He says, "I can't afford to have it knocked down $500. I have got additional expenses." And I thought I knew all of the expenses he had. . . . I asked, "What additional expenses?" And he said, "I guess you have never heard of Linsky."[3]

Q: Do you know a person by the name of Linsky?
A: Well, I did, sir.
Q: Who was Linsky?
A: He was Deputy Chief of Patrol for Area 6.

Fischer then described how he left Braasch's home and contacted Barry and arranged to meet him at a restaurant in the Old Town section of the 18th District. Webb asked Fischer to relate what was said.

Fischer leaned forward and said, raising his voice slightly:

"I asked Ed, what made him reach out on his own to find out about the package. I said, 'You know that I have been handling it for over two years, and I thought that that was my job, so to speak,' and I was just curious as to what made him do this thing on his own in light of Braasch's conversation that Ed Barry had, had volunteered to do this, and Ed said to me, he says, 'I didn't volunteer to do it.' He says, 'Braasch instructed me to do it.' "

To the jury, this conversation may not have seemed peculiar, but Webb knew that for Fischer it represented the moment of betrayal. Even now, Fischer still felt the sting of what he had learned that day. Braasch had lied to him and had used these lies to abandon a relationship that Fischer thought had been growing stronger through the years. It marked the end of the friendship between Braasch and Fischer and planted the seeds of Braasch's downfall.

During the twenty-seven months in which Fischer operated the "big club" and the gambling package he had collected $165,000. Eighty-five thousand dollars had ended up in Braasch's pockets. Fischer had received $25,000.

It was time for cross-examination. Tired, but still poised, Fischer looked away from Webb to see who would confront him first. David Schippers, Barry's attorney, stood up and walked to the rostrum, carrying a handful of yellow sheets of paper on which he had scribbled his notes. He looked thoughtfully at them for a few moments and then began his cross-examination. It was surprisingly short. He concentrated on trying to establish that Barry had not been involved in the "big club," and that Fischer had knowingly consorted with organized crime figures. He also questioned Fischer about his grant of immunity and the promises made to him by the government. It was an unim-

3. See Chapter 6.

pressive cross-examination, not because Schippers was incapable of grilling Fischer but simply because his approach was obviously a part of the overall defense plan which would leave to Cotsirilos the main task of impeaching Fischer.

Cotsirilos started his cross-examination by trying to establish that Fischer was a thoroughly corrupt individual who did not need the alleged involvement of a respected commanding officer to take bribes.

Q: (Cotsirilos) In connection with your duties at Area 2 Auto Theft [his assignment after being promoted to lieutenant in March 1967], did you collect on a weekly basis from a man named Ostrowsky $200 a week as protection money?
A: (Fischer) Yes.
Q: When did you start collecting that money, sir?
A: It was—as I recall, it was some time in the middle of 1970—
Q: For how long a period did you collect $200 a week then from Ostrowsky?
A: Until December of 1971.
Q: A fair estimate would be something like 20 months?
A: Well, O.K., 20 months.
Q: At about $800 a month?
A: Yes, sir.
Q: Sixteen thousand dollars.
A: If that is what it comes out to. Yes, sir.[4]

Cotsirilos reminded the jury that Fischer had been making nearly $20,000 a year in salary, that his wife was an executive secretary, that they had no children, and that he had admittedly collected $25,000 for himself while working for Braasch. In all, Cotsirilos pointed out, Fischer had received more than $40,000 in bribes.

Cotsirilos then reviewed with Fischer each visit he had claimed to have made to Braasch's home, apparently in an attempt to set him up for later testimony by Braasch that Fischer had been lying about going to his home so frequently. While much of this cross-examination might have seemed meaningless to someone who was not familiar with defense tactics, Webb recognized its importance. He listened carefully, took notes, and thought about how he would handle Braasch when he testified.

Cotsirilos devoted considerable time to Fischer's alleged conversations with

4. Fischer later modified this testimony, reducing the amount collected but did admit that he collected other money from different sources.

Gold and his subsequent talks with Braasch. He questioned Fischer about each of the ten members of the "big club," carefully highlighting the fact that none of the owners had testified at the trial. Then he came to the initial meeting which Fischer had with Davidson the previous December.

Q: (Cotsirilos) Didn't Mr. Davidson at that time tell you that they had enough on you to put you in jail?

A: (Fischer) No, sir, he didn't say that.

Q: Did he say anything to that effect?

A: No, sir.

Q: Did Mr. Davidson tell you that he wanted you to tell him all about the 18th District?

A: Yes, sir, he did say that.

Q: Did you say that you have nothing to say about the 18th District or that you couldn't say anything in regards to corruption?

A: Words to that effect, yes, sir.

Q: Did they tell you that they wanted you to talk about Braasch?

A: No, sir.

Q: Did they tell you if you didn't that they would put you in jail?

A: No, sir.

Q: During the entire forty-five minutes you denied any knowledge of any corruption in the 18th District, isn't that right?

A: Yes, sir.

Q: When you left, sir, you rode back with Mitchell Ware in his car?

A: Yes, sir.

Q: Did Mitchell Ware ask you again to tell him if there was corruption in the 18th District?

A: Not quite that way, sir. Not if.

Q: Did he ask you to tell him anything about Braasch?

A: What Mitchell said to me—

Q: Just answer my question. Did he ask you to tell him about Clarence Braasch, yes or no?

A: He did not speak those words, no.

Q: Did you say to him, in effect, "If I were to say anything about Braasch in regard to corruption, it would be a bunch of lies"?

A: No, sir, I never said that.

Q: Did you ever use the words that it would be lies if you were to implicate Braasch?

A: No, sir.

Cotsirilos was nearing the end of his cross-examination and returned to his main theme—that Fischer was a thoroughly depraved man.

A: (Cotsirilos) Do you know a man named Marcus Cohen?

A: (Fischer) Yes.

Q: What is Marcus Cohen's business?

A: He runs a junk yard.

Q: Did you ever have any contact with Marcus Cohen when you were at Area 2 Auto Theft?

A: Yes, sir.

Q: Did Marcus Cohen ever try to give you any money?

A: He sure did.

Q: Did you take that money and turn him in?

A: I inventoried the money and returned it to him.

Q: Did you report him to your superiors?

A: Yes, sir.

Q: And after you reported these facts, did you proceed to take a periodic payment from Marcus Cohen?

A: Did I?

Q: Yes.

A: Take a payment?

Q: Yes.

A: Not personally, no, sir.

Q: Did anybody take a payment from Marcus Cohen for you and turn it over to you?

A: Partially, yes.

Q: So that you reported a man—he was a businessman, wasn't he?

A: Yes.

Q: You reported a businessman as trying to corrupt you and then you took his money through someone else, is that right?

A: That is one way to state it.

A minute later, Cotsirilos, his voice shaking with emotion, wound up his questioning.

Q: (Cotsirilos) Was anybody there in the office of Commander Braasch when you went to his office and discussed the matters that you have testified to from this witness stand?

A: (Fischer) No, sir.

Q: Was anyone within earshot of Commander Braasch and you when you arrived in his home and you delivered what you said you delivered?

A: Not to my knowledge.

Q: As a matter of fact, everything that you have done in regard to Commander Braasch is a matter that is completely private between you and him, according to your testimony, is that right?

A: Yes, sir.

Q: And these nine documents that you say were made up at the time that the occurrences took place, you did not think about or come upon them until four months after you started talking to the Government?

A: True.

Fischer had not lost his composure once. Although Cotsirilos had not been able to trip him up on any important points, he had been able to stress the defense's main contention that Fischer had lied to save himself and to avoid what otherwise would have been certain imprisonment.

Webb had known that it was inevitable that Fischer would be attacked for his own corruption, but Braasch could not base his defense solely on the cross-examination of Fischer. Braasch would have to take the stand and tell a convincing story before the jury would disbelieve Fischer.

Fischer had been on the stand for the better part of four days. The major part of the government's case had been presented. Although there would be other witnesses, they would add nothing new to the case. It was only natural that the jury and the spectators would become increasingly restless as the days passed, waiting in anticipation for the defense.

This is how Webb had wanted it. A slow winding down after Fischer's testimony would impress the jury with the government's thoroughness and provide the best chance for the prosecution to argue that it had tried to put before the jury all of the important evidence.

The prosecution's case finally ended. During the seven weeks of testimony more than fifty tavern owners had testified and seven former officers had given evidence against their colleagues and friends. Yet it could be fairly said that the whole story had not yet been heard.

A Defense of Reputation

On September 24 Clarence Braasch took the stand. He seemed almost oblivious to what was at stake. He looked at the jury as if he were about to deliver a prepared lecture. As he listened to his attorney's questions, he hardly moved except to occasionally finger the rim of his glasses. In this gesture, however, there was no trace of nervousness.

Braasch began his testimony by describing his early life and his entrance into the Chicago Police Department. Born in Chicago on November 9, 1926, he attended elementary and high school there, graduating from the latter in 1944. He joined the army in 1946 and served two years. After his discharge he held a succession of jobs which gave no hint of the career to follow. Briefly, he worked for his father (he did not describe the nature of the business) and later as an installer of dial equipment for Western Electric. In 1952 he joined the Chicago Police Department.

Throughout the years he had diligently pursued his education, completing his undergraduate work at Northwestern University and receiving a Master's degree in public administration from the Illinois Institute of Technology in 1963. During this time he also supported a growing family which eventually consisted of his wife, three daughters, and a son. In addition, his mother- and father-in-law had lived in his home for almost twenty-five years.

Braasch confined himself to a recitation of the facts and offered no insights into the reasons for his decision to become a police officer, his personal ambitions, or his philosophy of life. With everything at stake, he chose to keep this information to himself, a closed book which he would not open.

During his early years on the force Braasch concentrated on traffic work and spent most of his time in accident investigation. In 1959 he was assigned to the Detective Division. A year later, eight years after he had joined the force, he was promoted to sergeant. At this time nothing extraordinary had occurred which would foreshadow his imminent rapid rise through the ranks.

Less than a year after his first promotion he received another one, this time to lieutenant of police. In one more year he was promoted to captain. In June 1963, after completing a course at the Northwestern Traffic Institute, he became a detective commander and was placed in charge of the auto theft section of the Detective Division. He was now one of the youngest police officers in the history of the department to hold the title of commander,[5] a position he had attained in only three years after his first promotion.

From 1963 to 1966 Braasch headed the auto theft section. It was a good time for the department. Wilson was superintendent and the department had been upgraded in both facilities and manpower. The department's national reputation also rose. However, a sore spot remained: the 18th District, where vice

5. There were persistent rumors that Braasch was helped by his father-in-law, John Trinka, who was head of the Chicago park district and politically well connected. Trinka was a familiar name to Webb. He remembered that he was mentioned by the anonymous telephone caller who had spoken with Davidson in July 1972 (see Chapter 6). In April 1976 Trinka pled guilty to charges of extracting payoffs from individuals desiring advantageous boat slips in Lake Michigan.

and organized crime operated openly and beyond control. Maurovich had not lived up to Wilson's expectations and now Holzman wanted out of the department. Wilson needed someone to take over and bolster police effectiveness in that area. He turned to Braasch, one of his rising young stars (Thanasouras was another one and was about to become commander of the Austin District), a natural leader, educated, austere, and strong-willed.

Braasch described police operations in the 18th District in great detail. He explained that the district force comprised more than five hundred officers, including three watch commanders holding the rank of captain, three tactical units of ten men each, a neighborhood relations unit, and a vice squad. In his account Braasch concentrated on emphasizing the heavy responsibility of a commander, thereby lending support to one of his defenses, that the job was so large that no matter how conscientious, he could not be expected to know everything that was happening.

Braasch also described the vice squad and its areas of authority. He emphasized that more than five hundred businesses in the district had liquor licenses and that all had to be controlled and investigated by only a small group of vice officers with the assistance of the uniformed patrol. Because it was a sensitive job, he had selected Robert Fischer as his vice coordinator, a man with whom he had worked in the auto theft unit and who had done a "good and faithful job."

Braasch spoke with authority and gave everything he said the kind of credibility that can come only from someone who is used to giving orders.

As Braasch described his grand jury appearance, Cotsirilos used this opportunity to enable Braasch to reaffirm his innocence. Cotsirilos read portions of this testimony, pausing after each section to ask Braasch if he still stood by it. Braasch's responses were short and confident.

Cotsirilos then led Braasch through a point-by-point denial of Fischer's testimony, including a rejection of Fischer's claim that he had been at Braasch's home at least twenty times. Braasch testified it was only six or seven, and he described some of the visits, as if trying to demonstrate that his memory was better than Fischer's.

During lunch Webb began to think about his cross-examination. Early in the trial he had noticed that Cotsirilos, during his cross-examination of the tavern owners, had spent inordinate time asking questions about the number of times the taverns had been raided. In questioning the police officers Cotsirilos had asked about the report review procedure whereby Braasch was required to make a written recommendation each time a licensed establishment was investigated or involved in a crime. From these earlier questions Webb thought he now knew what Braasch would use to support his denials that he knew anything about the corruption in the district.

Webb set about carefully laying his trap. However, he could not spring it unless Braasch walked into it. If it was going to happen, it would come before the day was over.

When court reconvened Braasch testified about the Napier incident. He related how his father-in-law, John Trinka, had received a call from Joe Morang, a *Tribune* reporter, who had talked about Napier. When Braasch heard about it, he contacted Barry, who told him that he had heard Napier was "shacking up with a stripper from the Club 19 and that for a period of three or four days, some weeks earlier, [he] had been absent from home and had used as an excuse the fact that he was working on a case." The alleged affair with Sheer Folly was also mentioned. On the basis of this conversation with Barry, Braasch stated, he ordered Napier's transfer. Braasch also denied ever having any conversations with Napier about the parking tickets or that he had told Napier, "You are making plenty of money."

Cotsirilos next walked over to his table and picked up a thick batch of papers, which were marked Defendants' Exhibit No. 38. Braasch looked at the documents and described them as reports he had prepared in connection with incidents or arrests on a licensed premises. He explained: "The report was to indicate if there was involvement by management or agent of management in the incident of the arrest and, if so, a recommendation for action; if not, a recommendation for no action against the licensee." There were thirty-four reports, covering the period between September 1966 and May 1970. Each contained a recommendation for action against the licensee. Cotsirilos raised his voice for the next question: "In each of those thirty-four instances, is the liquor licensee one of those listed in the indictment in which you were charged, sir?"

Braasch, as always, looked at the jurors. "I believe so, sir. Yes, sir."

Cotsirilos next handed Defendants' Exhibit 39 to Braasch, and he identified the documents as vice summary reports. One was included for each period (four weeks) beginning with the first period of 1967 and ending with the fourth period of 1970, except for one period in 1968, which Braasch explained was missing and could not be located. Cotsirilos asked Braasch to state, by category, what they reflected.

"Raids by vice units: gambling, 1967, 110 raids. 1968, with that one period missing, 112 raids. 1969, 131 raids and the four periods of 1970 [the portion of the year he was commander before his promotion], 32 raids."

Braasch then computed the total number of raids involving violations of the liquor laws at 166. The vice squad's grand total of raids during this period was 2,674.

Braasch stated that during his command of the district there had also been a significant increase in prostitution raids, an increase in the number of narcotics raids, a slight increase in gambling raids, "and the liquor law raids ran roughly the same across the board."

The implicit question raised by this testimony was this: If Braasch was involved in protecting taverns, why had he recommended action against thirty-four taverns belonging to the vice club? If he was involved in protecting gambling, why had the number of gambling raids increased under his command? The answer Braasch hoped to hear from the jury was that all of this took place because he was a conscientious commander and innocent of the charges in the indictment.

Braasch described his many honors—the Mayor's Youth Award, the Greater North Michigan Avenue Association Award for outstanding police service, an award for public relations work, and an award from the National Civil Service League for his contribution to a public safety program that led to a reduction of traffic fatalities for two consecutive years.

Whatever effect it had on the jury, the testimony about the awards had no effect on Webb. He was concentrating totally on the preparation of his cross-examination. Braasch had done what he had hoped. He had fallen into a trap of his own making. Webb was determined he would not escape.

Cotsirilos was finished. Webb stood up. The courtroom was silent.

The first order of business was the transfer of Lowell Napier. Braasch again related the conversation with Trinka, in which Trinka informed him of what Morang had said about Napier. Braasch then admitted that he had also talked later to Morang about Napier.

Q: (Webb) Did you ask Joe Morang where he had been when he learned or had found out that Lowell Napier had engaged in misconduct? Did you ask him that question?

A: (Braasch) No, I did not.

Q: Did you ask Joe Morang if the misconduct which he was referring to was misconduct on the part of Napier that he, himself, had personally observed? Did you ask him that question?

A: No, sir, I did not.

Q: When you received the information from Joe Morang about the misconduct of Lowell Napier did you initiate your own investigation to determine what that misconduct may have been?

A: Yes, sir.

Q: And you initiated that investigation because you were required to do so under general order No. 6316 of the Chicago Police Department, is that correct?

A: 6316, I am not quite sure if it was in effect during that period of time. It might have been 6721.

Q: In any event, the general orders were, in substance, the same in connection with the obligation on the district commander to conduct his own investigation at the time he learned of misconduct by one of his police officers?

A: At the time he learned of alleged or suspected misconduct. Yes, sir. I made that investigation and I did not consider that this fell within the purview of that order.

Q: Would you tell the Court and the jury why that information about Napier's misconduct did not fall under that general order?

A: It lacked any specifics, any substance.

Q: Sir, is it not a fact that under that regulation you are required to report that to IAD within an hour, regardless of whether you believe it to be founded or unfounded? Is that not a fact?

A: No, sir, there are exceptions to the rule.

Q: Would you please examine Article 7, which sets forth certain exceptions and see if you can find any exceptions which would have alleviated you from your responsibility to report this type of misconduct to the IAD?

A: There is no exception in Article 7.

Q: Now upon finding out that Lowell Napier was involved with Sheer Folly, you yourself did not discipline Napier while he was in the 18th District, is that correct?

A: No, sir.

Q: You found that Joe Morang's information was of no substance, was that correct?

A: It lacked substance and specificity.

Q: When Edward Barry told you that Lowell Napier was involved with Sheer Folly, did you conduct your own independent investigation to see if that information had any substance?

A: No, sir, I did not.

Q: That also is the type of misconduct which should have been reported to IAD under General Order 6713; is that correct?

A: No, sir. An off-duty incident, we generally don't pry into a man's affairs, his love life, unless it interferes with his duty.

Q: But it caused you to transfer him from the district?

A: Yes, it did.

Until this point Braasch had conducted himself exactly as he had on direct examination. He looked at Webb during the question and then turned to give his answer to the jury. His testimony on the Napier incident sounded a little off key, but nothing in Braasch's manner indicated that he was worried.

Q: (Webb) Sir, did you feel that Lowell Napier was, in fact, one of the best vice officers you had in the 18th District? Is that true or is that false?

A: (Braasch) I wouldn't think so, no, sir.

Q: Sir, do you know what a rating report is?

A: I certainly do.

Braasch had looked at Webb during this answer. A crack in the armor, perhaps.

Q: If a police officer is rated between 76 and 85, that means that he—that is a good rating as to the characteristics he is being rated for, provided on the face of the form; is that correct?

A: I believe so, yes.

Q: A rating of 86 to 89 on any given characteristic or trait would be an excellent rating; is that provided on the face of the form?

A: I believe so.

Q: If a police officer is outstanding, he will be rated somewhere between 90 and 100; is that on the face of the form, to the best of your recollection?

A: I believe so, sir . . .

Q: Sir, is it not a fact that while Lowell Napier worked under you, that you approved an overall rating of Napier as a police officer of 90?

A: You have the card there and I would just assume that is so.

Q: To the best of your recollection, is that how Lowell Napier was rated when he worked under you?

A: I can't recall how he was rated.

Webb showed Braasch the rating card. Braasch looked at it for a few seconds and then admitted that indeed 90 was Napier's rating. Braasch now avoided Webb's eyes.

Q: (Webb) Did you contact Mr. Napier's next commanding officer to inform him of the misconduct that Napier was prone to engage in?

A: (Braasch) No, sir, I did not.

Q: Were you taught during your training as a Chicago police officer that
when you find out that one of your police officers is engaging in misconduct
that you just transfer him rather than report it or try to do anything about it?
Were you taught that during your police training?

A: No, sir, I was not taught that.

Q: Sir, isn't it a fact that about a week before you fired Lowell Napier, you
had a conversation with him over the telephone in which you lost your temper
and told him he was making money on the street? Did that conversation take
place?

A: I have already denied that, sir.

Webb thought he detected a sign of belligerence.

Q: I am asking you if it took place.

A: I deny it again.

Q: And I am asking you now if the reason why you transferred Lowell
Napier was not because he was shacking up with a stripper by the name of
Sheer Folly, but because you had lost your temper with a patrolman and that
was not something that you cared to do?

Mr. Cotsirilos: Objection, your Honor, to the argument.

The Court: Sustained.

It did not matter to Webb that the court had sustained an objection to his
obviously rhetorical question. He had finished with the Napier incident. As he
went back to his table to organize his notes for the next series of questions,
he noticed out of the corner of his eye that Braasch was sitting more rigidly,
not looking at his lawyer or the jury, but into space.

Webb now turned to the subject of Robert Fischer.

Q: (Webb) And after Fischer became your vice coordinator in the 18th
District, is it accurate to say that you continued to impose a great deal of trust
in him because of the outstanding judgment you felt he possessed?

A: (Braasch) Yes, sir.

Q: During that period of time that he was your vice coordinator, in rating
him on his performance as a police officer, you gave him one of the highest
ratings that can be given to a subordinate, is that correct?

A: Yes, sir.

Q: Did you not make the following statements about Robert Fischer while
he was your vice coordinator in the 18th District: that "he possessed outstanding judgment and was very industrious; he set a very high standard for himself

and others; he required almost no supervision and that he always accepted and carried out responsibility with very little supervision and his ability to handle face to face relationships was superb." Did you make comments similar to those about Robert Fischer while he was your vice coordinator in the 18th District?

A: I most certainly did.

Q: Did you also say that he never avoided unpleasant tasks?

A: I did.

Q: Was one of those responsibilities and unpleasant tasks collecting money from Bill Gold and Dan Glitta?

Mr. Cotsirilos: Objection.

The Court: Sustained.

The day was drawing to a close and Webb did not want to have the most important part of his cross-examination interrupted. Consequently, he spent the remaining minutes questioning Braasch about the number of times Fischer had been at his home. Braasch was now tired and irritable, but he stuck to his position that Fischer had visited his home only occasionally.

The next morning Webb took Braasch through the sequence of events which he had sworn to the grand jury was the only time when he had ever heard reports that there was a "club" in the 18th District. Braasch testified that he recalled seeing a Wiedrich column in 1969 which mentioned that a "club" existed in a near north side district (it was not specified, but the 18th District was the most likely one considering the context of the article) and that he had sent Barry to inquire where Wiedrich had gotten the information. Barry, according to Braasch, reported that Wiedrich would not reveal his source. Braasch testified that he also had met with a representative of a community association who was a tavern owner, but that this person said he knew nothing about payoffs. Braasch admitted that this was the entire extent of his inquiry.

Webb tried next to get Braasch to concede that even after Fischer had left the 18th District they had maintained a close relationship. Braasch denied it although Webb repeatedly cited specific instances which indicated that Fischer had indeed maintained close contact with Braasch (as he would have had to do in order to make the monthly deliveries).

Q: (Webb) In the summer of 1968, in confidence you told Robert Fischer something you had never related to anybody else about the fact that you had been offered the job of superintendent of police in Detroit, Michigan.

A: (Braasch) I think a number of people were aware of that.

Webb was determined to get a specific answer. Braasch was becoming increasingly evasive.

Q: (Webb) My question is: Did you tell Robert Fischer that?
A: (Braasch) I don't recall.

Braasch would not look at Webb.

Q: (Webb) Well, then, do you recall telling Robert Fischer that you had been interviewed for a job as superintendent of police in a hotel in Chicago?
Braasch seemed surprised.

A: (Braasch) No, sir. I don't recall telling him that.
Q: (Webb) Sir, were you interviewed for the job as superintendent of police in Detroit in a hotel here in Chicago?
A: Yes I was.

Webb looked at Braasch. He no longer had the same sense of assuredness. It was time. Only Webb knew for what. Without any warning he changed the subject.

Q: (Webb) Were you familiar with an organization called the Vice Control Division?
A: (Braasch) Yes, sir.
Q: And the Vice Control Division has the authority to operate all over this city and in all police districts, is that correct?
A: That's correct, sir.
Q: Now, you, as the district commander of the 18th District, had no supervisory control over those police officers that were assigned to the Vice Control Division downtown at 11th and State, is that correct?
A: That's correct, sir.
Q: However, those Vice Control Division police officers did have the authority to come into the 18th District, did they not?
A: Yes, they did.

Webb picked up Defendants' Exhibit 39 and approached Braasch.

Q: (Webb) Tell the Court and jury how many arrests for liquor law violations were made by your 18th District vice squad during the period of time that you were the district commander.
A: (Braasch) I would have to have time to total up the number.

Q: I am sorry, sir, doesn't it reflect, the one figure you have on there is 166, isn't that the total figure?

A: Well, that is the number of raids.

Q: Now these—the letters which I believe are Defendants' Exhibit 38, which are also in evidence, for purposes of asking you questions, sir, would it be fair to call these Commander comment letters?

A: All right, sir.

Q: Any time there is an arrest in the 18th District by any police officer on an establishment which holds a City of Chicago liquor license in the 18th District, you, as the District Commander, were required under that order [General Order 6570] of the Police Department to prepare a Commander comment letter?

A: Yes, sir.

Q: That was true whether or not the arrest on the liquor establishment was by a vice officer of the 18th District, by a member of the Vice Control Division downtown or by a uniformed police officer in the 18th District, is that correct?

A: Yes, sir.

Q: Under the general order, those comment letters would be sent downtown, first to the Vice Control Division to their analytical section so that they could be reviewed, is that correct?

A: They went to the Vice Control Division.

Q: It was not your decision to make, as to whether or not any licensee in the 18th District should or should not lose his liquor license?

A: That is right, sir.

Q: You are aware, are you not, that after your Commander comment letter goes to the Vice Control Division, if they want to, they can forward that to the Chicago Liquor Commission. Are you aware of that?

A: Yes, sir.

Q: However, the Vice Control Division does not have to do that and they can more or less file your letter right there at the Vice Control Division, without sending the letter on to the Chicago Liquor Commission?

A: Yes, sir.

Q: Mr. Braasch, either yourself or . . . your attorney . . . [you did subpoena, did you not] the Commander comment letters that had been prepared on the 53 bars named in Count 1 of this indictment . . . during the period of time that you were district commander, from August 1, 1966 until May 30, 1972?

A: Yes, sir.

Q: Is it not true that what you did prior to testifying was to review all of the Commander comment letters that you received from the police department pursuant to the subpoena, and cull out and separate those Commander comment letters in which you recommended action be taken against the licensee?

A: Yes, sir.

Q: While you were the district Commander of the 18th District . . . you almost always recommended action be taken against the premises when the arrest was for prostitution; is that correct?

A: If there was involvement of the licensee. That was the determining factor.

Q: In reviewing the Commander comment letters that you received from the police department, in which you recommended no action, did you notice that there was only one letter which recommended no action where there was an arrest for prostitution?

A: No, I did not notice that . . .

Webb now asked Braasch to examine the thirty-four letters recommending action against taverns belonging to the vice club.

Q: (Webb) Would you count those up and tell the Court and the jury out of the total thirty-four letters written during your four-year period recommending action, how many of them were for prostitution?

A: (Braasch) I believe I counted thirteen . . .

Q: Prostitution constitutes sixty percent of your work?

A: Yes, sir.

Q: Is it fair to say that all of the arrests made by your vice officers during the period of time that you were the district Commander, approximately sixty percent of those arrests were for prostitution?

A: Yes.

Q: Sir, would you look at those thirteen letters and tell the Court and the jury how many of those arrests that resulted in your writing a letter were made by your 18th District Vice Squad in those fifty-three bars [the taverns named in the indictment]?

A: There were none, sir.

Q: Your 18th District Vice Squad never made one prostitution arrest in four years in any of those fifty-three bars that resulted in a letter from you recommending action?

A: That appears to be the case, yes, sir.

Q: Every one of those thirteen arrests during those four years was made by the Vice Control Division from 11th and State downtown; isn't that a fact?

Mr. Cotsirilos: Objection, your Honor.

The Court: He may answer the question.

A: Yes, sir.

Braasch now sounded irritated and annoyed. He refused to look at Webb or the jury.

During the next few minutes Webb forced Braasch to admit that only two of the thirty-four letters reflected arrests made by the 18th District vice squad and both had occurred before April 1967. For the last three and one-half years of his command Braasch's vice squad had not made a single arrest in any of the bars belonging to the vice club.

Webb returned to his table and picked up government Exhibit 118. He handed the materials to Braasch and asked him to review them during the noon recess. Braasch looked at the documents. They were Commander comment letters concerning the fifty-three bars which were club members during the period of his command. Then Judge Bauer interrupted and announced that it was time for the noon recess.

After lunch the courtroom was abuzz while Webb and the other participants waited for Judge Bauer to enter the courtroom. Webb's cross-examination had apparently perked up the spectators.

When Braasch returned to the stand Webb started immediately on Exhibit 118.

Q: (Webb) Now, is it correct that in every one of those Commander comment letters on the fifty-three bars in the indictment . . . you recommended no action because of insufficient involvement of the licensee?

A: (Braasch) Except for one . . . one doesn't directly affect—it wasn't an incident that occurred on a licensed premises. . . .

Q: Now, how many arrests took place in those bars that you recommended no action be taken? . . .

A: There are a total of forty-two; forty-one of them relate to incidents that occurred on a licensed premises.

Q: And you recommended no action on these forty-one?

A: Yes.

Webb could feel his heart pounding, but his voice was clear as he asked the climactic question.

Q: (Webb) Those forty-one incidents or arrests that took place in those bars, how many of those arrests were made by your 18th District Vice Squad?

Braasch was as calm as ever, but his eyes were glassy and his gaze was directed at an empty part of the courtroom.

A: (Braasch) None, sir.

Although the cross-examination was truly over, Webb knew that one more question could not hurt and might help the jury further understand the depth of Braasch's deception during direct examination.

Q: (Webb) Sir, did you ever make any inquiry or any investigation while you were the district commander to see what was the reason why from March of 1967 until May of 1970 there was never any 18th District Vice Squad arrest in any of those fifty-three bars?

Braasch was beyond explaining or evading.

A: (Braasch) No, sir.

With that, Webb looked at Judge Bauer and said, "I have no further questions, Judge."

Cotsirilos spent only a few minutes with Braasch on redirect. Braasch pointed out again that he had recommended action against the vice club bars in thirty-four cases, but only two of the arrests had been made by his vice squad. The others had been made by the Vice Control Division for relatively serious offenses which would have made it difficult for him to recommend no action without causing suspicion. In any event, his recommendation did not mean that a bar owner would lose his license.

Cotsirilos also asked Braasch about the Wiedrich column and Braasch replied that Barry had told him that Wiedrich had said the column talked only about a west side district.

Finally, Braasch said that he had not actually received an offer to be Superintendent of Police in Detroit, but had only been interviewed for the job and, furthermore, it was a not a secret.

Braasch stepped off the stand and walked to his chair. His testimony was complete, but the trial was not over. For six weeks he had waited to testify. Now he would wait for a verdict.

The End of an Era

Seven other defendants testified. All were minor participants in the vice club. They asserted their innocence and denied any involvement in corruption. The prosecution spent hardly any time on cross-examination. Either the jury believed they received their monthly shares or it did not.

For such a long trial, rebuttal testimony by both sides was brief. The highlight occurred when Joe Morang took the stand and testified that Braasch never asked him what Napier had done. Fischer also took the stand again to testify that Braasch knew about Sheer Folly four months before Napier's transfer.

On this almost anticlimactic note the evidentiary portion of the trial ended. It was Wednesday, September 26. Because of the Jewish New Year, Judge Bauer told the jurors that they would not have to return until the following Monday to hear closing arguments and the instructions. Court was adjourned.

Webb had four days to plan his closing argument. Although Braasch was the main defendant, it was important that the jury be convinced of the guilt of all defendants. Webb had to prepare a summation that would review the evidence against each of the defendants individually. He knew that it would be the longest closing argument he had ever given.

On Monday, October 1, Webb rose to deliver the prosecution's summation. He was hopeful that the jury would convict Braasch, but he also knew that he had to be a convincing and influential guide. He could not afford to lead the jurors down the wrong path through any error of judgment.

"I don't think there is any question that the evidence that has been presented during the course of this trial has established a rather shocking and deplorable scheme of police corruption in the 18th Chicago Police District. I think the evidence has established that each and every one of the defendants on trial engaged in that conduct. . . . The witnesses that took the stand during the course of this trial—the police officers themselves, who were involved in the corruption, and the fifty-some bar owners—one factor that was similar to all is that none of them wanted to testify. However, because of court orders entered granting them immunity from prosecution, they were ordered into the courtroom and gave testimony in this case."

Webb had prepared a chart to help the jury understand the evidence. The chart outlined the positions of the defendants in the conspiracy and the functions performed at each level of the conspiracy. At the top were Braasch and the vice coordinators, Fischer, Barry, and Geraghty. The second level contained those responsible for collection, and the third level was occupied by the defendants who received money. Fischer had testified about the supervisory level; Cello, Rifkin, Mascolino, and Napier about the collection level; and DuShane about the receiving level.

Before Webb began his detailed discussion of the evidence, he first explained the prosecution's legal theory of the case, that extortion did not require overt threats but rather, when committed by a public official, all that was needed was the use of the power of the badge. Webb also knew that the theory of a conspiracy was often difficult for a jury to understand, particularly the principle that evidence against one co-conspirator was evidence against another once the existence of the conspiracy was established. Webb spent the next twenty minutes carefully relating how that conspiracy theory applied in this case.

Then Webb embarked on the arduous task of reviewing the evidence. The jury paid close attention, hearing now for the first time all of the evidence of the past eight weeks compressed into a cohesive and shattering narrative. An hour passed. Then another. Throughout his long discourse, Webb repeatedly returned to Braasch, showing the jury how he had lied and the reasons for his lies. He discussed Napier's testimony, Braasch's claim that he knew only what he read in the newspapers, and his denial of a close relationship with Fischer.

In this way Webb methodically destroyed Clarence Braasch's defense. The evidence and Braasch's testimony allowed Webb to expose the lies through logic and common sense, a method which also supported the conclusion that Fischer told the truth.

By the end of the day Webb had completed reviewing the evidence against all of the defendants. Again he returned to Braasch, now comparing his demeanor to Fischer's, who, despite two days of cross-examination, had never become ruffled or evasive. Braasch, when testifying on direct examination had been "very cool, very calm, always looking at [the jury] to see if he could get some type of reading." However, on cross-examination, he had grown tense. "He lost his coolness. He was very surly on occasions." He had not looked at Webb. "Do you want to know the reason?" Webb asked and moved closer to the jury box.

"When you are on the stand and you manufacture a story . . . you have got to stay two or three steps ahead of the person cross-examining you. It took all of his concentration. He couldn't even look at me. He was trying to figure out where I was going and what I was going to do. . . . When Clarence Braasch got off of the witness stand, his testimony was not in the same condition as it had been before cross-examination. So when you go back to the jury room, when these defense attorneys tell you that the Government witnesses were not telling the truth, reflect back on the way they acted on the witness stand. It can be a very strong indicator.

"I think this case stands for a very important principle. That principle is that no man is above the law, not even public officials whose duty it is to enforce the laws. . . . These people cannot be elevated above the law any more than you or I can; because if they are, our legal system is meaningless.

"Power does corrupt, but public officials must learn what the Chicago police officers must learn; that power does not have to corrupt. There is no reason why Chicago police officers cannot perform their duties as police officers, without taking money from businessmen in the community in which they work. . . . I do not think there is any question that evidence has established that power, authority was abused and misused by these defendants for certain illegal purposes to benefit themselves. Such conduct cannot be tolerated any longer. The power and authority that we give out to law enforcement officers must be exercised within the confines of the law. If it is not, they have to be held accountable for it just as anybody else does. Police corruption has got to stop; and as to these twenty-three defendants, it is going to stop when you find them guilty as charged in this indictment."

Webb sat down, his work finished. He was exhausted.

All of the defense attorneys were expert speakers and knew what it took to sway a jury. It was never possible to know exactly what factors ultimately would convince a jury to reach a particular decision. The trial was not over.

As before, the burden of the defense fell on Cotsirilos. In his argument, delivered two days later, he argued that Fischer was a thoroughly depraved man who had admitted taking money for years and who now was lying to save himself. Cotsirilos referred to his own chart, checking each reason why Fischer could not be believed—he was crooked, he took money from bookies, he took money from stolen auto operators, and he had denied the charges when he was first brought to the U.S. Attorney's office by Mitchell Ware.

When Cotsirilos came to Braasch, he became emotional.

"Now I ask you if you were going to judge between this man and this man [indicating Fischer] on the question of credibility and that is all you have, which of the two men are you going to believe? You add to that, ladies and gentlemen, whatever other factual points you can think of as you go back there to the jury room. . . . Braasch is not a man who lived in fancy houses. He lives with his in-laws. He lives an average life, driving an average car. He does not take trips to Switzerland or Acapulco. What more can a person do in a criminal case, where he is charged, other than to deny the charge and to stand up and say, 'I did not do it,' where there is only one witness against him. What more can a man do but to take the witness stand and say, 'I did not do it. I tell you under oath, I did not do it and I am willing to be cross-examined no matter to what extent.' "

Webb knew that Cotsirilos's argument was devoid of logic. It was not Cotsirilos's fault; the evidence dictated that kind of argument. Webb could hope only that the jury would see through what Cotsirilos was doing, see that he was talking around the evidence, as when he exclaimed, "Where is McDermott? Where is Maurovich?" Webb shook his head. Surely, Cotsirilos knew that Maurovich and McDermott were beyond reach because of the statute of limitations.

Toward the end Cotsirilos vitriolically railed against the government's use of immunity, appealing to the jury's sense of fairness, but avoiding any discussion of Braasch's guilt or innocence.

"Ladies and gentlemen of the jury, if you can find it in your hearts and in your conscience to see the likes of Cello, Rifkin, Napier, Mascolino, and Fischer go free, while they have sold their souls in order that they go free, and convict men like Clarence Braasch, then our system of justice is broken down completely. If the fifty-three tavern owners who prey on the weaknesses of men can be granted mass immunity in a room, along with those police officers, and exchange their freedom for the freedom of men like Braasch, I say to you . . . that the system of justice that we live under no longer incorporates a concept of fair play that we have cherished so dearly. You cannot contaminate and pollute the presumption of innocence and the system of justice that we have by granting immunity to a mass of people like this, in order to get a group of men that are victims rather than proper defendants. . . .

"You are the only safeguard against this twentieth century rack and screw. You are the only safeguard for someone speaking out and saying that 'we will not let the domino theory, where three little men can bring in a Fischer, a Fischer can bring in a Braasch, a Braasch can bring in someone else and then they even throw the name of Daley in and then it goes to the highest reaches of Government and one of the men in the highest reaches of Government today[6] is complaining and says that immunity is a terrible thing and should not be granted.

"We think that at the conclusion of this case, . . . on the basis of the law and on the basis of credibility . . . and on the basis of the other level of evidence, that is this rampant use of immunity, [to demand that you] sign a verdict of not guilty. We have the right to plead for it. We have the right to claim it and we do claim it as a proper verdict in this case."

Farrell Griffin had been given the rebuttal assignment, but what was there to rebut? Little of Cotsirilos's argument concerned the evidence. Only the

6. Richard Nixon.

attorneys for the minor defendants had concentrated on the evidence. All had decried the use of immunity. Griffin felt that he must tell the jury why, without immunity, the corruption would still be continuing unchecked.

"They [the police] had . . . too good a thing going and it all hangs on silence. They cannot come in and start talking about each other. If I come in and squeal on you, you can squeal on me. They depend on silence. That is built into their system, and besides that it has been working for years. . . . Only by giving this immunity to all of these tavern owners could you see the dimensions of the impact on Chicago, you see all of the taverns affected on the near north side. I will grant it is only ten percent. Isn't that heinous in itself? Ten percent of those taverns, those number of years. You needed to know that. You needed to see the size of that. That is why tavern owners had to be immunized. . . .

"In Watergate, a number of people have been immunized, a number of people have been charged and pled guilty. Without immunity, do you think we would have heard about charges of political corruption? Do you think it's worth it? Do you even remember the names of those bagmen? Are they important or is correcting that problem that is important? It is letting some bagmen go, although it is the price that has to be paid. . . .

"Yes, it is absolutely necessary and that is why it was done. No, nobody likes giving crooked cops immunity. Nobody likes surgery. If it has to be done, to heal society now, it is done. . . . We exposed it [the corruption] and it can't live in open air. It can't live in front of you because when you see it and return a verdict of guilty, you demonstrate just what it is and you show it can't live in the open. You paid a price, the bagmen have gone free. . . . It is for you to determine that in the face of what was achieved it was worth the price."

When the courtroom emptied late in the afternoon of October 3, 1973, the marshal escorted the jurors to the jury room for deliberation. At the end of the next day the jury was still deliberating. At first, Webb and the other prosecutors had talked about the trial at length, but now there was nothing left to discuss. Time only to wait and worry. Not to worry that they had failed to put an effective case before the jury, but rather to worry that, in spite of everything, Braasch might be acquitted. Webb knew that if this happened, the investigation would have been a waste of time. Defenders of the police would say it had been a witch hunt, and there would be little reason for the public to be inspired to do something about its corrupt police department.

The next day the jury informed the marshal that a verdict had been reached.

The once again crowded courtroom watched the familiar, impassive faces of the jurors, sitting in their plastic swivel chairs as their foreman handed the verdict forms to the clerk, who gave them to Judge Bauer to review. He turned them back to the clerk for reading.

The prosecutors, the defendants and their lawyers, the jurors, and the gallery waited with anticipation as the clerk began to read the verdicts. He had a strong clear voice and the sound of the verdicts resonated in the silent courtroom. It took him several minutes to read the forms. When he was done it was clear that all of the defendants had been treated similarly, except for Sergeant Howard Pierson and Patrolmen William F. Demke, Thomas M. Lazar, and Confessor Troche. When the verdict on Troche was read a woman in the back of the courtroom shouted, "Oh, thank God," and ran from the courtroom. Troche followed and took her into his arms.

Only these four officers had been acquitted. They had been the defendants against whom the least evidence, most of it circumstantial, had been presented. The other defendants had been convicted on all counts. They took the verdicts calmly, although their families were weeping. Clarence Braasch had pursed his lips in a tight smile when the clerk began reading, but the smile had disappeared by the time the clerk had finished the long recitation.

The sentencing was delayed and the guilty defendants were allowed to remain on bond. The judge stood up and walked out of the courtroom. Relatives of the defendants rushed forward to comfort them. Braasch, always the man apart, walked out of the courtroom alone.

On the following Wednesday, five days later, while reports of the Braasch trial continued to be displayed prominently in the local newspapers, another story appeared, taking over the lead column. The headline read simply, "Superintendent Conlisk quits."

Daley made the announcement from his office. Conlisk was not present. Conlisk issued a statement a short time later.

The decision was mine and mine alone. . . . My six years as police superintendent was both challenging and rewarding. There has been significant progress in those years in achieving the department goal of serving and protecting the people of Chicago. . . . I wish success in the future years to my successor, whomever he may be.[7]

The United States Attorney, James Thompson, also issued a statement.

In a city known as the city of clout, there is no more time for halfway measures. As a replacement we don't need somebody who has grown up in the system and will be

7. *Chicago Tribune*, October 11, 1973.

just a repeat of the last one. We don't need a blue ribbon man who will take over at the top while the rest of the system remains the same. We need a knowledgeable man who will have a free hand. The mayor must say, "Hands off him."[8]

Daley did not immediately appoint a new superintendent. He turned instead to Deputy Superintendent James Rochford, whom he asked to be acting chief until a final decision could be made. Rochford, not disclaiming interest in a permanent appointment, said:

I have never violated my public trust. I never will. I abhor dishonesty among policemen. There is a strong clamor not only by the public but within the department to get rid of corruption, and I intend to devote all my energies to that.[9]

What those energies would be, no one knew.

During the next few weeks, however, one thing stood out. When Braasch was sentenced to six years in prison, few paid much attention. Clarence Braasch, the man, was already forgotten.

8. *Ibid.*
9. *Ibid., November 2, 1973.*

Chapter 11

The Closing Circle

Didn't Frank tell you about the Captains?

—David Holder,
April 1974

I don't want to be indicted and thrown into jail because my mind
isn't clear and I can't remember things.

—Mark Thanasouras,
June 13, 1974

The conviction of Braasch and the vice squad officers had an immediate effect
on the case against the uniformed club officers. A few days after the end of
the Braasch trial, all the defendants decided to plead guilty.

Webb breathed a sigh of relief. The summer spent prosecuting Braasch and
the others had been physically and mentally exhausting. He had been devoted
to the investigation of corruption in the 18th District, but had never intended
to make a career out of prosecuting crooked police officers. He wanted to move
on to other matters.

Webb's decision to leave the police investigation left a void in the 18th
District investigation. No one assumed the slack. For example, a key officer
who was still uninvestigated and uncharged was Captain John O'Shea, who
had succeeded Braasch as commander of the 18th District. The failure of the
prosecution to determine if he was involved in corruption had been due primarily to his vice coordinator's decision to stand trial rather than plead guilty
and cooperate. Although Geraghty (the vice coordinator) had been convicted
and sentenced to prison, he could still be granted use immunity. With Webb
off the case, this possibility went by the boards.

240

At the time, it seemed realistic to make a decision not to bother further with the 18th District. James Rochford, acting superintendent, was now insisting that there would be a serious effort to rid the department of corruption. Rochford, generally believed to be a man of considerable integrity, announced on November 9 that he was asking the department's entire seventy-five man command staff to submit to lie detector tests to prove themselves free of corruption and crime syndicate involvement.

Although Rochford's announcement sounded like the beginning of a sincere effort to reform the department, there were other indications which suggested that the proposed lie detector tests were little more than a public relations gimmick. Rochford would not state what specific action would be taken if any officer flunked the test, insisting only that the consequences would be severe. His hedging was understandable since a failure to pass a lie detector test was insufficient by itself to justify an officer's discharge, suspension, or demotion in rank. The authority to impose these sanctions belonged to the Police Board, which could act only on positive evidence after a full-scale hearing.

Another problem with the proposed tests involved the questions which were to be asked. Rochford suggested only four questions inquiring broadly into whether the officer had been directly or indirectly associated with organized criminal activity and corruption and whether he had knowingly condoned any organized corruption within his command. These general questions were limited to activities within the past three years. Since the federal investigation had begun in early 1970 and had been pubic knowledge for more than two years, one might suppose that the highest-ranking officers probably had made a special effort to remain "clean" until the scandal blew over. Thus, Rochford may not have expected to find much evidence of corruption in the high command through these tests.

Rochford anticipated questions about the time period and remarked that he had made this decision because of the Illinois statute of limitations for felony crimes.[1] Apparently, Rochford believed that if a member of his command staff had been involved in corruption before 1970, but had since refrained from illegal activity, it should not be cause for alarm.

The questions also suggested how Rochford viewed the problem of police corruption. Although he did not say why he was limiting the questions to organized corruption and organized criminal activity, it was not unreasonable to conclude that either he thought everyone would flunk if asked whether they had ever extorted money or taken a bribe, or, worse, believed that officers

1. *Chicago Tribune,* November 9, 1973.

should not be penalized or deprived of sensitive posts if they occasionally took money as long as it was not part of an organized "club" or "package."

Despite the legitimate questions concerning Rochford's sincerity in deciding to give lie detector tests, the announcement was received favorably. Most commentators, including the independent Chicago Crime Commission, praised the idea. Since it had never been done before, it sounded more daring and innovative than it really was and lulled the public into believing that Rochford was indeed serious about ferreting out corruption.

On January 30, 1974, George Bliss, a respected investigative reporter for the *Chicago Tribune,* wrote, "A Chicago Crime Commission investigation has indicated 20 to 50 percent of the Chicago Police Department's command staff failed lie tests last November dealing with their activities."[2] Rochford immediately labeled the report a "damned lie." The names of the flunking officers were never made public and, as far as anyone could determine, the men remained in the department and retained responsible positions. The tests had turned out to be only a gesture.

Rochford, like his predecessors, also ordered large-scale transfers and shifts of assignment. The ineffectiveness of this approach was reaffirmed when the Austin District investigation returned to the headlines and began to close the circle which had remained open since 1970.

The Rebirth of an Idea

Since the Braasch indictment had been returned in December 1972, everyone had paid close attention to the 18th District and ignored the 15th (Austin). Beigel was gone and when Davidson informed Becker in the spring of 1973 that he too would soon be leaving the Justice Department for private practice, Becker felt abandoned. Becker had been in the FBI for fifteen years and had seen prosecutors come and go with little concern, but this time it was different. With Davidson leaving, Becker believed it was only a matter of time before the investigation would collapse.

But Becker could not turn away from Austin, where the entire investigation had begun and where he still felt there was unfinished business. In February 1973, just two months after the return of the Braasch indictment, he went to Michael Mullen, to whom the investigation finally had been assigned, for help.

Becker strongly believed that Thanasouras, like Braasch, had been the kingpin of massive corruption. Even if no one else was interested, he wanted to continue pushing. He was not concerned about the effect which success or

2. *Ibid.,* January 30, 1974.

failure in the Austin investigation would have upon his career. He had never aspired to a supervisory position in the Bureau and was satisfied to work on interesting and worthwhile matters. For this reason, he was determined not to stop until he was certain nothing more could be accomplished in Austin.

At first, Mullen was not eager to get involved. He could not be faulted for his initial lack of interest since everyone in the office was talking about Braasch. Listening to Becker talk about two years of frustration did not encourage the young prosecutor to plunge headlong into an investigation which seemed to offer little chance of success. Only after Becker's repeated insistence that there were still some fruitful avenues to follow did Mullen decide that the investigation ought to be pressed.

There were several possibilities. Becker's experiences with Holder indicated that he would never be the first Austin cop to testify against his colleagues. He was too scared and too involved in the conspiracy of silence. Approaching Demet was also pointless. Completely destroyed by the investigation, he was content to sit out his time in jail and be finished with the whole terrible ordeal.

This left only two other officers who might yet cooperate. Frank Bychowski had been Thanasouras's first vice coordinator in Austin and had "taken the Fifth" in December 1971 during the original grand jury proceedings. He was still police chief of Bayfield, Wisconsin, and enjoying his "retirement" years. He was content to stay away from the Chicago investigation but Mullen and Becker decided it was time to bring it to him. However, the evidence against Bychowski was flimsy, consisting primarily of informant information and Marty Lindstrom's[3] statement that Bychowski and Demet had solicited payoffs six years earlier.

Charles Eckenborg had been a member of the Austin vice squad throughout the Thanasouras command. Becker had not found much evidence against him although everything indicated that he at least had known what was going on around him. Rumors proliferated throughout the district, corroborated by informants, that Eckenborg, who had been a close friend of Bychowski, had also made collections.

By May Mullen was ready to subpoena Bychowski and Eckenborg to the grand jury. Because the primary target was Bychowski, Becker contacted him first and asked if he would speak with Mullen prior to testifying. Bychowski agreed, but said he wanted to bring his attorney with him. This was a reasonable request and might be advantageous since it was often easier to negotiate a deal for immunity with an attorney.

Bychowski's attorney was James Demopolous, that perennial nemesis of the

3. See Chapter 5.

prosecutors. And he represented Eckenborg as well. This was not surprising since Demopolous had always claimed to represent most of the Austin vice officers who had served under Thanasouras.

At the scheduled time Bychowski, Eckenborg, and Demopolous arrived at Mullen's office. Becker introduced Mullen to Demopolous. Demopolous was friendly, and Bychowski, with his nicely developed paunchy waistline, acted the part of the retired police officer. He was obviously enjoying not having to worry about crime in the big city of Chicago. Eckenborg was smaller and younger and also a bit rotund. After the initial introductions neither Bychowski nor Eckenborg said anything. Eckenborg, however, looked worried.

Demopolous did all the talking, but said little. He challenged Mullen to tell him what the two officers had done wrong. It was impossible for Mullen to speak directly with Bychowski and Eckenborg or even to elicit any reaction from them. Obviously programmed for silence, they maintained classical stone-faced expressions throughout the meeting.

Mullen thought, as Beigel had, that Demopolous should not be representing the vice officers as well as Thanasouras. The same conflict-of-interest problem persisted. Mullen turned to Demopolous. "Jim, perhaps we can have a few minutes alone."

"Sure, Mike."

Becker took Bychowski and Eckenborg into the hall. After they had left and the door was shut, Mullen said quietly, "Jim, I know you once discussed this with Beigel, but for your own sake you should not be representing these two officers when you have represented other vice officers and Thanasouras."

"I don't represent Thanasouras," Demopolous said, the smile quickly fading from his face.

"But you did once and, anyway, you certainly represent Demet. We gave him use immunity and he wouldn't talk."

"Your use immunity was a travesty and grossly improper."

"There is no point in arguing. Bychowski and Eckenborg might well be in a position to give evidence against others who are also your clients. Under those circumstances, how can you justify representing them? You can't advise them solely on their best interests. The same thing goes for Holder. If he had talked, he would have implicated Eckenborg and, perhaps, Bychowski, and who knows who else. A neutral observer might believe that you tell these men not to cooperate to protect Thanasouras, or to avoid having the embarrassing situation of one client testifying against another."

Demopolous was now quite angry and stood up, gesturing wildly with his hands. "Nobody tells me whom I can or can't represent. These men retained me to advise them and that's just what I'm going to do. I don't tell them not to talk. That decision is up to them. But neither you nor anyone else is going to force me to withdraw."

"Have it your way, Jim. Remember one thing, though. If you persist in these tactics, we will not sit by and do nothing. If necessary, we will bring it to the attention of the court."

"I don't care what you do."

There was little sense in continuing the meeting. Mullen told Bychowski and Eckenborg they could leave. They would have to return, however, to appear before the grand jury.

Mullen sent an application to the Attorney General for approval to grant Bychowski immunity. It was a calculated risk. Based on what had happened when Holder and Demet had been granted use immunity, it was unlikely that Bychowski would persist in refusing to testify and risk going to jail for contempt. On the other hand, it was also unlikely that he would tell everything he knew before the grand jury. Mullen recalled that Beigel had excused Holder early during his questioning so as not to provoke him into lies and thereby destroy his credibility. That had been a year ago.

Now there was no more time to move cautiously. Mullen planned to grill Bychowski intensively and if he did not cooperate and was caught in a lie, he would be prosecuted. With Demopolous on the scene, conservative measures were obviously not going to work.

On the day of the subpoena Mullen brought Bychowski into court to face the judge. Demopolous was not with him. Instead, he was accompanied by Jeffrey Schulman, whom Demopolous had asked to appear in his place. Demopolous had other matters which demanded his attention. He had just been married and was honeymooning in Greece.

Demopolous must have been fairly confident about Bychowski to send a replacement. Still, Bychowski seemed much more nervous than he had been in Mullen's office a few weeks earlier. Because everything in the investigation was riding on what Bychowski would tell the grand jury, Mullen decided to pull out all the stops.

After Bychowski was given the formal order of immunity, Mullen told Schulman that he hoped Bychowski would decide to cooperate since, by doing so, he had everything to gain and nothing to lose. Schulman nodded his head in agreement, but said nothing. Mullen felt that Schulman would not advise Bychowski what course of action to take. Bychowski would have to decide on his own. At least, thought Mullen, Demopolous was not there to help him.

For three hours Bychowski waited to appear before the grand jury. As he waited and probably reflected on what he was facing, he became more nervous. He had a good life now, with few cares. Keeping quiet could end it all if he was sent to jail for contempt. If he lied, he might be indicted. With time to think and without anyone by his side to pressure him (Schulman had left and had not returned) he finally decided that he did not want to appear before the grand jury. He would accept the immunity and cooperate.

Bychowski had one stipulation which he insisted be met. One of his closest friends was Charles Eckenborg. "I've known Charlie for years," Bychowski said, "and he's in trouble because of me. I brought him to the Austin District. You have got to give him the same deal I am getting."

"Can he help us?" Mullen asked, not really caring as long as Bychowski would cooperate.

"Sure," Bychowski said. "He can corroborate some of the things I will say and he also made collections after I did. You'll be able to use him."

The two officers had finally decided to testify against their colleagues. Almost two years had passed since Becker had first spoken with Holder. Now it was not he who had agreed to cooperate, but others whose attorney had not seen fit to be present on the day of reckoning. It was Demopolous's fatal error.

The Final Collapse

While Webb began his preparation for the Braasch trial Mullen and Becker remained in the background, debriefing Bychowski and Eckenborg. Bychowski was, as expected, the principal source of information. He had served as Thanasouras's vice coordinator in Austin until November 3, 1969, and had been privy to most of the vice corruption existing in the district. As Becker spoke with Bychowski, he realized that all of the efforts to convince Holder to cooperate had been misdirected. While Holder had replaced Bychowski as vice coordinator when Bychowski retired to Bayfield, his term in this position had been brief (November 1969 to April 1970) because of the state indictment. Bychowski had been the direct link to Thanasouras, not Holder. In many ways Bychowski could be compared to Fischer and Holder to Cello or Mascolino.

Because the 18th District investigation had been broken open by convincing the commander's right-hand man to testify, Mullen and Becker now felt satisfied since they had persuaded Thanasouras's chief aide to cooperate. Unlike Fischer, however, Bychowski was not particularly articulate and provided information only in response to specific questions. Mullen talked with him at great length. Finally Bychowski warmed up and appeared to respond candidly, if not in great detail.

Eckenborg was also relatively close-mouthed. He had stayed in the Austin

District after Thanasouras had been transferred, serving under Victor Vrdolyak and the new vice coordinator, James Pacente. His main involvement in
the corruption had occurred during 1969 when Bychowski had asked him to
help out in the collections.

The statements of Bychowski and Eckenborg described the basic corruption
in the Austin District. It was well organized. After listening to Bychowski and
Eckenborg, Becker realized that what Braasch and his vice squad had done
had not been unique to the 18th. The Austin District breakthrough confirmed
that corruption in the Chicago Police Department was indeed widespread. The
"clubs" were traditional mechanisms of corruption, not confined to one area
of the city or a few crooked cops.

Bychowski described two basic methods of payoffs in the Austin District.
First, the vice officer club was financed by collections from more than twenty-
five taverns. Its purpose, which was no longer incredible in the light of
Fischer's testimony, was to insulate Thanasouras from complaints by lower-
ranking officers that they were not getting a fair shake on corruption money.
Bychowski named the taverns. (The shakedowns for which Holder had been
indicted turned out to be unassociated with this club, and had been independent forays, perhaps explaining why he had been so scared to talk.) Becker had
interviewed many of the tavern owners whom Bychowski named as members
of the club. All of them had either lied or said nothing. A few had even
appeared before the grand jury in December 1971 and denied any payoffs.

The second major source of revenue had been, not surprisingly, gambling
money. The size of the payoffs had never approached those made to the "big
club" and the syndicate in the 18th because Austin was a quieter neighborhood
with fewer gambling parlors. Still, the payoffs amounted to approximately
$2,000 a month and were split between Bychowski and Thanasouras. Bychow-
ski also supplemented his illegal income by taking a double share of the tavern
club proceeds.

During one conversation with Mullen and Becker, Bychowski remarked in
passing that he had once received $1,000 from the owner of the Cafe Chablis
and had given it to Thanasouras. Apparently, this owner had experienced some
difficulty in obtaining his license and Thanasouras had decided to take advantage of the situation. Bychowski believed that the payment he had delivered
to Thanasouras had been only part of the total paid, but did not know when
and how the rest had been passed. Becker took this information, along with
the names of the tavern club members, and began interviewing the owners to
build a case which would hopefully parallel the indictment returned against
Braasch and his vice officers.

The interviewing was routine as Becker, armed with specific information for the first time, found that he could with almost remarkable ease get the tavern owners to admit paying the police. He was not prepared, however, for the information he obtained in connection with the Cafe Chablis shakedown.

When Bychowski had mentioned the payoff, Becker had not been surprised that Thanasouras would personally participate in planning the shakedown of a specific tavern. He had not been as cautious as Braasch, often permitting his own men, especially Holder, to act high-handed and provoke attention. Still, Becker had never thought that Thanasouras would use the services of someone outside the department to collect money from a tavern owner. When Becker heard the name from the owner of the Cafe Chablis and his attorney, who had assisted in arranging the payment, he could not believe it. He immediately told Mullen, who pointed out that the information explained several strange events of the past several years. The bagman had been James Demopolous.

Demopolous, who had returned from his honeymoon, received a subpoena to testify before the grand jury. The date of his appearance was August 21, the same day that Webb was putting several of the 18th District tavern owners on the stand and a week before Lowell Napier would testify about Braasch's knowledge of the vice club.

When Demopolous took the stand Mullen informed him of his rights. Demopolous was no longer his usual bubbly and abrasive self. Although he was outwardly calm and self-possessed, he was also solemn and unusually deferential, as if he wanted to convince the grand jury that he was not only honest, but a model of dignity and grace.

Q: (Mullen) Do you know Mark Thanasouras?

A: (Demopolous) Yes, I do.

Q: For how long have you known Mark Thanasouras?

A: Possibly seven years. . . .

Q: And was your relationship business or social, or both?

A: It was more social than business.

Q: Do you know Sam Crispino, who is the owner of Crispino's Cafe Chablis at 6500 West North Avenue?

A: No, sir.

Q: Do you know Peter Boznos?

A: Yes, sir.

Boznos had represented Crispino in his attempts to obtain a liquor license and had finally agreed to cooperate after he became convinced that the government had the evidence necessary to implicate him.

Q: (Mullen) What dealings have you had, if any, with Peter Boznos?

A: (Demopolous) As I told you before in our interview, Mr. Mullen, I have had possibly two dealings in the past with Mr. Boznos.

Because Demopolous had represented many vice officers, Mullen had invited him to the office for a talk before submitting to formal interrogation. The meeting, however, had been unproductive. Demopolous had vehemently denied any criminal activity although he had not seemed surprised by the accusation.

Q: (Mullen) Were these professional, business or social?

A: (Demopolous) These were professional dealings. . . .

Q: Did you ever give $2,000 to Mark Thanasouras?

A: No, sir.

Q: Did you ever give any amount of money to Mark Thanasouras?

A: Well, again, as we said in our interview before we came into this grand jury, socially I have known Mark Thanasouras and I still know him socially; we have gone out when I was single. Now, if you would be specific, and I'm not being cute, as far as money, one dollar is money. I don't know, I would say, off the bat, no, if you're speaking of any great sums of money.

Q: Have you ever given more than fifty dollars to Mark Thanasouras?

A: No, sir.

Q: Did you ever receive $2,000 from Peter Boznos at any time?

A: Never received any money from Peter Boznos.

Q: Did you receive $2,000 from Sam Crispino?

A: I don't know Mr. Crispino.

Q: Are you familiar with the Rex Restaurant?[4]

A: Yes, I am.

Q: How frequently have you been at the Rex Restaurant?

A: Many times.

Q: Did you ever meet Mr. Peter Boznos at the Rex Restaurant?

A: Not that I can recall. . . .

Q: Did you receive a package under the table from Peter Boznos or another individual with Peter Boznos in the Rex Restaurant in or around February, 1969?

A: What do you mean "under the table"?

Q: Literally, under the table.

4. This was the restaurant where Dino Sanichas used to work and where he had first met Sergeant Fahey.

A: Definitely not. . . .

Q: You are familiar with Section 1623, Title 18, which is entitled "False Material Declarations before a Grand Jury"?

A: Yes, sir, I am and I don't believe you have to remind me of telling the truth.

Demopolous left the grand jury room, his testimony concluded. The casualness with which he claimed to have treated his first knowledge that someone was accusing him of being a bagman for Thanasouras could not have been very convincing to this grand jury, which now had more than a year of experience and had heard and rejected many more plausible stories.

On August 23, 1973, just two days after Demopolous's testimony before the grand jury, three indictments were returned. The first charged Thanasouras and Demopolous (and Bychowski as an unindicted co-conspirator) with conspiracy to extort $3,000 from Sam Crispino. Demopolous was also charged with lying to the grand jury during his August 21 appearance.

The second indictment alleged that fourteen officers who had served on the Austin vice squad, including Thanasouras, Holder, and Demet, had conspired to extort money from twenty-eight taverns between 1965 and 1969. The total amount collected had been almost $300,000. Ironically, the group had been named the "Friendship Club" by its organizers.

The third indictment alleged that Thanasouras, Holder, Demet, and Leroy Levy, a sergeant, had extorted $300 per month from the Blue Dahlia, a notorious Austin District nightspot, for four years, ending only when Thanasouras was demoted in 1970.

Although the Friendship Club indictment was closely analogous to the indictment returned eight months earlier against Braasch and the 18th District vice squad, it did not cause the same public commotion. Because Thanasouras had been demoted and had subsequently resigned in early 1971 after he had "taken the Fifth" before the grand jury, the news of his illegal activity did not have the shock value of the Braasch indictment. Moreover, the Austin District, with its rapidly changing racial character and lack of exciting night life, did not evoke the same titillating curiosity that information about corruption in Chicago's most famous nightclub district did. Finally, the indictment had to compete with daily stories of the Braasch trial, which was growing more exciting with each passing day.

Nevertheless, these three cases marked the conclusion of a long and hard struggle by Becker to build a case against Thanasouras and to show that corruption had been widespread under his command. Although Thanasouras had been out of the public eye for some time, he had once been a "child protégé" of the department. Those who compared the careers of Thanasouras and Braasch would realize that there was something seriously wrong with a police department which chose to elevate this kind of man so quickly into positions of substantial authority. Even more discouraging, these two commanders had achieved their rapid advancement under O. W. Wilson, Chicago's legendary "reform" superintendent.

After the return of the three indictments defense attorneys filed the inevitable pretrial motions. At that time it was still uncertain what would happen in the Braasch trial. Although the prosecutors had consistently won convictions, it could not yet be said that the indicted and untried were so overawed by the government's success that they immediately wanted to plead guilty and throw themselves on the mercy of the court. This hope that resistance might yet carry the day for the beleaguered and battle-worn police was epitomized by David Holder. Still silent, he had not even gone to trial in the original March 1972 case. He had been granted one continuance after another. Now he had to fight not one, but three indictments.

The convictions of Braasch and his co-defendants in October changed everything. One of the department's brightest young stars had been unceremoniously snatched from the sky. Police resistance collapsed. The seven officers indicted as part of the uniformed club in the 18th District had pled guilty. Several weeks later, on January 14, 1974, David Holder ended his four-year fight against investigations, state and federal, and pled guilty to all of the charges against him.

Holder was sentenced to three years in prison. After the indictments of Demopolous and Thanasouras, Holder had retained a new attorney but made no move to work out a bargain which would lighten his sentence in return for information. Holder now continued to maintain his silence, if not his innocence. Three years was a stiff sentence and reflected the growing judicial impatience with crimes of corruption. Holder, however, was determined to carry the day on behalf of the conspiracy of silence. Even though Thanasouras had now been indicted, Holder went quietly to jail.

As another consequence of the Braasch conviction, two Austin vice officers pled guilty. The rest seemed prepared to proceed with their defense. However, since the Friendship Club trial would not begin until March, Mullen expected that others might soon give up the fight.

The Demopolous-Thanasouras trial was scheduled to begin on February 4. Mullen spent the preceding week preparing his star witnesses, Frank Bychowski and Peter Boznos, and carefully grooming the owner of the Cafe Chablis,

Sam Crispino, whose memory was good but whose heart fluttered like a rabbit's in a constant state of nervous agitation. Although Crispino had given Becker and Mullen a physical description which matched Demopolous perfectly, he could not pick out his photograph. Mullen, however, was not worried. Even if Crispino failed to identify Demopolous in court as the man at the Rex Restaurant who had taken the $2,000 payment, Boznos would certainly identify him. Mullen believed that this would be sufficient for the jury to convict.

On February 4 Judge William Lynch entered his courtroom ready to begin the trial against Thanasouras and Demopolous. The last few years had not been good to Thanasouras. He was pale, fuzzy-eyed, and walked with a limp. Demopolous was dressed as usual in a tight-fitting dark suit with his black straight hair matted down. He fidgeted nervously with some papers in his briefcase, as if preparing to argue a motion on behalf of a client.

When Lynch asked if everyone was ready to proceed, George Collins, Thanasouras's attorney, stepped forward and said that he would like a conference in chambers. "Is there a problem?" Judge Lynch asked.

"No problem, Your Honor. We just want to discuss disposition of the case insofar as my client is concerned."

Mullen and Becker were taken completely by surprise. Collins had never mentioned the possibility of a guilty plea before. Perhaps Thanasouras was ready to cooperate, thought Mullen. But if that were the case, Collins would have talked with him earlier.

In chambers, Collins stated that his client wanted to plead guilty. The decision to plead had been Thanasouras's alone and reflected his desire to acknowledge his guilt to all of the charges against him and trust his fate to the court's sense of fairness.

Mullen did not know whether to be relieved or disappointed, but there was nothing he could do. Arrangements were made for Thanasouras to enter his guilty pleas and Lynch put off Demopolous's trial for sixty days.

Mullen and Thanasouras appeared before Judge Bauer a week later. Bauer, before whom the Friendship Club indictment was pending, had been designated to handle the sentencing. Mullen explained that if Thanasouras had gone to trial, the evidence would have documented his involvement in a scheme that had resulted in the extortion of $275,000 from taverns and bookies in Austin. Collins made no attempt to dispute the evidence, nor did he try to minimize the gravity of the crimes. Instead, he referred repeatedly to Thanasouras's poor physical condition. He said that Thanasouras, although only in his early forties, was suffering from failing eyesight, diabetes, back ailments, poor leg muscles, and other assorted maladies. When he finished, Bauer sentenced Thanasouras to three and one-half years in prison and fined him $20,000. Several days later Thanasouras was taken to the federal prison at Terminal Island.

Thanasouras's guilty plea broke the ice. By the time the Friendship Club trial began on March 9, several other defendants, including the perpetually suffering George Demet, had pled guilty. Only five vice officers were left to be tried: Robert Eadie, James Gartner, James Psichalionos, Eugene Manion, and Holder's old partner, Masanabu Noro, who was trying to repeat his earlier success when he escaped prosecution on the state charge in 1970 after the State's Attorney had claimed he could not find his major witness.

The guilty pleas, especially that of Thanasouras, robbed the trial of the spark that had propelled the Braasch case. When Bychowski took the stand and testified how taverns could purchase protection from harassment by joining a "friendship club" for $75 to $100 a month and that he had obtained permission from Thanasouras for the organization and operation of the shakedowns, the absence of Thanasouras made the trial seem like a trumped-up exercise designed to punish only the least culpable. All of the defense arguments in the Braasch case, which had been to no avail, now suddenly assumed a startling effectiveness and force. No commander was present to satisfy the jury's desire to convict the ringleader if the little guys also were to be punished.

As the trial moved into the last of its three weeks, Mullen and Becker could see that convictions were by no means certain. The defendants had been clearly on the periphery. It would not be surprising if the jury felt sorry for them and acquitted.

Eugene Pincham led the defense team. During closing arguments he ridiculed the testimony of Bychowski and Eckenborg, emphasizing that they were the primary collectors and arguing that they were seeking to implicate innocent men to make things easier on themselves. The other defense attorneys followed his lead. Richard Kuhlman, Gartner's lawyer, asked the jury, "Couldn't they find someone to testify against Jimmy Gartner other than two confessed criminals?"

The case went to the jury on March 26. After nine hours of deliberation, the jury returned with its verdicts. The clerk announced that Noro and Eadie were guilty as charged. When the Manion acquittal was read, four of his eleven children let out a loud cheer which was cut off by an icy stare from Judge Bauer. Psichalinos jumped up and down and hugged Pincham when he was acquitted. When Gartner heard that he had been found not guilty, he slid down in his chair. He had been acquitted once before in a case in which Louis King, the owner of The Scene and a witness against Demet, had testified. Twice he had survived prosecution.

Since three of the five defendants had been acquitted, it was easy to forget that the major defendants, Thanasouras, Holder, and Demet, had pled guilty along with nine of the vice officers. The acquittals achieved a conspicuousness they did not deserve. Gartner added fuel to the fire by openly criticizing the government for harassing him. He told reporters after the trial that "My only regret is that I didn't see Tom Becker here for the verdict because I wanted to ask him if he would leave me alone now."[5]

Manion was also vociferous and self-righteous. He talked freely with reporters and appeared on local television to vent his spleen against the injustice he claimed had been done him by the federal government. But he did not defend the police. Indeed, he was quite willing to speak about what he thought was wrong with the department. He told a *Tribune* reporter:

I always knew the stuff was going on, too. But I didn't know who—or how. In fact, there is a lot that stinks in the Department. Especially for a cop who wants to do his job. Take a case I had in 1966—a case involving two minors who got in a tavern fight. Well, the kids' attorney comes to me—right there in the courtroom—and asks me to take a bribe to forget it. I tell her to forget it. She tells me she can do the same thing with the judge, that it will just cost her a little more, and she goes into the judge's chambers. Out walks the judge, he takes my name and assignment, and dismisses the case. I look at him and say "That stinks," and the judge and the State's Attorney go bananas. They try to haul me back in the chambers, but I cut out and go back to my station. When I get there, my watch commander is on the phone with the State's Attorney. He hangs up and tells me, "Listen, why do you want to make trouble? This is the way things go here."[6]

In many ways Manion had a right to be bitter, but not about his indictment. There had been evidence that implicated him in the sharing of the club's proceeds. However, while the other defendants had been disciplined for "taking the Fifth" before the grand jury, Manion had been suspended because he did not live in the City of Chicago, a violation of an ordinance governing city employees which was honored more in the breach than in the observance. The department would obviously do anything to give the impression of reform.

Becker was disappointed by the result of the trial, not just because three defendants had been acquitted when he believed the evidence showed they were as guilty as the others, but also because the press had paid little attention

5. *Chicago Tribune,* March 27, 1974.
6. *Ibid.,* March 31, 1974.

to the case's significance. Not one reporter had pointed out the obvious similarity between the patterns of corruption in Austin and the Rush Street area. This similarity was particularly enlightening since the social and racial characteristics of the two districts were entirely different. In Becker's mind, the existence of the same type of corruption in both places was a clear indication that corruption in the Police Department was more pervasive than anyone had realized. There were 21 other police districts. No one knew how many officers in those districts had enriched themselves at public expense.

Neither Becker nor Mullen could afford the luxury of reflecting too long on the results of the vice club trial. They had to prepare for the Demopolous trial on April 9, less than two weeks away. Now that Thanasouras had pled guilty, that trial would pose tricky problems, particularly because it no longer really mattered that Crispino had paid $1,000 out of the $3,000 to Bychowski at the Austin District station. Bychowski could not testify directly against Demopolous, and if he appeared, the defense would probably succeed in an objection to his testimony as irrelevant. Mullen decided to avoid any potential difficulty by not calling Bychowski to the stand although he recognized that the jury would then be given only half of the Cafe Chablis story.

Boznos was Mullen's first witness. He told the jury how he had been granted immunity from prosecution and that he knew he could be indicted for perjury if he lied. He then told about his involvement with the Cafe Chablis and how he first had been retained by Crispino in 1968 to rperesent him in its purchase and to advise him on how to obtain a liquor license.

Boznos prepared the application for the liquor license and submitted it on January 28, 1969. During the next two weeks Crispino was interviewed by the 5th Licensing Unit of the Police Department, as is customary. But no license was issued. Shortly after the interview, Boznos said, he received a telephone call from someone who claimed to be an Austin District vice officer, who would not give his name.

"I was asked if I was the attorney for Samuel Crispino, and I replied that I was, and I was asked if I was representing him in his liquor license application. And I answered yes, and I was told that my client, Mr. Crispino, would not obtain a liquor license because of the background facts of his family, specifically his brother's death some two or three years prior to this point in time, and that based on that, that the Austin District was going to refuse to issue a license to Mr. Crispino.

"I argued with the caller, tried to show him that Mr. Crispino had no prior record, never had been in trouble before, and I was then told by the caller that if my client wanted to proceed with his liquor license application, he would have to pay $5,000 to someone from the Austin District.

"I talked with the caller—kept talking with the caller, and I eventually told him that Mr. Crispino would file a suit against the City because he was completely qualified to have a liquor license. The caller told me that this would take at least two or three months and there was no guarantee that Mr. Crispino would get it in the courts.

"I then argued with him further, and the caller said the price then would be $3,000 and I was asked to relate this information to my client, Mr. Crispino, and he was to make the decision as to whether or not to proceed along these lines.

"The caller then also told me that if Mr. Crispino would agree to some— to the payment of this money, he was to go to the Rex Restaurant at midnight on a certain night and to pay these moneys or see someone.

"Then the caller asked me if I knew James Demopolous, and I said that I did, and he said that Mr. Demopolous would be present that night at the restaurant."

Boznos met Crispino a few days later at the Rex Restaurant shortly before midnight. They sat down at a table in the lounge, ordered coffee, and waited. Soon, Demopolous entered the restaurant and came over to the table. Boznos introduced him to Crispino. Demopolous sat down and put his hands under the table. Crispino did the same. Boznos said it was noisy in the lounge and for that reason he could not make out what was being said. He did not see being passed the envelope which Crispino previously had shown him. After a few more minutes Demopolous got up and left. A short while later Crispino received his liquor license.

Demopolous's attorney, George Callaghan, attempted on cross-examination to establish that Boznos and Thanasouras had been good friends for years. Boznos denied this, although admitting that he had known Thanasouras for twelve or fourteen years and had been his fraternity brother. Boznos also conceded that he had known that the events at the Rex in February 1969 were criminal, but had not reported them to the authorities.

Callaghan also pointed out that although Boznos knew Thanasouras, he had made no attempt to contact him after receiving the anonymous phone call from the alleged Austin vice officer. Mullen did not know why Boznos had not contacted Thanasouras, but considered it insignificant because Crispino would corroborate Boznos on what had happened at the Rex. This was the only relevant evidence for the jury to consider.

Another part of Callaghan's cross-examination of Boznos concerned the date of the meeting at the Rex. Callaghan was intent on establishing that the meeting had occurred no earlier than the last week of February. Boznos would say only that the meeting could have occurred then. He could not be more specific. On redirect examination Boznos told Mullen that it was his best recollection that the meeting had occurred sometime during the last two weeks of February.

Mullen next called Sam Crispino to the stand. Crispino was so nervous that his voice scarcely rose above a whisper. Every muscle in his body was like a coiled spring. His discomfort was so noticeable that Judge Lynch felt constrained at one point to interject: "You can sit back in that chair and relax and you won't be so tense. The acoustics in this courtroom are excellent and don't worry about the microphone. Speak up and don't worry about these lawyers. I will protect you from them."

When Mullen asked Crispino when he had gone to the meeting at the Rex Restaurant, he said, "I don't recall the date. It had—in the time of maybe the last three weeks in February." Mullen then asked him if the meeting occurred before or after he received his license on February 26, and Crispino replied, "Before."

Crispino told the jury how he had brought to the meeting a package containing $2,000 in cash. He corroborated Boznos's testimony about the sequence of events which ended with Crispino giving the package under the table to the man who had entered and who had sat down with him and Boznos.

During Mullen's direct examination of Crispino, Callaghan stood off to the side of the courtroom, leaving Demopolous sitting alone at the defense table. The reason for his behavior became clear when Mullen reached that portion of his questioning concerned with the identification of the man to whom Crispino had given the $2,000. As the nervous Crispino stood up, he looked everywhere except the obvious place, the defense table. He even looked at the jurors. Then, in a quivering voice, he pointed to a man seated in the first row of the gallery and said, "To my best recollection, I am not positive, but the man in the first row there." Judge Lynch asked the identified man to rise and state his name. He stood and said, "Gregory Vlamis."

Mullen and Becker immediately realized what had happened. Crispino had been afraid to identify Demopolous. Although Crispino had never been able to pick out the photograph of the man to whom he had given the envelope, he had described him to Becker. Vlamis did not fit this description. Demopolous did. The prosecutor's suspicions received some support when, upon questioning by the judge, he learned that Vlamis was a friend and associate of

Demopolous. Mullen wanted to question Valmis, but Lynch thought he ought to have counsel first. A public defender was appointed. After conferring with Vlamis, he told the judge that his client would refuse to answer any questions on the ground of the privilege against self-incrimination.

Mullen did not believe that this misidentification would be fatal to his case. The description Crispino had given to the FBI corresponded closely with the physical build of Demopolous. Furthermore, Boznos had already placed Demopolous at the Rex and had testified that this was the only occasion that he had ever been there with Crispino. By circumstantial inference, the jury could only conclude that Crispino was referring to Demopolous despite his misidentification in court. Crispino had also testified that the man was not Thanasouras and that he had been told by Boznos that the man was an attorney.

Callaghan and Demopolous must also have concluded that Crispino's failure to make a positive identification in court would be insufficient to persuade the jury to acquit. As soon as Demopolous took the stand in his own behalf, Callaghan began a new line of questioning.

Q: (Callaghan) More particularly, were you in the Rex Restaurant in February, 1969, with a man named Peter Boznos and a man named Sam Crispino?

A: (Demopolous) No, sir.

Q: Mr. Demopolous, will you tell us please whether or not you left this country some time in February of 1969?

A: Yes, sir, I did. I was in Europe.

Q: When did you leave?

A: I left on the 25th of February, 1969, in the afternoon.

This was the sum total of Demopolous's major defense. Mullen could not believe it. The evidence was clear that Crispino had received his liquor license on February 26. Consequently, unless the payment was made on the 25th, Demopolous's testimony was irrelevant.

The jury would have to decide whether to believe Boznos or accept the alibi defense. Crispino's inability to identify Demopolous had not been helpful, but his corroboration of what Boznos had said about the meeting probably would neutralize the effect of his failure. Furthermore, Demopolous had admitted being Thanasouras's friend and acting as his consulting attorney when he had appeared before the grand jury. Callaghan also had been unable to construct an alibi defense that covered enough of the time period involved. Finally, he had not presented a convincing reason as to why Boznos might lie.

On the evening of April 12, after only a brief deliberation, the jury reached its verdict. When the clerk said "Guilty," Demopolous stared straight ahead. He was allowed to remain on bond pending sentence and appeal. On April 25 Lynch sentenced him to eighteen months in prison despite Callaghan's pleas that the certain disbarment which would follow was punishment enough. Demopolous, former attorney for Thanasouras and his vice squad, went to prison, joining many of the officers he had previously represented.

It now seemed that the Austin District investigation could be closed.[7] Mullen and Becker had exposed the same kind of corruption as had existed in the 18th District. The convictions had demonstrated that organized corruption was more than an aberration confined to a single police district.

With the convictions of Braasch and Thanasouras, the FBI and the U.S. Attorney's office were no longer interested in continuing to invest massive amounts of manpower in the further investigation of police corruption. Although other small cases were still being pursued, particularly in the Town Hall District against the vice coordinator and some of his officers, they were mostly a repetition of the previous cases and shed no new light on the patterns of corruption in the department.

Nevertheless, Becker was not quite ready to stop. Thanasouras had always been a tantalizing source of information. Although Braasch had made no move to cooperate (his appeal was still pending), Thanasouras was in prison and in ill health. Until Becker was positive that obtaining his cooperation was not in the cards, he would not mark "Closed" on his file.

The Closing Circle

Becker did not have long to wait. Shortly after the end of the Demopolous trial, David Holder began writing to the U.S. Attorney, complaining about his fate in general and jail in particular. "Why am I rotting in here?" he wrote plaintively. This question hardly needed an answer, but his second letter caught Mullen's attention. In it he asked, "What about the Captains? Didn't Frank tell you about the Captains?"

Was it possible that Bychowski had not told the government everything? If so, it was hard to believe. He had been questioned thoroughly. If he had any other information about corruption in Austin, he should have disclosed it. However, Holder seemed insistent that something had been missed and that if he had to stay in jail, others should join him.

---

7. The Blue Dahlia case never went to trial. The last defendant, Levy, was very sick. Ultimately, the charges against him were dropped because of his illness.

Mullen called Bychowski back to Chicago and asked him what he knew about corruption among the captains in the Austin District. "Oh," Bychowski said innocently, "you must mean the watch commanders. Didn't I tell you about them? I must have forgotten."

Although this hardly sounded plausible, Mullen decided not to make an issue of Bychowski's curious lapse of memory since it was true that no one had asked him specifically about the watch commanders.

The story gradually unfolded. Like Braasch, Thanasouras had been concerned about flak from his subordinates about gambling payoffs in which they did not share. He had satisfied his vice officers by allowing them to organize the "Friendship Club." Similarly, to mollify his watch commanders, he decided to give them money directly. Bychowski did not know about these payments first-hand because Thanasouras had handled them himself. If good cases were to be made against the watch commanders, Thanasouras would have to agree to testify.

When Holder realized that he would soon be the only officer who had not talked, he contacted Becker and asked if he could still make a deal. It was almost too late. He had been convicted and sentenced. Mullen could promise only a favorable letter to the Parole Board. Holder had little choice. He decided to cooperate. The first vice officer in the investigation to be accused became one of the last to point the finger.

With Holder now in the prosecution's camp, Becker grew hopeful that Thanasouras would decide to make a deal with the government, particularly when he realized that protecting one's fellow officer at all costs was no longer the prevailing police morality.

On May 28, 1974, Thanasouras's attorney, George Collins, filed a motion in federal court asking for a reduction in sentence. He claimed that Thanasouras had been marked for death by the Black Panthers since word had gotten out that he had been in charge of the police details notorious for their brutality during the riots after the assassination of Martin Luther King in 1968. Prison officials were sufficiently worried that they transferred him to the placid surroundings of the Lexington, Kentucky, correctional facility, a preferred haven for white-collar criminals.

Thanasouras was still not satisfied. Within a week Collins was in touch with Mullen. He wanted to make a deal. This is what Becker had been hoping for. Thanasouras should be in a position to give evidence against the watch commanders and possibly about corruption elsewhere. The price for his cooperation would be small, possibly an earlier release from prison and a reduction of the heavy fine imposed by Judge Bauer.

On June 7 Thanasouras was brought back to Chicago. For a week he talked to Becker and Mullen. He made many accusations of corruption among deputy superintendents but could or would not give first-hand evidence. Nevertheless, he provided a wealth of information about how corruption worked in the department and specific details about the activities of many officers, including the four captains who had served as his watch commanders. On June 13 Thanasouras was granted immunity from further prosecution by Chief Judge Robson.

The last significant supporter of the conspiracy of silence had finally talked. The years of looking over his shoulder had brought Thanasouras to the point of exhaustion. He was no longer the happy-go-lucky bon vivant of the department, the darling of the Greek community, and a man of unlimited future. When he had appeared earlier before Judge Robson to receive his immunity, he said, "I don't want to be indicted and thrown into jail because my mind isn't clear and I can't remember things."

Thanasouras, however, was a resilient individual. With renewed hope that he would soon be back on the streets, his previously faulty memory miraculously improved. He gave a detailed statement of his nefarious accomplishments in the Austin District. With respect to the Friendship Club and the gambling payoffs, he told Mullen that he had made no attempt to rigidly segregate the money received. Although he received little from the tavern shakedown funds and had been content to take his one-half share of the gambling payoffs, he still provided a monthly stipend to the watch commanders of $100 to $150 from the Friendship Club proceeds after the vice officers had taken their shares.

During the next three months Mullen and Becker spent countless hours interrogating Thanasouras. At the same time, Mullen also struggled to find an acceptable legal theory for prosecuting the watch commanders. Their payoffs did not readily come under the purview of the Hobbs Act because they were not directly related to the Friendship Club operation. Finally, however, he decided that because the money had come from the same pot as the tavern proceeds and because the watch commanders had known about the club's existence and had agreed not to harass the member tavern owners, they could be prosecuted as if they had been active participants in the Friendship Club.

On October 16, 1974, the grand jury indicted the four watch commanders. This time the press took more notice of the Austin investigation because of who had been charged.

Edward Russell was sixty-four, retired, and had served in the department for thirty-six years, receiving numerous awards. He had spent most of his career as a foot patrolman and detective before advancing to command rank in the 1950s.

John Foley was a fifty-five-year-old World War II army veteran who had joined the department in 1947. By 1962 he had become a captain and, like many aspirants for higher positions, had attended college during the Wilson regime. He had testified as a character witness for Frank Gill. His statement to Beigel and Webb about why Gill had not arrested the minor had led the two lawyers to look for and find the witness who was to destroy Gill's carefully planned defense.

Matthew McInerney, age fifty-three, had also joined the department in 1947 and had been a protégé of O. W. Wilson during the early sixties. During his career he had held every type of police job, ranging from traffic officer to patrol cop to detective. In recent years he had been commander of the General Assignment Unit in the Wood Street District. At the time of the indictment he was the commander of the important Monroe Street District.

John O'Shea, age fifty-nine, had been assigned to the Austin District when Wiedrich had first reported the existence of a $100-a-month club. In 1970 he was transferred to the 18th District after the beginning of the federal investigation in Austin. Ironically, he replaced Braasch as commander of the 18th after Braasch had been promoted. When his vice coordinator, Geraghty, was convicted during the Braasch trial in part on the testimony of Rifkin that the vice club had continued in full force under O'Shea's command, he was transferred to Shakespeare and demoted to watch commander.

Watch commanders were in charge of the day-to-day police operations in the districts. The indictment of these four men, particularly O'Shea, illuminated the total bankruptcy of "reform by transfer." The absurdity of the idea that corruption could be solved by transfers and minor demotions was now clear. Internal shake-ups in command, a corrective action favored by Conlisk and Rochford, would no longer suffice to guarantee that the corruption problem was being handled.

The indictment of these four officers brought the total number charged during the investigation to more than seventy. Only nine had been acquitted. Although the statistics were impressive, Becker believed that the true success of the investigation did not lie in the number of officers indicted and convicted but in the breakup of the conspiracy of silence and the demonstration that corruption could be investigated successfully.

Nevertheless, the indictments still dealt with only two districts, even though the charged officers had served throughout the department during their careers. Becker thought that it would be a fitting conclusion to the investigation if a case could be made which involved corrupt activities that had not been directed by Thanasouras or Braasch.

Such a case took shape when Thanasouras told Becker and Mullen about his tenure in the Shakespeare District beginning in 1970. Thanasouras had been transferred to this district to serve as watch commander after Conlisk had ousted him as commander of Austin in the wake of the state indictments of Holder and Noro. He had stayed in Shakespeare until subpoenaed before the grand jury in December 1971, when Conlisk had transferred him downtown in an effort to diffuse the impact of the first grand jury.

No sooner had he arrived in the Shakespeare District than he began receiving monthly payments. At first, he knew only that his money represented a part of the "captains' share." Making a few discreet inquiries, Thanasouras learned that gambling in the district was principally controlled by Andy "The Greek" Louchious and a hermaphrodite named Lottie Zagorski. Thanasouras also discovered that the officer who had given him his first monthly allotment also made the collections from the bookies. Thanasouras told Becker his name was Forsberg. Thanasouras, however, did not know who received the rest of the money or for whom Forsberg worked.

Forsberg had retired in early 1972 and was not easy to locate. Fortunately, however, he had remained in Chicago. When Becker finally found him he did not seem surprised that the investigation had caught up with him, and willingly cooperated in exchange for immunity. Forsberg told Becker how he had collected from Andy "The Greek" and another bookmaker for many years. Even after he had retired he had continued making the collections. As to what he did with the money, he named a Shakespeare watch commander, Thomas P. Flavin, as the immediate recipient. The name sounded familiar, but Becker could not immediately place it. He looked through his files and found that, like Foley, Flavin had been a character witness for Frank Gill. Gill had worked with Flavin when he was a field lieutenant in the Shakespeare District.

Forsberg could not tell Becker what Flavin had done with the money— although he assumed that he was sharing it with others. The collections had stopped in May 1974 but, interestingly, not because of the federal investigation. The protection payments were reduced when Zagorski died in June 1973 and stopped entirely in May 1974 when Louchious fell dead from a stroke while watching the Kentucky Derby.

A review of the Shakespeare command structure at that time revealed that this alleged corruption had gone on in part under the command of John McInerney, currently a Deputy Superintendent of Police and a cousin of the recently indicted Matthew McInerney. He was called before the grand jury, as was his vice coordinator, Thomas Simpson. Simpson appeared twice and was granted immunity, but his testimony was of questionable value. As for John McInerney, nothing could be found to link him to the Flavin collections or any other wrongdoing. If he had been involved in the same way as Braasch and Thanasouras, no evidence could be found. The most that could be said was that the current Deputy Superintendent for Patrol had been commander of a district where gambling collections had continued unimpeded for at least four years. Ironically, McInerney had been promoted to deputy superintendent in the same shake-up that had included Braasch's promotion and O'Shea's assignment as commander of the 18th District. As for Simpson, he had been sent to a new district as part of the same shake-up. It was, of course, the 18th.

Mullen could not indict Flavin under the Hobbs Act because gambling payoffs had never been used as a basis for a Hobbs Act violation. After painstaking investigation, however, he and Becker were able to develop sufficient evidence to establish that the gambling operations which funded the payoffs met the requirements of a recently enacted Organized Crime Act gambling statute which made it a federal crime to conduct and manage a gambling enterprise which is illegal under state law as long as it involved five or more people and had been in continuous operation for more than thirty days. With a violation of this statute established, Mullen could invoke the little-used federal obstruction of justice statute under the same Organized Crime Act to indict Flavin for having taken money to protect the illegal gambling business. In the indictment he also included ten counts charging that Flavin had violated federal income tax laws by not reporting the illegal income which he had received.

This indictment was returned on February 11, 1976, six years after Holder and Noro had been indicted by a Cook County grand jury, more than four years after Thanasouras had first appeared before a federal grand jury, more than three years after Braasch had been indicted, and eighteen months after Thanasouras had been granted immunity by Judge Robson.

It was now a new era. When the investigation had begun, Nixon was President. His massive landslide reelection had ocurred a month before Braasch had been indicted. In the beginning there had been those who had complained that the police investigation was nothing more than an attempt by Nixon to embarrass Daley. These criticisms and other charges of political motivation had long since faded into oblivion. Too many cops had been convicted. Too much had happened. Although this investigation never achieved the national scope of a Watergate, it had made its mark on the citizens of Chicago. After six years it would be difficult to find a Chicagoan who would not admit that corruption was a serious problem in law enforcement.

In other respects little had changed. Rochford, whom Daley had appointed superintendent, had made certain cosmetic changes. The Braasch conviction had forced Conlisk's resignation. The public catharsis afforded by the abdication of a superintendent as a result of an investigation by an outside agency had been so great that it was impossible to sustain public interest in a scandal that seemed to drag on for years. Whatever changes were made in the department, they were not apparent to the outside world. Gradually the police corruption story ceased to be a page-one item. When Thanasouras testified at a pretrial hearing on the Flavin indictment, the story was buried in the back pages of the Chicago newspapers.

By the spring of 1976 the investigation was rapidly becoming a part of Chicago's history. James Thompson had resigned as U.S. Attorney the year before to run for Governor of Illinois. His successor, Samuel Skinner, talked more about investigating federal agency abuses than local police corruption.

The cases against Flavin and the watch commanders, however, were still to be tried. Neither of the cases was particularly strong. Thanasouras was not expected to make a good witness. He was snide, flippant, and so heavily involved in corruption that Mullen knew it would be difficult to present him credibly to a jury. But no one seemed to care.

In August 1976 Beigel met Becker for lunch. They had not seen one another for more than a year.

"It was too bad about losing the watch commander and Flavin cases," Beigel said after the two men had exchanged news about their lives during the past year.

"I suppose. But Thanasouras was awful on the stand, insincere and too easily riled on cross-examination. He was no Fischer. But now it's over. I've been transferred to another squad. Inserra retired to private business. I like what I'm doing now, interstate theft. It's a change of pace. Maybe my request for reassignment to L.A. will come through."

"Well, you certainly spent long enough on the police investigation."

"It could have been longer. There were so many missed opportunities."

"What do you mean?"

"Other districts, information given by Thanasouras. All worth pursuing. But now, especially with the last two verdicts, nothing will be done."

"I wouldn't let it bother you. The investigation lasted longer than anyone had a right to expect. Times change, after all. Finding corruption in government is no longer any big deal."

Becker looked sad. "I just don't know if any of it did any good. Nothing seems to have changed."

"You can't tell. People talk about corruption nowadays. They never did that much before. Still, five years ago, our investigation was an idea whose time had come. Now it is an idea whose time has passed."

"Then nothing has changed, has it?"

"I don't know, Tom. Maybe you're right. The other night there was a talk show on the radio. One guest was an ex-cop who has written a book, a kind of primer for the policeman who wants to know how to take a bribe. Another guest was a lawyer who had once been a cop. The moderator asked him what he thought of the whole federal investigation. He said only a few cops were ever charged with corruption compared with the many thousands of honest police officers who serve us faithfully each day, unsung and unheralded."

"I'm right. Nothing has changed. Why did we even bother?"

"We wanted to do it."

Becker laughed. "That's it, nothing more?"

"It was reason enough for us."

Epilogue

But that is the beginning of a new story—the story of the gradual
renewal of a man, the story of his gradual regeneration, of his
passing from one world into another, of his initiation into a new
unknown life. That might be the subject of a new story, but our
present story is ended.

—Fyodor Dostoevsky,
Crime and Punishment

An investigation ends, but the lives affected by it go on. More than sixty police
officers went to prison. Some are back in the outside world. David Holder is
driving a truck. George Demet is looking for a job which will give him and
his family a decent income. Mark Thanasouras is making plans to enter the
tavern business.

Many officers, given immunity by the government, never went to jail, but
their lives were also changed by the investigation. Skippy Cello and Sal Mascolino are security officers for a large corporation. James "Keep-It-All" Murphy works in a hospital. Lowell Napier owns a gas station in Kentucky. Eddie
Rifkin is president of a protective service. Frank Bychowski is still chief of
police of Bayfield, Wisconsin. Robert Fischer left Chicago and his wife behind
to look for a job under an assumed name, still fearful of organized-crime figures
whom he had named during the Braasch trial. He had difficulty finding employment, was on and off welfare, and at last word is bitter about his ruined
career.

One officer's life changed very little. Charles DuShane, the "house mouse"
of the 18th District, was reinstated by the police force, the beneficiary of a
United States Court of Appeals decision that the department improperly used
Rule 51 to fire officers who had refused to testify before the grand jury.

267

The police corruption investigation was not the end of Conlisk's troubles. After resigning as superintendent he remained on the force as chief of traffic, outside the public eye. In early 1975 a Cook County grand jury began an investigation into illegal police surveillance of local political groups and citizens. Conlisk was called before the grand jury. In November the grand jury ended its investigation, saying that layers upon layers of silence in the department hierarchy had prevented the gathering of sufficient evidence to indict those responsible for the substantial abuses uncovered. In its report the grand jury presented to the court a petition alleging that Conlisk should be held in contempt because he had tried to thwart the grand jury's work with "filibusters and subterfuges instead of truths." Examples included his refusal to tell the grand jury the extent of his formal education without consulting a lawyer and his reading of a 2,038-word statement defining "burglary" when asked if he was aware of burglaries committed by police spies. Nothing was done with the petition although, in May 1976, State's Attorney Bernard Carey said he still intended to press vigorously for sanctions against Conlisk. As of March 1977, however, he had done nothing.

In March 1976 a police officer interviewed the owner of a small tavern on the far northwest side in connection with his application for a 4 A.M. closing time. During their conversation the officer told the owner that he would have trouble getting permission because of reports of frequent disturbances at the tavern. The worried tavern owner said, "What can I do, Officer?"

"I'll be back the day after tomorrow and we can discuss it then."

The tavern owner had followed the federal investigation and believed he was being set up for a shakedown. He called the FBI. An agent was assigned and, with the owner's agreement, a recording device was placed on the premises.

When the officer returned, he said casually, "I've checked with my boss and you are going to have trouble."

"How much will it take to clear up the problem?"

The officer hesitated and looked at the tavern owner for a few seconds before responding. "We don't take money any more." Before the tavern owner could say anything, the officer turned around and walked out.

From the federal penitentiary in Montgomery, Pennsylvania, a letter came to Judge Richard B. Austin.

Dear Judge Austin:

With your honor being fully aware of the circumstances surrounding my case, I would like to say that I'm not a habitual criminal as my record will bear out. I would like to emphasize that more serious crimes, some similar to mine, have been lodged against the citizenry of this country, and I would like to bring reference to some of the Watergate figures who served only a few months in prison and were given a second chance and returned to society and their families. Am I to believe that only first time offenders such as myself are to feel the full wrath of the law? I have shamed my parents and family by my apparent indecorousness and my position which I loved as a child is now lost to me forever.

I have served approximately four months in prison here in Allenwood in the hope that I would receive a parole after one-third of my sentence which would be in July of this year. However, I was told that in accordance with the guidelines on severity of crimes, extortion falls within the range of offenses for which this kind of parole is not possible.

I truly don't believe that this is what your honor intended for me. Now I come to you once again and ask for your reconsideration on your previous ruling on reduction of my sentence. However, if your honor intends for me to serve my time in its entirety then I have no recourse, none at all.

Respectfully,
Walter F. Moore

In October 1976 the campaign for Governor of Illinois between James Thompson and Michael Howlett was drawing to a close. Mayor Daley, campaigning for Howlett, criticized Thompson for his part in the police corruption investigation. A reporter listened to Daley's remarks, which seemed to indicate that Daley believed the police cases should not have been brought. He asked Daley if he thought the tavern owners had lied. Daley replied, "What do you think?"

Afterword: What Should Be Done

Those who do not learn by history are condemned to repeat it.

—George Santayana

Anyone who has watched, no matter how closely, an investigation of police corruption that has lasted six years must be wary of suggesting general solutions. The investigation described in this book was of people, not systems. No one could or should have expected that the result would be institutional reform of the police. Nevertheless, the system was exposed.

Police corruption is a complex phenomenon which does not readily submit to simple analysis. This is clearly seen through a review of the "victimless crimes" problem which many view as a prime cause in the growth of police abuse.

Victimless crimes include gambling, prostitution, vagrancy, possession of narcotics or drugs (not for sale), and certain minor traffic offenses. Although these offenses technically have victims, it is generally accepted that a "victimless crime" is any illegal act in which the "victim" does not consider himself to have been victimized or one in which the "victim" has received some sort of service or pleasure, for example, narcotics, prostitution, gambling.

Public servants who are charged with enforcing these laws often face an insoluble dilemma. While a police officer may easily feel moral or righteous indignation when facing a bank robber, murderer, or rapist, it is hard for him to be equally aroused when arresting someone for gambling or for possession of a small amount of drugs. Many observers of police work believe that a police officer is more likely to "look the other way" when investigating a victimless crime.

Some support for the belief that victimless crimes encourage police corrup-

270

tion has emerged from other investigations of police corruption as well as the one described in this book. In them, the large majority of corrupt acts by police involve payoffs from both the perpetrators and "victims" of victimless crimes. The Knapp Commission in New York found that although corruption among police officers was not restricted to this area, the bulk of it involved payments of money to police from gamblers and prostitutes.[1]

Any police officer who is tempted to make additional money through the use of his police power is likely to find that the most acceptable way of accomplishing his objective is to take money from those whom he feels no special moral compulsion to arrest. The police officer who is about to arrest a small-time bookie, a prostitute, or a homosexual will be more tempted to take money and forget the arrest than he would when offered money by a suspected burglar, bank robber, rapist, or murderer.

This corruption is not, however, confined to isolated violations of the law. Some victimless criminal activities are highly organized. The success of illegal gambling may be in part attributable to the effective organization resulting from the necessity to lay off bets which one bookie cannot afford to handle himself. When victimless criminal activity is organized, police corruption tends to be similarly structured. Police who take money from bookmakers or pimps are usually part of a "club." The distribution of payoffs then occurs within the police structure in a hierarchical manner and has many features similar to the handling of money within organized crime.

Because of the apparent close connection between victimless crimes and police payoffs, it may seem that a quick solution to police corruption would be to legalize all victimless crimes. But the problem of police corruption is, unfortunately, not so easily handled.

For instance, it is quite possible that the legalization of gambling and prostitution would not eliminate corruption, but rather rechannel it. During prohibition liquor could be obtained as long as police and other law enforcement officials were willing to cease enforcing the law in exchange for money paid by bootlegging organizations. When prohibition was repealed, police corruption associated with bootlegging disappeared, but corruption associated with liquor licensing and permits to sell grew. This rechanneling of corruption is less likely to occur, of course, in states which authorize the sale of liquor only through state outlets. However, in those states which allow the sale of liquor by bars and nightclubs, the potential for corruption of public officials is present whether or not it involves the police. Similar developments might be expected

1. Knapp Commission Report, 1973, pp. 1–3.

if prostitution and gambling were civilly rather than criminally regulated.

The problem of police corruption is, therefore, part of a broader problem associated with governmental regulation. If the activity is regulated primarily through the criminal law, corruption will be more prevalent among the police who are charged with enforcing those laws. If the regulated activity is a civil matter, corruption is more likely to occur among those authorized to approve the activity through licenses.

There are, of course, other reasons for regulating certain activities besides the fact that, without it, the activities will have some adverse effect on the public morals. For example, regulation often occurs when too many people want to engage in an activity which, by its nature and economics, is better limited to a specific group. This includes licensing of interstate carriers, bars, TV stations, and taxis. Regulation may also be used as a method of collecting revenues, for example, metered parking and fines for minor traffic violations. Whatever the reason for regulation, corruption may occur.

Even if it is accepted that there is no single panacea to the problem, it is still important to examine what can be done with the police institution to reduce the possibility of corrupt enforcement without simply passing off the problem to another governmental institution.

Recruitment, Selection, and Promotion Practices

Although the existence of police corruption is a consequence of institutional issues rather than "rotten apples" in an otherwise healthy barrel, this does not lessen the importance of focusing on how the recruitment, selection, and management of police personnel resources may contribute to the development of police corruption.

Any actions taken to revitalize this process, so that it acts as a barrier against the development of police corruption, must be designed to disrupt the entrenched, self-serving bureaucracy. That bureaucracy often supports the development of internal corruption by allowing the payment of money to join the police force, to receive better shift assignments, to obtain choice vacation time, to guarantee promotions, and to insure assignments which yield opportunities for participation in other forms of corruption.

Police departments must find ways to enable their personnel selection, recruitment, and management processes to minimize the development of an environment in which officers find corruption to be the best alternative.

Heisel and Murphy have pointed out that most modern police departments still lack "viable, adequately staffed, sufficient support personnel units that can maximize the agency's human resources."[2] They attribute this to factors such as the failure of police management to determine their human resource objectives, the inability to describe a specific function for a personnel administrator without the presence of these objectives, the unwillingness of many police administrators to delegate authority to an individual with specific personnel responsibility, the scarcity of fiscal resources for personnel management functions, and the adherence by police departments to traditional practices which mitigate against the institution of new personnel polices.

A necessary first step in the creation of a police personnel system which will assist in the control of police corruption is an independent management system. The administrator of this personnel system should be responsible only to the police chief to prevent influence from line personnel.

While the placement of the personnel manager and the personnel office at a staff level may protect against corruptive influences from line officers, it does not protect against corruption of the personnel management function by the police administrator himself. To implement a system of checks and balances which protects against this possibility, the police administrator must be selected without influence by the police department and the entrenched political bureaucracy. The selection of a police chief should not be based solely upon "emergence from the ranks," but also upon an open recruitment process which insures the availability of candidates who are free from any previously existing corruptive practices. In retrospect, while other faults may be found with the selection of O. W. Wilson as Chicago Police Superintendent after the Summerdale scandal, the mechanism used to select him, namely an independent commission free from political authority, was excellent. The recruitment of an "outsider" was a wise choice. Had other things been done, he possibly could have reduced the influence of previous corrupt police practices.

Heisel and Murphy also suggest that a police department has two options in the selection of its full-time personnel officer, namely the selection of a staff police officer who will require additional training in personnel management or a civilian, competent in personnel management but without a specific police background. Since the overriding principle is the disruption of an entrenched, self-serving bureaucracy which supports the continuation of police corruption, the personnel manager should be a civilian with personnel management experience, most likely in industry or government, who can learn the police mission

2. W. Donald Heisel and Patrick V. Murphy, "Organization for Police Personnel Management" in *Police Personnel Administration,* edited by O. Glenn Stahl and Richard A. Stanfenberger (Police Foundation, Philadelphia, 1974), pp. 1–16.

and then apply previously acquired management skills. The selection of a staff
police officer for this position involves a greater risk since it may lead to the
perpetuation of traditional practices often associated with police corruption.

Traditional police personnel classification patterns have also supported the
development of police corruption. Lutz and Morgan[3] point out that the personnel and command structures of most police departments have borrowed heavily from the armed forces. They had not recognized the need for specialist
classifications because they have relied almost totally upon a promotional
structure which moves people up the administrative hierarchy without con-
comitant career development training. Lutz and Morgan quote a top police
executive, Samuel G. Chapman:

The time-honored, uninspiring path of promotion sees an administrator fish-laddering
his way up through the ranks without being prepared in anything more than a "by
chance" manner for the new and difficult responsibilities of successive demands. The
consequence is that many of today's police commanding officers are simply promoted
policemen, not professional administrators carefully prepared for demanding roles in the
complex enterprise that is the hallmark of contemporary police work.[4]

While describing this phenomenon, neither Chapman nor Lutz and Morgan
mention the often devastating effect which this promotional pattern has upon
the maintenance of police corruption. A corrupt patrol officer, promoted
through the ranks, will bring with him the very corrupt attitude that should
be eliminated. Worse, that attitude, moved to a higher level, is even more
damaging as a result of the support which greater administrative power gives.

Increased training as officers move up the promotional ladder generally
neglects questions of attitude. The patterns of corruption which have been
already set are not altered by training which focuses on the acquisition of new
skills. A dual approach is required in which not only is promotion available
to those who have received increased training, but also entrance into the law
enforcement system at higher levels is made attractive to those outsiders who,
because of specialized training received elsewhere, qualify for important positions in the police hierarchy without beginning at the level of patrol officer.

Lutz and Morgan also describe another characteristic of existing police
personnel practices which has a negative influence upon morale. The current
position classification system is not usually based upon a principle of "equal
pay for equal work" but rather on "equal pay for all those who happen to have

3. Carl W. Lutz and James P. Morgan, "Jobs and Rank" in *Police Personnel Administration,* pp.
17–44.
4. *Ibid.,* pp. 24–25.

the same rank."[5] This rank and pay system has a negative influence on many police officers who see others with the same rank and pay performing less hazardous and less responsible work. This situation does not usually lead to a belief that the other officer should be receiving less money, but that the individual who perceives himself as performing responsible work should be receiving more money. Since this is not available through the traditional pay structure, this may make that officer more susceptible to involvement in corrupt practices. This is particularly true among members of vice squads, where work is often hazardous and difficult. Yet the compensation is the same as for patrol officers of the same rank whose work is often oriented toward service rather than "law enforcement."

Before any progress can be made in dealing with this aspect of police corruption, police departments must dispense with promotional systems which allow increased pay only through "management promotion" without due regard for competence and technical skills. Otherwise, it will be impossible to bring those with high-level "technical skills" into the police department at appropriate levels of the hierarchy regardless of their previous involvement in the promotional system.

The development of a group of applicants with the broadest possible range of socio-economic backgrounds, skills, and origins of interest should also be encouraged. Baker and Danielson[6] argue that current law enforcement recruitment trends mitigate against this possibility because of the relative scarcity of positions in comparison to the large number of applicants seeking them. Most police departments tend to "close down" recruitment for long periods of time. The individual who has the specialized skills required for a position may be denied access to the police system.

In the past the most likely source of police applicants has been the "lower economic classes." There the role of police officer is often seen as a status symbol which carries with it a degree of authority which is attractive. A recruitment and selection process that limits itself to these groups is more likely to attract those individuals who have a social and cultural background similar to the criminals they are required to seek out. One high-ranking New York City police official believes that a large number of corrupt policemen are "content merely to take random petty graft. These petty grafters do not think

5. *Ibid.*, p. 27.
6. Bruce R. Baker and William F. Danielson, "Recruitment" in *Police Personnel Administration,* pp. 59–68.

of themselves as corrupt. They view their behavior as part of the prevailing police culture."[7]

This "police culture" may be merely an extension of the "community culture" from which most policemen have come. The failure of the selection and recruitment process to attract a diversified group of individuals encourages not only the development of a "community of interest" between the police officer and the criminal, but also the continuance of the relationship between the "police culture" and police corruption.

To break down this process, Eisenberg and Murray[8] have suggested the use of at least two recruitment and selection criteria which might serve as the basis for a preferential "bonus points" scheme that, when applied to all applicants previously judged to be eligible, would support the development of the broadest possible police personnel structure. The first criterion is based upon the desirability of attracting police personnel who are representative of the population they serve. While this is commonly assumed to refer to the recruitment of "minorities," its adoption could also lead to the recruitment and selection of a greater number of applicants who do not view police work as a chance to bring status to a life which otherwise would be considered "average" or "blue collar." If police work were not available, many officers would find themselves in jobs not traditionally considered professions.

The second criterion for which "bonus points" might be available would be the presence of a prior work history which indicates that the recruit has certain skills which are needed. These might include experience in dealing with people, specific training in highly valued areas, and bilinguality where the jurisdiction has a significant proportion of non-English-speaking people.

If modern police departments are to attract qualified individuals for the important tasks at hand, they must develop a system of recruitment which is open at all times and is based upon an aggressive policy of recruitment designed to find the individuals whose skills are needed in police work, regardless of the level of past experience.

Breaking the Conspiracy of Silence

The conspiracy of silence that exists among police officers, whether or not they are directly engaged in corruption activities, prevents meaningful investigations of police corruption and ultimately its control and reduction. This

7. William H. T. Smith, "Deceit in Uniform," *Police Chief,* September 1973, pp. 20–21.
8. Terry Eisenberg and James G. Murray, "Selection" in *Police Personnel Administration,* pp. 69–100.

conspiracy is based upon the development and implementation of a "code" which defines, within a specific police department, the "norm" of practices, whether legal or illegal, which are accepted as part of a police officer's behavior.[9] The conspiracy of silence then "says" that any activities which fall within the code are not to be shared with outsiders. Where practices exist that in the civilian's view would be "corrupt," but in the police officer's view are within the code, the conspiracy of silence reinforces their continuance.

During the investigation of corruption in the Chicago Police Department it was clear that all possible manifestations of police corruption existed. Furthermore, all of them, with the possible exception of "premeditated theft," were within the code and subject to the conspiracy of silence. They included the following:[10]

(1) Mooching—the act of receiving gratuities (such as free meals) as a consequence of being in an underpaid profession or in return for possible favoritism;

(2) Chiseling—an act in which a police officer demands free admission or discounts to activities not necessarily connected with police duties;

(3) Favoritism—the practice of using courtesy cards to gain immunity from police action such as in traffic arrests;

(4) Prejudice—when a police officer gives less than impartial or neutral attention to groups, particularly minority groups, whose influence within the political structure is not likely to cause trouble for the officer;

(5) Shopping—the practice of picking up small items at a store, within the patrol officer's jurisdiction, where the door has been left accidentally unlocked during nonbusiness hours;

(6) Extortion—demands made by a police officer for support of police activities or police functions; the payment of cash will, in turn, prevent trouble from the police officer for the person making the payment;

(7) Bribery—the unsolicited payment of cash by an individual to a police officer to avoid prosecution;

(8) Shakedown—the practice by a police officer of appropriating expensive items for personal use and then attributing their loss to criminal activity which has taken place at the same time but did not include the appropriated items;

9. Ellwyn L. Stoddard, "A Group Approach to Blue-Coat Crime," in *Police Corruption: A Sociological Perspective,* edited by Lawrence W. Sherman (Garden City, N. Y.: Anchor Books, 1974), p. 277–304.
10. *Ibid.,* pp. 286–287.

(9) Perjury—the action of a police officer who lies to provide an alibi for fellow officers who have engaged in activities covered by the "code"; and

(10) Premeditated theft—activities which might include a planned burglary on the part of a police officer.

Wherever the code recognizes any of these activities as acceptable, even though illegal, the conspiracy of silence will provide protection to involved officers.

In most police departments initiation of a police officer into the conspiracy of silence begins shortly after that officer's entrance into the department. New police officers are screened by current practitioners of the code to determine whether they might participate. In some departments initiation into the code has begun before the officer's entrance through requiring "payment" for an appointment to the police department.

The initiation of a recruit into the code and the conspiracy of silence is not necessarily a brief process. Practitioners of the code are very careful, constantly balancing the knowledge given to the potential recruit about the code with an assessment of whether he is willing to become a committed participant.

Not all police officers in departments where corruption occurs become practitioners, but the careful screening process guarantees that those who decline to participate do not gain access to information damaging to the officers involved. These nonparticipants, while they remain outside the conspiracy of silence, do not have the potential to damage those who are code practitioners and members of the conspiracy of silence.

If a code does exist in a law enforcement agency, one of the major factors which protects it from attack is secrecy. This factor is compounded by public acceptance of the traditional view of illegal behavior as only an individualistic, moral problem.[11]

This public acceptance leads most community members to place a low priority on the problem of police corruption. This lower priority is reinforced by their concern, often realistic, that the police will retaliate if more rigid controls are imposed.

If the police "have carefully practiced prejudice, the chances are slim that the persons against whom these illegal practices were committed possess either the social or political power to break the 'code' before the system could retaliate."[12] This was clearly seen during the Chicago investigation. The vic-

11. *Ibid.,* p. 301.
12. *Ibid.*

tims of police abuse normally did not possess sufficient power within the political structure to call attention to the corrupt practices or were so financially insecure that they could not withstand the harassment which would occur if they did.

How does a police administration and a public concerned about the continuation of police corruption break the conspiracy of silence? This problem is not an easy one to solve since, as Smith points out, the conspiracy of silence is

animated by intense loyalty to the group and mutual protectiveness against outsiders; and it operates through pure pressure. To violate the code means to be ostracized, to be cast out of the group, if not worse. In practice, the code leads to a perversion of ethics. It shields the corrupt policeman from exposure and condemns any colleague who would expose him. Even the most upright officer is effectively muzzled, and justifies his silence with the rationalization that he himself is honest and is, after all, not his brother's keeper.[13]

To undermine the conspiracy of silence, it is not sufficient to call attention to its existence and hope that it will disappear as a result of public exposure. Police and political authorities must take more positive action.

The key law enforcement strategy has been to strengthen its own "internal security" mechanisms. While this step is to be applauded, particularly in view of the experiences in Chicago where the Internal Investigative Division was notorious for its lack of pursuit of corrupt policemen, it does not offer an effective solution to the conspiracy of silence problem.

Members of internal security are usually recruited from the ranks of the police force. This procedure raises the possibility that those officers, by the time they are transferred to internal security, may already have been practitioners of the code and members of the conspiracy of silence. If this is the case, internal security will be ineffective since it will become part of the conspiracy of silence.

To avoid the internalization of the code and the development of the conspiracy, internal security divisions must be staffed with officers who are recruited from outside the ranks of ordinary police work. This might be carried out through a series of communications and relationships between local, state, and federal law enforcement agencies. Personnel could also be recruited entirely from outside the ranks of law enforcement. While this may appear more difficult, it requires only that individuals, at the time of their initial recruitment into police work, be immediately assigned and trained as specialists in internal

13. Smith, "Deceit in Uniform," p. 220.

security. However, this will not be practical until the police revise their concepts of recruitment and selection so that entering officers can be placed at levels of the police bureaucracy higher than "entering" patrolmen and compensated accordingly.

In addition to strengthening internal security, other police organizations[14] have adopted programs designed to encourage officers to cooperate with investigators and tell all they know. These programs have been deliberately publicized within police departments to shake confidence in the conspiracy of silence. Questions must be raised about this approach since, pending further research, it is not clear how this may interrupt the "efficiency" of law-abiding officers and the conduct of regular and acceptable police activities. Although it is true that a corrupt policeman is the greatest enemy of honest policemen, it is not clear whether a program which encourages "honest" policemen to turn against "corrupt" policemen would be successful. If the code is operating effectively, it is unlikely that honest policemen will have sufficient information to lead to the arrest and conviction of dishonest policemen. Any program that attempts to encourage dishonest policemen to turn against their co-conspirators could not possibly offer the financial remuneration and esprit de corps that dishonest practices provide.

On the other hand, since dishonest policemen are more likely to have relevant information regarding illegal police activities, any strategy for effectively breaking the conspiracy of silence must be directed at them. Use immunity can be a very potent weapon. However, its effectiveness is dependent upon the availability of "substantive" evidence against those who are given immunity. If used properly, the pressure on the witness can be unbearable. To effectively implement this strategy, prosecutors must also assume the responsibility of developing a system which will provide protection from harassment and retaliation to those who agree to cooperate. Use immunity will also be more effective when it is combined with a strengthened internal security operation which will uncover a sufficient number of corrupt police officers through investigation.

Breaking the conspiracy of silence must also take into account the relationship between the political bureaucracy and the police bureaucracy. Police corruption often mirrors corruption which exists at other levels of the political hierarchy. There is often little incentive on the part of the political structure to break the conspiracy of silence because it deprives corrupt police officers of the support of the political bureaucracy.

14. *Ibid.,* p. 221.

Law Enforcement Only

From its earliest beginnings a policed society has always functioned through a consensual, if not openly verbalized, agreement between the governed (the public) and the governing (the police) which influences the scope of police activities. Through the years, this agreement has been subject to the changing attitudes of the governed or the governing. Police activity which is within the scope of this agreement, whether legal or illegal, is accepted by the public.

The concept of the police officer as social service provider is within the existing consensual agreement between the community and the police. In conferring power upon the police officer in situations which are not "law enforcement" but are still within the public's definition of "keeper of the peace," the public sets up a situation in which it supports, both directly and through its apathy, an environment in which it is easier for the police officer to become corrupt. Conferring upon the police officer a job description which calls for activities beyond the scope of law enforcement, accompanied by enormous discretionary power, helps to create a setting ripe for the invasion of corruptive influences.

Any solution to the problem of police corruption requires that society reexamine its role definition for the police and consider whether sanctioned police activity should conform more strictly to existing laws which govern criminal behavior.

If the police role is narrowed, society will need to develop other alternatives for taking care of those problems which are now given to the police as "keepers of the peace." These activities are diverse and include, for example, the "statutory" crimes of juveniles (such as runaways), most conflicts arising out of marital disharmony, the monitoring of many civil regulations, numerous law enforcement activities such as traffic control, and the broad social work function which dominates the daily routine of today's law enforcement officer.[15] Returning the police officer to a strictly "law enforcement" role will narrow the scope of his discretionary power and will in turn reduce his latitude to exact "favor" for activities which are not governed by law and which therefore provide a fertile soil for corruption.

15. Harold Russell and Allan Beigel, *Understanding Human Behavior for Effective Police Work* (Basic Books, New York, 1976), pp. 3–13.

Reorganizing the Police System

As urban areas have expanded since World War II, all governmental bureaucracies, including those of law enforcement, have grown. As a result, implementing accountability for police action becomes more difficult and corrupt practices are more easily able to flourish. The massive size of many police departments prevents easy detection of corrupt activities and precludes effective countermeasures.

Controlling police corruption requires a greater accountability of the police bureaucracy by the public and appropriate political authorities. Numerous methods have been introduced to increase accountability of police systems. They have included the use of the judicial system, citizens' groups, civilian review boards, and the press and public opinion. None has been successful in controlling police corruption.[16]

The close relationship between prosecutors and the police also reduces the possibility that those statutes which might have an impact upon police corruption will be used to the fullest extent. Prosecutors, without putting aside other legitimate areas of concern, have insufficient investigative resources outside the police to control police corruption. Finally, the politicalization of the judiciary in many large metropolitan areas and its generally nonactivist position do not make it a viable resource in the battle against police corruption.

Citizens' groups have been unsuccessful because of a tendency to develop their own "militant" agenda which is pushed to the point where the entire program, good and bad, is rejected. These groups also lack the broad political base necessary to acquire the support necessary to effect meaningful reform.

Civilian review boards have also been used to increase police accountability. However, they usually do not possess sufficient investigatory power to look at police corruption as a whole. Instead, they act on a case-by-case basis. Since they act only on citizens' complaints, it is difficult for them to take a leading reform role.

Although the emergence of an investigatory press has brought into the limelight several police corruption scandals, it is clear that many of the reporters rely primarily upon the police for their information. Because of the conspiracy of silence, it is difficult for them to mount the kind of attack necessary to expose police corruption. The press is also vulnerable to accusations that their exposures of police corruption are motivated by a selfish interest to sell news-

16. Alan Edward Bent, *The Politics of Law Enforcement* (Lexington, Mass.: D. C. Heath, 1974), pp. 71–74.

papers. The credibility of their reports is often suspect.

The influence of public opinion has been relatively minimal because of the pronounced apathy of the public toward this problem as well as its apparent unwillingness to reexamine the role which it has assigned to the police and which has contributed to the development of police corruption.

With the failure of these indirect controls, most police departments have tended to rely on internal mechanisms for increasing accountability. This approach has also had its share of problems since many of the internal reforms have encountered resistance from the entrenched police bureaucracy. The political bureaucracy, which often views its fate as closely aligned to that of the police bureaucracy, has also offered, in many cities, little support for these internal accountability changes, perhaps because of its fear that "we are next."

In the light of this pessimistic overview, what should be done to increase the accountability of the police system and the awareness of the problem of police corruption?

First, there is an increased need to recognize the importance of an "independent" prosecutor's office with the authority to conduct investigations and to press charges against corrupt police officers. This has been started in some jurisdictions. As yet, however, such offices have been limited in effectiveness because of inadequate resources which cause them to rely on cooperation from internal police security or to depend on other police officers for the collection of data necessary to prosecute.

Second, strong action must be taken to control the developing militancy of police organizations which are rapidly approximating the status of "unions."[17] While police unions are controversial because of implications associated with the removal of employees' "rights," society must still recognize that as long as it encourages the militancy of these "unions," it is also contributing to reduced checks on "police power." On the other hand, if police departments developed effective personnel systems which objectively reviewed performance and introduced professional classifications which supported adequate compensation for skill, then the impetus for the development of "police unions" would lessen.

Third, and most generally overlooked, is the bureaucracy. While decentralization of investigatory and law enforcement functions, as exemplified within the federal bureaucracy, has many problems, particularly with regard to cooperation and duplication of effort, it has also contributed to the relatively low profile of "corruption" in these spheres. As the police bureaucracy grows along

17. *Ibid.*, pp. 76–81.

with the increasing population of metropolitan areas, it would be wise to consider a plan which would fragment large-city police departments and create independently controlled and smaller law enforcement units. Each would have specific functions related to the investigation of specific crimes and each would be responsible to a different part of city government. The development of computers, with the increased accessibility of information, makes this a more realistic plan than it has been in the past since the easy availability of information could reduce duplication of effort. The presence of a strong centralized authority, directly accountable to the public, could alleviate the problem of cooperation between the different units. The result of such a decision could also allow for more effective control of corruption by making abuses more difficult to hide.

Why Investigate Police Corruption?

While this book has described a "successful" investigation of police corruption, the question can be fairly raised, given the limited scope of the investigation, which focused primarily on police extortion from tavern owners, and the limited number of people convicted, why bother?

When a criminal investigation is undertaken which has as its goal the uncovering of illegal activity by local police, the number of those indicted and convicted will constitute only a small percentage of the officers involved in the types of activities being investigated. No matter how many are indicted and convicted, there will be no appreciable long-term impact on day-to-day police operations or the internal security mechanism unless efforts are undertaken by those in charge to institute major reforms. It is difficult to justify any investigation of police corruption by claiming that the investigation will have any lasting effect on the quality or integrity of local law enforcement.

At the same time, any investigation which produces significant results may alert the public to the need for reform of the police structure. In the case of a federal inquiry, where local officials may protest that the investigation has been initiated because of a political desire to embarrass those in power, the only required response is that, if wrongdoing has occurred, the federal intrusion into local affairs could have been avoided easily by an alert, aggressive, and honest local law enforcement apparatus. Many state laws are in existence which could be used to prosecute corrupt police officers. If local or state law enforcement officials have no desire to enforce these laws, it is inevitable that another governmental body will take action using whatever power and authority it possesses. Outside investigations will never eliminate police corruption, but it is also true that, without these investigations, public scrutiny will never be encouraged.

Paradoxically, the increasing activity of the federal government in investigating local police corruption may lead to the reexamination of certain traditional facets of the investigatory and judicial process. In this investigation, use of immunity and the implementation of the broad powers of the grand jury to subpoena witnesses and to command the production of books and records, which are subject to little or no court scrutiny, have seriously been questioned by commentators, politicians, and the public. While these practices are not new, they have rarely before been so heavily challenged.

An investigation into police corruption may have the positive benefit of revealing the existence of widespread police corruption. It may also ultimately result in the revision of the apparatus used in that investigation. It is even conceivable that reform in the procedures used in this investigation may be greater than those made in the institutions which are the subject of investigation.

When all is said and done and the public clamor which inevitably follows investigations of this type dies down, the only solution to police corruption is the institution of long-term reforms in the system of law enforcement which will make further investigations unnecessary. Until then, there will be more police corruption and more investigations.

Index